HUMAN DOCUMENTS OF THE
INDUSTRIAL REVOLUTION IN BRITAIN

HUMAN DOCUMENTS
OF THE
INDUSTRIAL REVOLUTION
IN BRITAIN

BY

E. ROYSTON PIKE

London
GEORGE ALLEN & UNWIN LTD
RUSKIN HOUSE   MUSEUM STREET

FIRST PUBLISHED IN 1966
SECOND IMPRESSION 1966
THIRD IMPRESSION 1968
FOURTH IMPRESSION 1970
FIFTH IMPRESSION 1973

ISBN: 0 04 942059 3 *Cased*
0 04 942060 7 *Paper*

PRINTED IN GREAT BRITAIN
in Plantin type
BY UNWIN BROTHERS LIMITED
OLD WOKING SURREY

INTRODUCTION

So many books have been written on the Industrial Revolution in Britain that it may be thought that there is hardly room for another. Should an apology be thought necessary, it may be said that the present volume is an attempt to go some way towards filling what must surely appear to be a somewhat surprising gap in the literature. Its aim and purpose is to enable the men and women—and, let it be said, the children and young people—who lived in and through the Industrial Revolution in this country and who had their part, large or small, in its development and helped to give it direction and impetus, to describe their experiences in their own words.

All the documents quoted are *original* documents, prepared and written and set down in print when the Revolution was actually going on. No doubt many of them are one-sided, some of them frankly partisan, most of them limited in their viewpoint. But then they are not what has been filtered through the minds and pens of historians, writing long afterwards in a calmer atmosphere and enjoying the not inconsiderable advantages of knowledge after the event. They are the raw material of history; and what they may perhaps lose in balanced reflection and considered judgment they much more than make up for in first-hand testimony, in the warmth of feeling engendered by personal experience.

There is something more. Throughout, in this compilation, this collection of real-life stories, the emphasis is on the *human element*. In making my selection from out of the enormous amount of significant material that is available, I have disregarded anything and everything that suggests that the men and women who were engaged in the Industrial Revolution may be looked upon as figures in a statistical table or points on a graph. Here is the rich red meat of human experience, in one of the most tremendously important, exciting and exacting periods of modern times, indeed of all time.

In these documents we may read what it was really like to live in that great age of revolutionary change. We may listen to what the people have to say, told in their own words and in their own inimitable way. To be a domestic worker compelled to exchange the free and easy conditions of his cottage employment, combined with some seasonal work in his own fields, for the regulated toil of the factory—a workhouse brat despatched in a cart with other unfortunates down the long road that had its terminus behind the grim walls of the apprentice-house—a child 'trapper' sitting in the dark for lonely and seemingly interminable hours in the gloomy recesses of a coal-pit—a woman dragging tubs of coal attached by a chain drawn round her naked middle—a cotton operative fined for whistling in the factory—a girl in Manchester working from before light to long after dark in a company of precocious young males—a Sheffield grinder coughing up his lungs—a London dressmaker kept at her needle for days and nights together with sometimes no more than a couple of hours in the twenty-four to call her own. . . . All these we may meet, and many another of the hosts of humble workers in that age of boundless opportunities for the fortunate few and of incessant and poorly rewarded labour for the vast majority, in a society almost entirely wanting in everything that makes for social welfare. If the rhetoric may be allowed, most of these pages are marked with human sweat, many are tear-stained, and not a few are bespattered with blood.

While in my selections I have drawn on a large and varied collection of books and pamphlets, by far the most numerous and important class come from what today we should call Blue Books —the minutes of evidence taken before Government or Parliamentary inquiries, committees, commissions of one kind and another, together with the reports and conclusions that were founded upon them. The bulk of these have never been reprinted, and are available only on the shelves of the very largest of our national libraries. Much of what the volumes contain is of interest only to the dedicated student of industrial techniques and administrative detail, but buried in their many hundreds of pages is many a gem of human interest, as the somnolent air of the committee room was disturbed by the sharp exclamations of indignation and disgust, of pain and misery. For a hundred years and more they have rested in the obscurity of the nation's archives—in some cases I have found the pages uncut—and the reader will be able to judge how well they have deserved their discovery and resurrection.

Not much need be said about the way in which the material has been arranged. To begin with, there is a section, or book or chapter, on *The Rise of the Factory System*, in which the old industrial order is shown giving birth to the new. This is followed by a collection of documents illustrative of *Factory Life and People*, in which I have drawn very considerably on the accounts of Dr Kay and Peter Gaskell, two authors who have been often referred to in all the histories of the social and economic life of the time but very inadequately represented in quotation. Then comes a section on *Child Labour*. This is by far the largest in the book, partly because of the exceedingly important part that children (even infants) and young persons played in building up the industries of modern Britain, but more because they were the first, and for a long time the only, objects of legislative 'interference'. Over a period of more than forty years their condition received the attention of Parliament, and the reports and minutes of evidence of the successive committees of inquiry are among the most valuable social documents of the time. Hardly second in importance, and not even second in human interest, is the section that follows, having for its subject *Woman's Place* in the new world that was coming to birth in such turmoil and anguish and disorder. Here we are given the most intimate pictures of women's life, in the factory and workshop, in the home, and, in all its disgusting detail, underground in the coal mines. From this it is a natural transition to *Sexual Relations*, in which that almost virgin subject of social investigation, the sex life of the working people, is examined and revealed. Then, under the heading of *The State of the Towns* will be found accounts of some of the most important of the centres of population in those parts of the country that were most affected by the series of revolutionary changes. Some of them, many in fact, make disgusting reading; but it is well to be reminded of the conditions of overcrowding, poverty, squalor and stench in which the industrial masses lived out their lives. It is good to be reminded, too, that there were fine flowerings of the human spirit on the urban dunghills.

These are the main sections, but there are numerous subsidiary headings. Each division has an introduction, which has been kept short since this book is not intended to be a history of the Industrial Revolution but rather something in the nature of a gloss. In a number of cases I have said something about the authors of the documents quoted, in order that the reader may judge their credentials and allow for possible partisanship and bias. If we are considering, say, the conditions of work in a cotton factory, we may well feel inclined to give greater weight to the evidence of one who actually worked in the factory than to one who looked at the factory from outside and may have visited it only as a member of a conducted tour. The headings given to the documents are mine, and editorial additions by way of explanation, etc., in the text are enclosed in square brackets. Full details of the source are appended to each extract.

The period covered by the survey is roughly that from the end of the eighteenth century to well on in the reign of Queen Victoria, when the Industrial Revolution, after having brought about a new social and industrial order, had at length been brought under some measure of public control, its worst excesses were being remedied, and the generation of hardbitten pioneers had given place to men of a much more socially responsible type.

What impression are the two hundred and fifty 'documents' assembled here, likely to make on the reader? Something resembling the impression they have made on my own mind perhaps—that the truth about the Industrial Revolution is nothing like so simple and clear-cut as the histories may have led us to suppose. There are many strange things in these pages, astonishing phrases, surprising descriptions, unexpected asides. Not all the masters were tyrants, and not all the tyrants were masters. And the things which are dealt with are still so very much alive that we must make allowance for the passions and prejudices of class and education, of employment and status. The final thought the documents have left with me is that the only really valid generalization about the Industrial Revolution is that no generalization is possible.

Here, then, is the Industrial Revolution in the raw, as it were —its glory and its grime, its tremendous achievement at the cost of so much human suffering and labour, its shame and its pride, and, let us not forget to acknowledge, its boundless promise of a better and brighter tomorrow.

E. R. P.

CONTENTS

CHILD LABOUR

CONTENTS

CONTENTS

CONTENTS

15

CONTENTS

CONTENTS

ILLUSTRATIONS

THE RISE OF
THE FACTORY SYSTEM

'Previously to 1760,' said Arnold Toynbee in one of those lectures delivered to an Oxford audience in 1881 that inaugurated the specialized literature of the Industrial Revolution, 'the old industrial system obtained in England.'

What was the 'old industrial system'? It has often been described, and almost as often in the most sympathetic terms. One of the best accounts, if by 'best' we mean 'readable', is that of Peter Gaskell, given in the opening chapter of his book, *The Manufacturing Population of England*, first published in 1833. Its peculiar quality will be appreciated from what is reprinted here (No. 1). Gaskell disclaimed any intention of painting an Arcadia, but there is none the less about his description a glow of nostalgic warmth.

How far Gaskell wrote out of personal knowledge and experience is hard to ascertain, since very little is known about him. He qualified as an apothecary in London in 1827 and in the next year was admitted to the membership of the Royal College of Surgeons. He seems to have lived in the neighbourhood of Stockport, in Cheshire, and it is reasonable to assume that it was then that he obtained his obviously considerable acquaintance with the poor and their problems. The most important thing about him is his book, which, as stated above, was published in 1833; a second edition, revised and slightly enlarged, appeared three years later, under the title of *Artisans and Machinery*. Gaskell died in 1841, at the age of 35, when he was living in Camberwell, then one of the more rural of the London inner suburbs.

Very possibly the book would have remained as obscure as the young surgeon who was its author if it had not attracted the attention of Frederick Engels, the friend and supporter, in more ways than one, of Karl Marx. When he was writing his book on

The Condition of the Working Class in England in 1844, first issued in Germany in 1845 and not in an English translation until 1892, Engels drew very heavily on Gaskell for his opening chapters on the recent history of the English working classes. He acknowledged his debt in a footnote, adding that in his opinion Gaskell was an unprejudiced witness to the evils of the factory system. How far the tribute was merited may be left to the reader to judge.

Richard Guest, one of the earliest historians of the Cotton industry, took a rather different view (No. 2). He thought that the factory population were far more actively patriotic than the domestic weavers, even though they were not such good sportsmen: they didn't give the hare a fair run. ... In No. 3 we return to Gaskell's lively pages for an account of the up-and-coming race of manufacturers. It is an unpleasant picture on the whole, but not all the 'new masters' were dissolute brutes, who varied their spurts of tremendous energy with bouts of heavy drinking and lustful pursuit of their mill-girls. The Bolton Barber, Sir Richard Arkwright (No. 4), was allowed, even by Sir Edward Baines, another historian of the Cotton industry, who was inclined to discount Arkwright's claims in the field of invention, to have been 'ardent, enterprising, and stubbornly persevering', and he well deserves to be called the Father of the Factory System. Nor was he exceptional in his pioneering activities. The success story of the Peels is another instance—one among many—of the rise to wealth and influence of men from lowly beginnings, who yet managed to achieve outstanding success without suffering a debasement of their moral character in the process. And when we read of the vulgar bedizened woman who, according to Gaskell, was the manufacturer's wife, we should do well to keep in mind the picture of the first Lady Peel, who became her husband's 'high-souled and faithful counsellor', as Samuel Smiles put it (No. 5).

Next we come to Robert Owen (1771–1858), whose account of the founding of the great cotton-spinning establishment at New Lanark shows the difficulties that confronted the new manufacturers and how they were faced and overcome. Many books have been written about this extraordinary little Welshman, and he deserves to be remembered, not only for his business successes and his humanizing of the relations of employer and employed but for his outstanding achievement in enlightened capitalism and practical socialism, the foundation of infant schools and other educational ventures, and the beginnings of the co-operative movement and trade unionism. If there was one thing that Robert Owen most firmly believed it was that circumstances make human character, and he devoted his long life to the improvement of the conditions in which the work-people lived, since only then might they be expected to become healthy and happy and wise.

I

Domestic Manufacturers

Prior to the year 1760, manufactures were in a great measure confined to the demands of the home market. At this period, and down to 1800 . . . the majority of the artizans engaged in them had laboured in their own houses, and in the bosoms of their families. It may be termed the period of domestic manufacture; and the various mechanical contrivances were expressly framed for this purpose. The distaff, the spinning wheel, producing a single thread, and, subsequently the mule and jenny, were to be found forming part of the complement of household furniture, in almost every house of the districts in which they were carried on, whilst the cottage everywhere resounded with the clack of the hand-loom.

These were, undoubtedly, the golden times of manufactures, considered in reference to the character of the labourers. By all the processes being carried on under a man's own roof, he retained his individual respectability; he was kept apart from associations that might injure his moral worth, whilst he generally earned wages which were sufficient not only to live comfortably upon, but which enabled him to rent a few acres of land; thus joining in his own person two classes, that are now daily becoming more and more distinct. It cannot, indeed, be denied, that his farming was too often slovenly, and was conducted at times but as a subordinate occupation; and that the land yielded but a small proportion of what, under a better system of culture, it was capable of producing. It nevertheless answered an excellent purpose. Its necessary tendence filled up the vacant hours, when he found it unnecessary to apply himself to his loom or spinning machine. It gave him employment of a healthy nature, and raised him a step in the scale of society above the mere labourer. A garden was likewise an invariable adjunct to the cottage of the hand-loom weaver; and in no part of the kingdom were the floral tribes, fruits, and edible roots more zealously or more successfully cultivated.

The domestic manufacturers generally resided in the outskirts of the large towns, or at still more remote distances. Themselves cultivators, and of simple habits and few wants, the uses of tea, coffee, and groceries in general but little known, they rarely left their own homestead. The yarn which they spun, and which was wanted by the weaver, was received or delivered, as the case might be, by agents, who travelled for the wholesale houses; or depots were established in particular neighbourhoods, to which he could apply at weekly periods. Grey-haired men—fathers of large families—have thus lived through a long life, which has been devoted to spinning or weaving, and have never entered the precincts of a town, till driven, of late years, by the depression in their means of support, they have gone there, for the first time, when forced to migrate with their households, in search of occupation at steam-looms.

Thus, removed from many of those causes which universally operate to the deterioration of the moral character of the labouring man, when brought into large towns . . . the small farmer, spinner, or hand-loom weaver, presents as orderly and respectable an appearance as could be wished. It is true that the amount of labour gone through, was but small; that the quantity of cloth or yarn produced was but limited—for he worked by the rule of his strength and convenience. They were, however, sufficient to clothe and feed himself and family decently, and according to their station; to lay by a penny for an evil day, and to enjoy those amusements and bodily recreations then in being. He was a respectable member of society; a good father, a good husband, and a good son.

It is not intended to paint an Arcadia—to state that the domestic manufacturer was free from the vices or failings of other men. By no means; but he had the opportunities brought to him for being comfortable and virtuous—with a physical constitution, uninjured by protracted toil in a heated and impure atmosphere, the fumes of the gin shop, the low debauchery of the beer-house, and the miseries incident to ruined health. On the contrary, he commonly lived to a good round age, worked when necessity demanded, ceased his labour when his wants were supplied, according to his character, and if disposed to spend time or money in drinking, could do so in a house as well conducted and as orderly as his own . . .

The domestic manufacturer possessed a very limited degree of information; his amusements were exclusively sought in bodily exercise, the dance, quoits, cricket, the chace, the numerous seasonal celebrations, etc.; an utter ignorance of printed books, beyond the thumbed Bible and a few theological tracts; seeking his stimulus in home-brewed ale; having for his support animal food occasionally, but living generally upon farm produce, meal or rye bread, eggs, cheese, milk, butter, etc.; the use of tea quite unknown, or only just beginning to make its appearance; a sluggish mind in an active body; labour carried on under his own roof, or, if exchanged at intervals for farming occupation, this was going on under the eye of, and with the assistance of his family; his children growing up under his immediate inspection and control; no lengthened separation taking place until they married, and became themselves heads of families; engaged in pursuits similar to his own, and in a subordinate capacity; and lastly, the same generation living age after age on the same spot, and under the same thatched roof, which thus became a sort of heir-loom, endeared to its occupier by a long series of happy memories and home delights . . .

The very fact of these small communities (for they were generally found in petty irregular villages, containing from ten to forty cottages), being as it were, one great family, prevented, except in a few extraordinary instances, any systematic course of sinning. This moral check was indeed all-powerful in hindering the commission of crime, aided by a sense of religion very commonly existing amongst them. In one respect this failed, however—and it was in preventing the indulgence of sexual appetite, in a way and at a time which are still blots upon the rural population of many districts . . . The mischief produced by this means was, however, of small amount. This premature intercourse occurred generally between parties, when a tacit though binding understanding existed. Its promiscuousness seldom went further. So binding was this engagement, that the examples of desertion were exceedingly rare—though marriage was generally deferred till pregnancy fully declared itself.

There can be no question, but the more widely inquiries are extended, the more obvious becomes the fact, that the domestic manufacturer, as a moral and social being, was infinitely superior to the manufacturer of a later date . . .

P. GASKELL, *The Manufacturing Population of England: Its Moral, Social, and Physical Conditions, and the Changes which have arisen from the Use of the Steam Machinery* (1833) ch. I.

2

Change Comes to Lancashire

The population of Lancashire, before the introduction of the Cotton Manufacture, was chiefly agricultural. In those days, the Squire was the feudal Lord of the neighbourhood, and his residence, or the Hall, as it was called, was looked upon in the light of a palace. He was the dictator of opinion, the regulator of parish affairs, and the exclusive settler of all disputes. On holidays the rustics were invited to the Hall, where they wrestled, ran races, played at quoits and drank ale. An invitation to the Hall was a certificate of good character; not to be invited along with his neighbours was a reproach to a man, because no one was uninvited unless he had been guilty of some impropriety. The Clergyman had scarcely less influence than the Squire, his sacred character and his superior attainments gave him great authority . . . He never met the elders of his flock without the kindest enquiries after the welfare of their families, and, as his reproof was dreaded, so his commendation was sought, by young and old.

Incontinence in man or woman was esteemed a heinous offence, and neglecting or refusing to pay a just debt was scarcely ever heard of. Twice at Church on Sundays, a strict observance of fast days, and a regular reading of the Scripture every Sunday evening, at which the youngsters, after putting off their best clothes, were always present, were uniform and established customs. The events of the neighbourhood flowed in a regular, unbroken train; politics were a field little entered into, and the histories of each other's families, including cousins five times removed, with marriages, births, deaths, etc., formed the almost only subjects of their conversations.

The Farmer was content to take on trust the old modes of husbandry and management practised by his forefathers for generations; and new improvements were received, or rather viewed, with dislike and contempt. There was little fluctuation in prices, little competition between individuals, and the mind became contracted from the general stagnation and its being so seldom roused to exertion. Men being mostly employed alone, and having few but their own families to converse with, had not their understandings rubbed bright by contact and an interchange of ideas; they witnessed a monotonous scene of life which communicated a corresponding dullness and mechanical action to their minds. The greatest varieties of scene which they witnessed were the market day of the village, and the attendance at Church on the Sabbath; and the *summum bonum* of their lives was to sit vacant and inactive in each other's houses, to sun themselves in the market-place, or to talk over news at that great mart of village gossip, the blacksmith's shop . . .

The progress of the Cotton Manufacture introduced great changes into the manners and habits of the people. The operative workmen being thrown together in great numbers, had their faculties sharpened and improved by constant communication. Conversation wandered over a variety of topics not before essayed; the questions of Peace and War, which interested them importantly, inasmuch as they might produce a rise or fall of wages, became highly interesting, and this brought them into the vast field of politics and discussions on the character of their Government, and the men who composed it. They took a greater interest in the defeats and victories of their country's arms, and from being only a few degrees above their cattle in the scale of intellect, they became Political Citizens . . .

The facility with which the Weavers changed their masters, the constant effort to find out and obtain the largest remuneration for their labour, the excitement to ingenuity which the higher wages for fine manufactures and skilful workmanship produced, and a conviction that they depended mainly on their own exertions, produced in them that invaluable feeling, a spirit of freedom and independence, and that guarantee for good conduct and improvement of manners, a conscious-ness of the value of character and of their own weight and importance.

The practical truth of these remarks must be obvious to every one who had served on the Jury at Lancaster, and compared the bright, penetrating shrewd and intelligent Jurors from the south of the county, with the stupidity and utter ignorance of those from its northern parts; and to every one who witnessed the fervour and enthusiasm with which the people in the manufacturing districts flew to arms, in 1803, to defend their firesides against a foreign invader. What crowding to the drills; what ardour and alacrity to learn the use of arms there then was, and how much stronger and more rapid the feeling of independence, both national and individual, is found among the highly-civilized dense manufacturing population, than among a scattered, half-informed Peasantry!

The amusements of the people have changed with their character. Athletic exercises of Quoits, Wrestling, Foot-ball, Prison-bars and Shooting with the Long-bow, are become obsolete and almost forgotten; and it is to be regretted that the present pursuits and pleasures of the labouring class are of a more effeminate cast. They are now Pigeon-fanciers, Canary-breeders and Tulip-growers.

The field sports, too, have assumed a less hardy and enterprising character. Instead of the Squire with his merry harriers and a score or two of ruddy, broad-chested yeomen, scouring the fields on foot, heedless of thorn or brier, and scorning to turn aside for copse or ditch, we see half a dozen Fustian Masters and Shopkeepers, with three or four greyhounds and as many beagles, attacking the poor Hare with such a superiority, both as respects scent and fleetness, as to give her no chance of escape, and pouncing on their game like poachers, rather than pursuing it with the fairness and hardihood of hunters.

RICHARD GUEST, *A Compendious History of the Cotton-Manufacture* (1823), pp. 31–39.

3

The New Masters and Their Women

Master cotton-spinners and weavers, at the commencement of this important epoch, were in many instances men sprung from the ranks of the labourers, or from a grade just removed above these—uneducated —of coarse habits—sensual in their enjoyments—partaking of the rude revelry of their dependants—overwhelmed by success—but yet, para-doxical as it may sound, industrious men, and active and far-sighted tradesmen.

Many of these might be found, after a night spent in debauchery and licentiousness, sobered down by an hour or two of rest, and by the ringing of the factory bell, going through the business of the day with untiring activity and unerring rectitude—surrounded too, as they were, by their companions, alike busily engaged under their inspection— again to plunge, at the expiration of the hours of labour, into the same vortex of inebriation and riot.

Meanwhile a great change was progressing in the homes of these men. The low and irregularly built farm-house, or the cottage attached to the mill, were exchanged for mansions erected purposely for them—larger, more commodious, and in the most modern order of domestic architecture, furnished in a style of shew and expense—if not of taste— sufficiently indicative of the state of the owner's purse and prospects; and to these were transferred the manners which had unhappily disgraced their late more humble residences.

They did not, it is true, introduce here their low and dissolute companions, in whose society a portion of their time was still spent. The reunions, however, which did occur, though of a different order, consisting generally of men of their own, or somewhat inferior standing, were fully as debased; and drink—drink was their only amusement and occupation.

Many of them had married before any such brilliant prospect as they now enjoyed had opened before them; and, of course, had married women of a similar grade with themselves. It is a singular fact that woman, plastic as she is in many of her relations, and readily as she accommodates herself to changes in worldly circumstances, yet, if suffered to pass a certain age, she shews her original coarseness much longer and much more unpleasantly than her husband. This is abundantly verified by an acquaintance with the families of those manufacturers whose wives have progressed with them through a successful career from a humble origin.

The husband will certainly not exhibit the polish of a well-bred gentleman, but his manners will be good, and his information, from a long course of shrewd observation of men and things, will be varied and extensive. He is, in consequence, fitted to move reputably in the rank in which his exertions and industry have placed him.

Not so his wife—vulgar in speech, or its vulgarity so badly patched up as to render it still more offensive—coarse in her habits, utterly illiterate, tawdry in her dress, and extravagantly vain of her fine clothes, her fine house, her fine carriage, her fine footman—she is an epitome of every thing that is odious in manners. One redeeming point must be granted her, and that is—she is profusely hospitable; though truth compels the confession, that she is led to this from a sense of vain-glory, not prompted by any nobler feeling or intention.

The influence of a mother's habits upon the character and disposition of her daughters, is of so durable and decided a nature, that no wonder can be felt, that many of them—highly cultivated as they have been—educated in the most expensive schools, and separated, for a time, from home—still show traces of the germ from which they have sprung . . . It was, however, upon the sons, younger brothers, and immediate male connexions, that the example set by these individuals exerted the most pernicious influence. The demand for hands necessarily led to the employment of all the male relatives of the master manufacturers at a very early age. His own sons were invested with considerable authority, when mere children—taken from school to superintend certain portions of the mills, and liberally supplied with money. The same remark holds good with reference to others, his relations. Boys, at an age when they should have been sedulously kept apart from opportunities of indulging their nascent sexual propensities, were thrust into a very hot-bed of lust, and exposed to vicious example, in addition to other causes, irresistibly tending to make them a prey to licentiousness . . .

The organized system of immorality which was pursued by these younger men and boys, was extremely fatal to the best interests of the labouring community. Chastity became a laughing stock and byeword. Victim after victim was successively taken from the mill—the selection being, in the generality of cases, the prettiest and most modest-looking girl to be found among the hundreds assembled there. One after another they yielded, if yielding it deserves to be called.

So depraved, however, was their idea of woman's honour already become, that an improper intimacy was rather esteemed creditable than otherwise. The miserable creature was pointed out by her companions, as being peculiarly fortunate in having attracted the notice of the young master, his nephew, brother, or cousin, as the case might be; while she, in her turn, displayed, with ostentatious parade, the ribbons, cap, or gown, (in reality the insignia of her infamy), which were considered by her as a rich reward for whatever favours she could bestow . . .

Nothing can more clearly shew the demoralizing effects of this pernicious intercourse than the fact, that a girl, who was known to have lived in a state of concubinage, found no difficulty in marrying subsequently amongst her equals . . .

P. GASKELL, *The Manufacturing Population of England* (1833), ch. 2.

4

The Father of the Factory System

Richard Arkwright rose by the force of his natural talents from a very humble condition in society. He was born at Preston on the 23rd of December, 1732, of poor parents; being the youngest of thirteen children, his parents could only afford to give him an education of the humblest kind, and he was scarcely able to write. He was brought up to the trade of a barber, and established himself in that business at Bolton in the year 1760. Having become possessed of a chemical process for dyeing the human hair, which in that day (when wigs were universal) was of considerable value, he travelled about collecting hair, and again disposing of it when dyed. In 1761 he married a wife from Leigh, and the connexions he thus formed in that town are supposed to have afterwards brought him acquainted with Highs's experiments in making spinning machines. He himself manifested a strong bent for experiments in mechanics, which he is stated to have followed with so much devotedness as to have neglected his business and injured his circumstances. His natural disposition was ardent, enterprising, and stubbornly persevering; his mind was as coarse as it was bold and active, and his manners were rough and unpleasing.

In 1767 Arkwright fell in with Kay, the clockmaker, at Warrington, whom he employed to bend him some wires, and turn him some pieces of brass. He entered into conversation with the clockmaker, and called upon him repeatedly; and at length Kay, according to his own account, told him of Highs's scheme of spinning by rollers. Kay adds that Arkwright induced him to make a model of Highs's machine, and took it away. It is certain that from this period Arkwright abandoned his former business, and devoted himself to the construction of the spinning machine . . .

The statement of Arkwright was, that 'after many years of intense and painful application, he invented, about the year 1768, his present method of spinning cotton . . .'. Being altogether destitute of pecuniary means for prosecuting his invention, Arkwright repaired to his native place, Preston, and applied to a friend, Mr John Smalley, a liquor merchant and painter, for assistance . . . His spinning machine was fitted up in the parlour of the house belonging to the Free Grammar School, which was lent by the headmaster to Mr Smalley for the purpose. The latter was so well convinced of the utility of the machine, that he joined Arkwright with heart and purse.

In consequence of the riots which had taken place in the neighbourhood of Blackburn, on the invention of Hargreave's spinning jenny in 1767, by which many of the machines were destroyed, and the inventor was driven from his native county to Nottingham, Arkwright and Smalley, fearing similar outrages, directed against their machine, went also to Nottingham, accompanied by Kay. This town, therefore, became the cradle of two of the greatest inventions in cotton spinning.

Here the adventurers applied for pecuniary aid to Messrs Wright, bankers, who made advances on condition of sharing in the profits of the invention. But as the machine was not perfected so soon as they had anticipated, the bankers requested Arkwright to obtain other assistance, and recommended him to Mr Samuel Need, of Nottingham. This gentleman was the partner of Mr Jedediah Strutt, of Derby, the ingenious improver and patentee of the stocking-frame; and Mr Strutt having seen Arkwright's machine, and declared it to be an admirable invention . . . both Mr Need and Mr Strutt entered into partnership with Arkwright.

Thus the pecuniary difficulties of this enterprising and persevering man were terminated. He soon made his machine practicable, and in 1769 he took out a patent . . . It is remarkable that the inventor, in his application for a patent, described himself as 'Richard Arkwright, of Nottingham, *clockmaker*'. He and his partners erected a mill at Nottingham, which was driven by horses; but this mode of turning the machinery being found too expensive, they built another mill on a much larger scale at Cromford, in Derbyshire, which was turned by a water-wheel, and from this circumstance the spinning machine was called the *water-frame* . . .

On the 16th December 1775 Mr Arkwright took out a second patent. for a series of machines, comprising the carding, drawing, and roving machines, all used in preparing silk, cotton, flax, and wool for spinning, When this admirable series of machines was made known, and by their means yarns were produced far superior in quality to any spun before in England, as well as lower in price, a mighty impulse was communicated to the cotton manufacture. . . . Cotton fabrics could be sold lower

1. Arkwright's first Cotton Mill at Cromford, Derbyshire (from *The Mirror* 1836)

New Lanark: the model factories in Robert Owen's time, and (below) a dancing class for young workers (*photos:* British Museum)

2. Carding, roving, and drawing in a Manchester cotton factory; drawn by
T. Allom; from E. Baines's *History of the Cotton Manufacture in Great
Britain* (1835) (*photo:* The Mansell Collection)

The Twist Factory of Messrs. Hyde, Wood, and Cook, Oxford Street,
Manchester; from E. Baines's *History of the Cotton Manufacture in
Great Britain* (1835) (*photo:* The Mansell Collection)

than had ever before been known. The demand for them consequently increased. The shuttle flew with fresh energy, and the weavers earned immoderately high wages. Spinning mills were erected to supply the requisite quantity of yarn. The fame of Arkwright resounded through the land; and capitalists flocked to him, to buy his patent machines, or permission to use them . . . Mr Arkwright and his partners expended, in large buildings in Derbyshire and elsewhere, upwards of £30,000, and Mr Arkwright also erected a very large and extensive building in Manchester, at the expense of upwards of £4,000. Thus a business was formed, which already, i.e. in 1782 (he calculated) employed upwards of five thousand persons, and a capital of not less than £200,000 . . .

The factory system in England takes its rise from this period. Hitherto the cotton manufacture had been carried on almost entirely in the houses of the workmen: the hand or stock cards, the spinning wheel, and the loom, required no larger apartment than that of a cottage. A spinning jenny of small size might also be used in a cottage, and in many instances was so used. But the water-frame, the carding engine, and the other machines which Arkwright brought out in a finished state, required both more space than could be found in a cottage, and more power than could be applied by the human arm. Their weight also rendered it necessary to place them in strongly-built mills, and they could not be advantageously turned by any power then known but that of water . . .

Although Arkwright, by his series of machines, was the means of giving the most wonderful extension to the system, yet he did not absolutely originate it. Mills for the throwing of silk had existed in England, though not in any great number, from the time of Sir Thomas Lombe, who, in 1719, erected a mill on the river Derwent, at Derby, on the model of those he had seen in Italy . . .

Arkwright commonly laboured in his multifarious concerns from five o'clock in the morning till nine at night; and when considerably more than fifty years of age,—feeling that the defects of his education placed him under great difficulty and inconvenience in conducting his correspondence, and in the general management of his business, he encroached upon his sleep, in order to gain an hour each day to learn English grammar, and another hour to improve his writing and orthography! He was impatient of whatever interfered with his favourite pursuits; and the fact is too strikingly characteristic not to be mentioned, that he separated from his wife not many years after their marriage, because she, convinced that he would starve his family by scheming when he should have been saving, broke some of his experimental models of machines.

Arkwright was a severe economist of time; and, that he might not waste a moment, he generally travelled with four horses, and at a very rapid speed. His concerns in Derbyshire, Lancashire, and Scotland, were so extensive and numerous, as to shew at once his astonishing power of transacting business and his all-grasping spirit. In many of these he had partners, but he generally managed in such a way, that, whoever lost, he himself was a gainer . . .

In 1785 Arkwright's patent was finally set aside; and those most useful machines, which, though invented by others, owed their perfection to his finishing hand, were thrown open to the public. The astonishing extension of the manufactures which immediately followed, shewed that the nullification of the patent was a great national advantage.

Arkwright continued, notwithstanding, his prosperous career. Wealth flowed in upon him with a full stream from his skilfully managed concerns . . . In 1786 he was appointed high sheriff of Derbyshire; and having presented an address of congratulation from that county to the King on his escape from the attempt of Margaret Nicholson on his life, he received the honour of knighthood. Sir Richard was troubled for many years with a severe asthmatic affection; he sunk at length under a complication of disorders, and died at his house at Cromford, on the 3rd of August, 1792, in the sixtieth year of his age . . .

SIR EDWARD BAINES, *History of the Cotton Manufacture in Great Britain* (1835), pp. 148–153, 182–185, 193–195.

5

The Success Story of the Peels

———

The founder of the Peel family, about the middle of the last century, was a small yeoman, occupying the Hole House Farm, near Blackburn, from which he afterwards removed to a house situated in Fish Lane in that town. Robert Peel, as he advanced in life, saw a large family of sons and daughters growing up about him; but the land about Blackburn being somewhat barren, it did not appear to him that agricultural pursuits offered a very encouraging prospect for their industry. The place had, however, long been the seat of a domestic manufacture—the fabric called 'Blackburn greys', consisting of linen weft and cotton warp, being chiefly made in that town and its neighbourhood. It was then customary—previous to the introduction of the factory system—for industrious yeomen with families to employ the time not occupied in the fields in weaving at home; and Robert Peel accordingly began the domestic trade of calico-making. He was honest, and made an honest article; thrifty and hardworking, and his trade prospered.

But Robert Peel's attention was principally directed to the *printing* of calico—then a comparatively unknown art,—and for some time he carried on a series of experiments with the object of printing by machinery. The experiments were secretly conducted in his own house, the cloth being ironed for the purpose by one of the women of the family. It was then customary, in such houses as the Peels', to use pewter plates for dinner. Having sketched a figure or pattern on one of the plates, the thought struck him that an impression might be got from it in reverse, and printed on calico with colour. In a cottage at the end of the farm-house lived a woman who kept a calendering machine, and going into her cottage, he put the plate with colour rubbed into the figured part and some calico over it, through the machine, when it was found to leave a satisfactory impression. Such is said to have been the origin of roller-printing on calico. Robert Peel shortly perfected his process, and the first pattern he brought out was a parsley leaf; hence he is spoken of in the neighbourhood of Blackburn to this day as 'Parsley Peel' . . .

Stimulated by his success, Robert Peel shortly gave up farming, and removing to Brookside, a village about two miles from Blackburn, he devoted himself exclusively to the printing business. There, with the aid of his sons, who were as energetic as himself, he successfully carried on the trade for several years; and as the young men grew up towards manhood, the concern branched out into various firms of Peels, each of which became a centre of industrial activity and a source of remunerative employment to large numbers of people . . .

Sir Robert Peel [1750–1830], the first baronet and the second manufacturer of the name, inherited all his father's enterprise, ability, and industry. His position, at starting in life, was little above that of an ordinary working man; for his father, though laying the foundations of future prosperity, was still struggling with the difficulties arising from insufficient capital. When Robert was only twenty years of age, he determined to begin the business of cotton-printing, which he had by this time learnt from his father, on his own account. His uncle, James Haworth, and William Yates of Blackburn, joined him in his enterprise; the whole capital which they could raise amongst them amounting to only about £500, the principal part of which was supplied by William Yates . . . Robert Peel, though comparatively a mere youth, supplied the practical knowledge of the business. William Yates, being a married man with a family, commenced housekeeping on a small scale, and to oblige Peel, who was single, agreed to take him as a lodger.

A ruined corn-mill, with its adjoining fields, was purchased for a comparatively small sum, near the then insignificant town of Bury; and a few wooden sheds having been run up, the firm commenced their cotton-printing business in a very humble way in the year 1770, adding to it that of cotton-spinning a few years later.

William Yates's eldest child was a girl named Ellen, and she very soon became an especial favourite with the young lodger. On returning from his hard day's work . . . he would take the little girl upon his knee, and say to her, 'Nelly, thou bonny little dear, wilt be my wife?' to which the child would readily answer, 'Yes', as any child would do. 'Then I'll wait for thee, Nelly; I'll wed thee, and none else.' . . . And after the lapse of ten years—years of close application to business and rapidly increasing prosperity—Robert Peel married Ellen Yates when she had completed her seventeenth year; and the pretty child, whom her mother's lodger and father's partner had nursed upon his knee, became Mrs Peel, and eventually Lady Peel, the mother of the future Prime Minister of England.

Lady Peel was a noble and beautiful woman, fitted to grace any station in life. She possessed rare powers of mind, and was, on every emergency, the high-souled and faithful counsellor of her husband. For many years after their marriage she acted as his amanuensis, conducting the principal part of his business correspondence, for Mr Peel himself was an indifferent and almost unintelligible writer. She died in 1803, only three years after the baronetcy had been conferred upon her husband . . .

The career of Yates, Peel & Co. was throughout one of great and uninterrupted prosperity. Sir Robert Peel himself was the soul of the firm; to great energy and application uniting much practical sagacity and first-rate mercantile abilities . . . In short, he was to cotton-printing what Arkwright was to cotton-spinning, and his success was equally great . . .

SAMUEL SMILES, *Self Help* (1859), ch. 2.

6

The Great Experiment at New Lanark

In the year 1784 the late Mr Dale [David Dale: 1739–1806], of Glasgow, founded a manufactory for spinning of cotton, near the falls of the Clyde, in the county of Lanark, in Scotland; and about that period cotton mills were first introduced into the northern part of the kingdom.

It was the power which could be obtained from the falls of water that induced Mr Dale to erect his mills in this situation; for in other respects it was not well chosen. The country around was uncultivated; the inhabitants were poor and few in number; and the roads in the neighbourhood were so bad, that the Falls, now so celebrated, were then unknown to strangers.

It was therefore necessary to collect a new population to supply the infant establishment with labourers. This, however, was no light task; for all the regularly trained Scotch peasantry disdained the idea of working early and late, day after day, within cotton mills. Two modes then only remained of obtaining these labourers; the one, to procure children from the various public charities of the country; and the other, to induce families to settle around the works.

To accommodate the first, a large house was erected, which ultimately contained about five hundred children, who were procured chiefly from workhouses and charities in Edinburgh. These children were to be fed, clothed, and educated; and these duties Mr Dale performed with the unwearied benevolence which it is well known he possessed.

To obtain the second, a village was built; and the houses were let at a low rent to such families as could be induced to accept employment in the mills; but such was the general dislike to that occupation at the time, that, with a few exceptions, only persons destitute of friends, employment and character, were found willing to try the experiment; and of these a sufficient number to supply a constant increase of the manufactory could not be obtained. It was therefore deemed a favour on the part even of such individuals to reside at the village, and, when taught the business, they grew so valuable to the establishment, that

37

they became agents not to be governed contrary to their own inclinations.

Mr Dale's principal avocations were at a distance from the works, which he seldom visited more than once for a few hours in three or four months; he was therefore under the necessity of committing the management of the establishment to various servants with more or less power.

Those who have a practical knowledge of mankind will readily anticipate the character which a population so collected and constituted would acquire. It is therefore scarcely necessary to state, that the community by degrees was formed under these circumstances into a very wretched society: every man did that which was right in his own eyes, and vice and immorality prevailed to a monstrous extent. The population lived in idleness, in poverty, in almost every kind of crime; consequently, in debt, out of health, and misery . . .

The boarding-house containing the children presented a very different scene. The benevolent proprietor spared no expense to give comfort to the poor children. The rooms provided for them were spacious, always clean, and well ventilated; the food was abundant, and of the best quality; the clothes were neat and useful; a surgeon was kept in constant pay, to direct how to prevent or cure disease; and the best instructors which the country afforded were appointed to teach such branches of education as were deemed likely to be useful to children in their situation. Kind and well-disposed persons were appointed to superintend all their proceedings. Nothing, in short, at first sight seemed wanting to render it a most complete charity.

But to defray the expense of these well-devised arrangements, and to support the establishment generally, it was absolutely necessary that the children should be employed within the mills from six o'clock in the morning till seven in the evening, summer and winter; and after these hours their education commenced. The directors of the public charities, from mistaken economy, would not consent to send the children under their care to cotton mills, unless the children were received by the proprietors at the ages of six, seven, and eight. And Mr Dale was under the necessity of accepting them at these ages, or of stopping the manufactory which he had commenced.

It is not to be supposed that children so young could remain, with the intervals of meals only, from six in the morning until seven in the evening, in constant employment, on their feet, within cotton mills, and afterwards acquire much proficiency in education. And so it proved;

for many of them became dwarfs in body and mind, and some of them were deformed. Their labour through the day and their education at night became so irksome, that numbers of them continually ran away, and almost all looked forward with impatience and anxiety to the expiration of their apprenticeship of seven, eight, and nine years, which generally expired when they were from thirteen to fifteen years old. At this period of life, unaccustomed to provide for themselves, and unacquainted with the world, they usually went to Edinburgh or Glasgow, where boys and girls were soon assailed by the innumerable temptations which all large towns present, and to which many of them fell sacrifices.

Thus Mr Dale's arrangements, and his kind solicitude for the comfort and happiness of these children, were rendered in their ultimate effect almost nugatory. They were hired by him and sent to be employed, and without their labour he could not support them; but, while under his care, he did all that any individual, circumstanced as he was, could do for his fellow-creatures. The error proceeded from the children being sent from the workhouses at an age much too young for employment. They ought to have been detained four years longer, and educated; and then some of the evils which followed would have been prevented.

If such be a true picture, not overcharged, of parish apprentices to our manufacturing system, under the best and most humane regulations, in what colours must it be exhibited under the worst?

Mr Dale was advancing in years; he had no son to succeed him; and it is not surprising that he became disposed to retire from the cares of the establishment. He accordingly sold it [in 1799] to some English merchants and manufacturers; one of whom undertook the management of the concern, and fixed his residence in the midst of the population. This individual [i.e. Robert Owen] had been previously in the management of large establishments, employing a number of work-people, in the neighbourhood of Manchester; and, in every case, by the steady application of certain general principles, he succeeded in reforming the habits of those under his care, and who always, among their associates in similar employment, appeared conspicuous for their good conduct. With this previous success in remodelling English character, but ignorant of the local ideas, manners, and customs, of those now committed to his management, the stranger commenced his task.

At that time the lower classes in Scotland, like those of other countries, had strong prejudices against strangers having any authority over them, and particularly against the English, few of whom had then settled in Scotland, and not one in the neighbourhood of the scenes under description . . . In consequence, from the day he arrived amongst them every means which ingenuity could devise was set to work to counteract the plan which he attempted to introduce . . . He, however, did not lose his patience, his temper, or his confidence in the certain success of the principles on which he founded his conduct.

Slowly and cautiously the population began to give him some portion of their confidence; and as this increased, he was enabled more and more to develop his plans for their amelioration. It may with truth be said, that at this period they possessed almost all the vices and very few of the virtues of a social community. Theft and the receipt of stolen goods was their trade, idleness and drunkenness their habit, falsehood and deception their garb, dissensions, civil and religious, their daily practice; they united only in a zealous systematic opposition to their employers.

Here then was a fair field on which to try the efficacy in practice of principles supposed capable of altering any characters. The manager formed his plans accordingly. He spent some time in finding out the full extent of the evil against which he had to contend, and in tracing the true causes which had produced and were continuing those effects. He found that all was distrust, disorder, and disunion; and he wished to introduce confidence, regularity, and harmony. He therefore began to bring forward his various expedients to withdraw the unfavourable circumstances by which they had hitherto been surrounded, and to replace them by others calculated to produce a more happy result. He soon discovered that theft was extended through all the ramifications of the community, and the receipt of stolen goods through all the country around. To remedy this evil, not one legal punishment was inflicted, not one individual imprisoned, even for an hour; but checks and other regulations of prevention were introduced; a short plain explanation of the immediate benefits they would derive from a different conduct was inculcated by those instructed for the purpose, who had the best powers of reasoning among themselves. They were at the same time instructed how to direct their industry in legal and useful occupations, by which, without danger or disgrace, they could really earn more than they had previously obtained by dishonest practices. Thus the difficulty of committing crime was increased, the detection afterwards rendered more easy, the habit of honest industry formed, and the pleasure of good conduct experienced.

Drunkenness was attacked in the same manner; it was discountenanced on every occasion by those who had charge of any department; its destructive and pernicious effects were frequently stated by his own more prudent comrades, at the proper moment when the individual was soberly suffering from the effects of his previous excess; pot and public houses were gradually removed from the immediate vicinity of their dwellings; the health and comfort of temperance were made familiar to them: by degrees drunkenness disappeared, and many who were habitual bacchanalians are now conspicuous for undeviating sobriety.

Falsehood and deception met with a similar fate: they were held in disgrace: their practical evils were shortly explained; and every countenance was given to truth and open conduct. . . .

Dissensions and quarrels were undermined by analogous expedients. When they could not be readily adjusted between the parties themselves, they were stated to the manager; and as in such cases both disputants were usually more or less in the wrong, that wrong was in as few words as possible explained, forgiveness and friendship recommended, and one simple and easily remembered precept inculcated, as the most valuable rule for their whole conduct, and the advantages of which they would experience every moment of their lives; viz.:—'That in future they should endeavour to use the same active exertions to make each other happy and comfortable, as they had hitherto done to make each other miserable; and by carrying this short memorandum in their mind, and applying it on all occasions, they would soon render that place a paradise, which, from the most mistaken principle, of action, they now made the abode of misery.' The experiment was tried; the parties enjoyed the gratification of this new mode of conduct; references rapidly subsided; and now serious differences are scarcely known . . .

The same principles were applied to correct the irregular intercourse of the sexes: such conduct was discountenanced and held in disgrace; fines were levied upon both parties for the use of the support fund of the community. (This fund arose from each individual contributing one-sixtieth part of their wages, which, under their management, was applied to support the sick, the injured by accident, and the aged.) But . . . the door was left open for them to return to the comforts of kind friends and respected acquaintances . . .

The system of receiving apprentices from public charities was abolished; permanent settlers with large families were encouraged, and comfortable houses built for their accommodation. The practice of employing children in the mills, of six, seven, and eight years of age, was discontinued, and their parents advised to allow them to acquire health and education until they were ten years old ... The children were taught reading, writing, and arithmetic during five years, that is, from five to ten, in the village school, without expense to their parents ...

During the period that these changes were going forward, attention was given to the domestic arrangements of the community. Their houses were rendered more comfortable, their streets were improved, the best provisions were purchased, and sold to them at low rates, yet covering the original expense, and under such regulations as taught them how to proportion their expenditure to their income. Fuel and clothes were obtained for them in the same manner; and no advantage was attempted to be taken of them, or means used to deceive them ... They were taught to be rational, and they acted rationally. Thus both parties experienced the incalculable advantages of the system which had been adopted. Those employed became industrious, temperate, healthy, faithful to their employers, and kind to each other; while the proprietors were deriving services ... far beyond those which could be obtained by any other means than those of mutual confidence and kindness ...

From ROBERT OWEN, *A New View of Society* (1831), Second Essay.

FACTORY LIFE AND PEOPLE

(a) LIVING CONDITIONS

As the factories multiplied, at first along the banks of streams and rivers and then, with the adoption of steam power, in populous towns, they called into being a new class of human society. It was in the towns of the industrial belt that stretched from Lancashire into Yorkshire, in the Scottish lowlands and in the valleys of South Wales, that the British proletariat was born.

Their existence, the conditions in which they lived and worked and died, aroused the wonder of the many who did not share their experiences, and the intense concern of a few brave spirits who had somehow become possessed of a social conscience. Such a man, to take a classic case, was the Manchester doctor, James Phillips Kay.

Kay was a Lancashire man himself, born in Rochdale in 1804, when the factory system was just getting into its stride. He studied medicine at Edinburgh, where he qualified a brilliant MD in 1827. He settled in Manchester, where he was medical officer to dispensaries at Ancoats and Ardwick, and here, as at Edinburgh, he made a close study of the ways of life of his poorer patients. It is recorded that in 1832 when the cholera first made its appearance, Kay was assiduous in his attendance on the sufferers, most of whom were in the grossly overcrowded and desperately insanitary quarters of the town. In that same year he published a small book, or pamphlet, on *The Moral and Physical Condition of the Working Classes employed in the Cotton Manufacture in Manchester*, which for factual detail must be given a high place in the literature of social investigation (No. 1). To meet the possible objection that he did not give the whole truth about the manufacturing population in general, Dr Kay included an 'advertisement', informing 'the Stranger, that the investigations on whose results the conclusions of this pamphlet are founded, were of necessity conducted in the township of Manchester only; and that the inhabitants of a great part of the adjacent townships are in a condition superior to that described'.

Sometimes Kay is hard to find in the reference books. This is because when he married in 1842 Miss Janet Shuttleworth, a Lancashire heiress, of Gawthorpe Hall, near Burnley, he was granted permission by royal licence to assume her name and arms. His philanthropic efforts came to the notice of the Government, and in 1835 he was appointed an assistant Poor Law Commissioner. This led to his taking an interest in education, and in 1839 he started the Battersea College for the training of elementary school teachers. He was made a baronet in 1849, and as Sir James Kay-Shuttleworth he has an honoured place in history as founder of the modern English system of popular education. He died in 1877.

Following the extracts from Kay's little work come some further passages from Gaskell (No. 2: the side-headings are the Editor's), and the other documents in this section add detail to the pictures so carefully drawn by our two doctors.

I

Manchester Cotton Operatives

The township of Manchester chiefly consists of dense masses of houses, inhabited by the population engaged in the great manufactories of the cotton trade. Some of the central divisions are occupied by warehouses and shops, and a few streets by the dwellings of the more wealthy inhabitants; but the opulent merchants chiefly reside in the country, and even the superior servants of their establishments inhabit the suburbal townships.

Manchester, properly so called, is chiefly inhabited by shopkeepers and the labouring classes. Those districts where the poor dwell are of very recent origin. The rapid growth of the cotton manufacture has attracted hither operatives from every part of the kingdom, and Ireland has poured forth the most destitute of her hordes to supply the constantly increasing demand for labour.

This immigration has been, in one important respect, a serious evil. The Irish have taught the labouring classes of this country a pernicious lesson. The system of cottier farming, the demoralization and barbarism of the people, and the general use of the potato as the chief article of food, have encouraged the population in Ireland more rapidly than the *available* means of subsistence have been increased. Debased alike by ignorance and pauperism, they have discovered, with the savage, what is the minimum of the means of life, upon which existence may be prolonged. They have taught this fatal secret to the population of this country . . .

When this example is considered in connexion with the unremitted labour of the whole population engaged in the various branches of the cotton manufacture, our wonder will be less excited by their fatal demoralization. Prolonged and exhausting labour, continued from day to day, and from year to year, is not calculated to develop the intellectual or moral faculties of man. The dull routine of a ceaseless drudgery, in which the same mechanical process is incessantly repeated, resembles the torment of Sisyphus—the toil, like the rock, recoils perpetually on the wearied operative. The mind gathers neither stores nor strength from the constant extension and retraction of the same muscles. The intellect slumbers in supine inertness; but the grosser parts of our nature attain a rank development. To condemn man to such severity of toil is, in some measure, to cultivate in him the habits of an animal . . .

Having been subjected to the prolonged labour of an animal—his physical energy wasted—his mind in supine inaction—the artizan has neither moral dignity nor intellectual nor organic strength to resist the seductions of appetite. His wife and children, too frequently subjected to the same process, are unable to cheer his remaining moments of leisure. Domestic economy is neglected, domestic comforts are unknown. A meal of the coarsest food is prepared with heedless haste and devoured with equal precipitation. Home has no other relation to him than that of shelter—few pleasures are there—it chiefly presents to him a scene of physical exhaustion, from which he is glad to escape. Himself impotent of all the distinguishing aims of his species, he sinks into sensual sloth, or revels in more degrading licentiousness. His house is ill furnished, uncleanly, often ill ventilated, perhaps damp; his food, from want of forethought and domestic economy, is meagre and innutritious; he is debilitated and hypochondriacal, and falls the victim of dissipation . . .

JAMES PHILLIPS KAY (later Sir James Kay-Shuttleworth), M.D., *The Moral and Physical Condition of the Working Classes employed in the Cotton Manufacture in Manchester* (1832), pp. 6–11.

2

England's Manufacturing Population

Personal Appearance. The vast deterioration in personal form which has been brought about in the manufacturing population, during the last thirty years, a period not extending over one generation, is singularly impressive, and fills the mind with contemplations of a very painful character . . .

Any man who has stood at twelve o'clock at the single narrow doorway, which serves as the place of exit for the hands employed in the great cotton-mills, must acknowledge that an uglier set of men and women, of boys and girls, taken them in the mass, it would be impossible to congregate in a smaller compass. Their complexion is sallow and pallid—with a peculiar flatness of feature, caused by the want of a proper quantity of adipose substance to cushion out the cheeks. Their stature low—the average height of four hundred men, measured at different times, and at different places, being five feet six inches. Their limbs slender, and playing badly and ungracefully. A very general bowing of the legs. Great numbers of girls and women walking lamely or awkwardly, with raised chests and spinal flexures. Nearly all have flat feet, accompanied with a down-tread, differing very widely from the elasticity of action in the foot and ancle, attendant upon perfect formation. Hair thin and straight—many of the men having but little beard, and that in patches of a few hairs, much resembling its growth among the red men of America. A spiritless and dejected air, a sprawling and wide action of the legs, and an appearance, taken as a whole, giving the world but 'little assurance of a man', or if so, 'most sadly cheated of his fair proportions'.

The Daily Round. The mode of life which the system of labour pursued in manufactories forces upon the operative, is one singularly unfavourable to domesticity.

Rising at or before day-break, between four and five o'clock the year round, scarcely refreshed by his night's repose, he swallows a hasty meal, or hurries to the mill without taking any food whatever. At eight o'clock half an hour, and in some instances forty minutes, are allowed for breakfast. In many cases, the engine continues at work during mealtime, obliging the labourer to eat and still overlook his work. This, however, is not universal. This meal is brought to the mill, and generally consists of weak tea, of course nearly cold, with a little bread; in other instances, of milk-and-meal porridge. Tea, however, may be called the universal breakfast, flavoured of late years too often with gin or other stimulants.

Where the hands live in immediate proximity to the mill, they visit home; but this rarely happens, as they are collected from all parts, some far, some near; but the majority too remote to leave the mill for that purpose. After this he is incessantly engaged—not a single minute of rest or relaxation being allowed him.

At twelve o'clock the engine stops, and an hour is given for dinner. The hands leave the mill, and seek their homes, where this meal is usually taken. It consists of potatoes boiled, very often eaten alone; sometimes with a little bacon, and sometimes with a portion of animal food. This latter is, however, only found at the tables of the more provident and reputable workmen. If, as it often happens, the majority of the labourers reside at some distance, a great portion of the allotted time is necessarily taken up by the walk, or rather run, backwards and forwards.

No time is allowed for the observances of ceremony. The meal has been imperfectly cooked, by some one left for that purpose, not unusually a mere child, or superannuated man or woman. The entire family surround the table, if they possess one, each striving which can most rapidly devour the miserable fare before them, which is sufficient, by its quantity, to satisfy the cravings of hunger, but possesses little nutritive quality . . . As soon as this is effected, the family is again scattered. No rest has been taken; and even the exercise, such as it is, is useless, from its excess, and even harmful, being taken at a time when repose is necessary for the digestive operations.

Again they are closely immured from one o'clock till eight or nine, with the exception of twenty minutes, this being allowed for tea, or baggin-time, as it is called. This imperfect meal is almost universally taken in the mill: it consists of tea and wheaten bread, with very few exceptions. During the whole of this long period they are actively and unremittingly engaged in a crowded room and an elevated temperature, so that, when finally dismissed for the day, they are exhausted equally in body and mind.

It must be remembered, that father, mother, son, and daughter, are alike engaged; no one capable of working is spared to make home (to which, after a day of such toil and privation, they are hastening) comfortable and desirable. No clean and tidy wife appears to welcome her husband—no smiling and affectionate mother to receive her children —no home, cheerful and inviting, to make it regarded. On the contrary, all assemble there equally jaded; it is miserably furnished—dirty and squalid in its appearance. Another meal, sometimes of a better quality, is now taken, and they either seek that repose which is so much needed, or leave home in the pursuit of pleasure or amusements, which still further tend to increase the evils under which they unavoidably labour.

Food and Drink. The staple diet of the manufacturing population is potatoes and wheaten bread, washed down by tea or coffee. Milk is but little used. Meal is consumed to some extent, either baked into cakes or boiled up with water, making a porridge at once nutritious, easy of digestion, and easily cooked. Animal food forms a very small part of their diet, and that which is eaten is often of an inferior quality. In the class of fine spinners and others, whose wages are very liberal, flesh meat is frequently added to their meals. Fish is bought to some extent, though by no means very largely; and even this not till it has undergone slight decomposition, having been first exposed in the markets, and, being unsaleable, is then hawked about the back streets and alleys, where it is disposed of for a mere trifle. Herrings are eaten not unusually; and though giving a relish to their otherways tasteless food, are not very well fitted for their use. The process of salting, which hardens the animal fibre, renders it difficult of digestion, dissolving slowly, and their stomachs do not possess the most active or energetic character. Eggs, too, form some portion of the operatives' diet. The staple, however, is tea and bread. Little trouble is required in preparing them for use; and this circumstance, joined to the want of proper domestic arrangements, favours their extensive use amongst a class so improvident and careless as the operative manufacturers.

House Furnishings. The houses of great numbers of the labouring community in the manufacturing districts present many of the traces of savage life. Filthy, unfurnished, deprived of all the accessories to decency and comfort, they are indeed but too truly an index of the vicious and depraved lives of their inmates. What little furniture is found in them is of the rudest and most common sort, and very often in fragments,—one or two rush-bottomed chairs, a deal table, a few stools, broken earthenware, such as dishes, tea-cups, etc., one or more tin kettles and cans, a few knives and forks, a piece of broken iron, serving as a poker, no fender, a bedstead or not, as the case may happen to be, blankets and sheets in the strict meaning of the words unknown —their place often being made up of sacking, a heap of flocks, or a bundle of straw, supplying the want of a proper bedstead and feather bed, and all these cooped in a single room, which serves as a place for domestic and household occupations.

Housing Arrangements. In those divisions of the manufacturing towns occupied by the lower classes of inhabitants, whether engaged in mill-labour alone, or in mill-labour conjointly with hand-loom weaving, the houses are of the most flimsy and imperfect structure. Tenanted by the week by an improvident and changeable set of beings, the owners seldom lay out any money upon them, and seem indeed only anxious that they should be tenantable at all, long enough to reimburse them for the first outlay. Hence in a very few years they become ruinous to a degree.

One of the circumstances in which they are especially defective, is that of drainage and water-closets. Whole ranges of these houses are either totally undrained, or only very partially . . . The whole of the washings and filth from these consequently are thrown into the front or back street, which being often unpaved and cut up into deep ruts, allows them to collect into stinking and stagnant pools; while fifty, or more even than that number, having only a single convenience common to them all, it is in a very short time completely choked up with excrementitious matter. No alternative is left to the inhabitants but adding this to the already defiled street, and thus leading to a violation of all those decencies which shed a protection over family morals.

It very frequently happens that one tenement is held by several families, one room, or at most two, being generally looked upon as affording sufficient convenience for all the household purposes of four or five individuals. The demoralizing effects of this utter absence of social and domestic privacy must be seen before they can be thoroughly understood, or their extent appreciated. By laying bare all the wants and actions of the sexes, it strips them of outward regard for decency —modesty is annihilated—the father and the mother, the brother and the sister, the male and female lodger, do not scruple to commit acts in the presence of each other, which even the savage hides from the eyes of his fellows . . .

Many of these ranges of houses are built back to back, fronting one way into a narrow court, across which the inmates of the opposite houses may shake hands without stepping out of their own doors; and the other way, into a back street, unpaved and unsewered. Most of these houses have cellars beneath them, occupied—if it is possible to find a lower class—by a still lower class than those living above them.

Foul Language. The brutalizing agency of this mode of life is very thoroughly displayed in the language employed by the manufacturing population, young and old alike. Coarse and obscene expressions are their household words; indecent allusions are heard proceeding from the lips of brother to sister, and from sister to brother. The infant lisps words which, by common consent, are banished from general society. Epithets are bandied from mother to child, and from child to mother, and between child and child, containing the grossest terms of indecency. Husband and wife address each other in a form of speech which would be disgraceful to a brothel—and these things may be imputed in a very considerable degree to the promiscuous way in which families herd together.

Smoking and Drinking. Tobacco is very largely consumed by the male and female labourers indiscriminately; hundreds of men and women may be daily seen inhaling the fumes of this extraordinary plant, by means of short and blackened pipes. Smoking, too, is an almost universal accompaniment to drinking—a pernicious habit, prevailing to a frightful extent in this portion of the population . . . In Manchester alone there are very near if not quite one thousand inns, beer-houses, and gin-vaults. Of these more than nine-tenths are kept open exclusively for the supply of the labouring population, placed in situations calculated for their convenience, decked out with everything that can allure them, crowded into back streets and alleys, or flaunting with the most gaudy and expensive decorations in the great working thoroughfares.

They are open at the earliest hour, when the shivering artizan is proceeding to his work, holding out to him a temptation utterly irresistible—and remain open during a considerable portion of the night ministering their poisons to thousands of debilitated creatures . . .

Nor is it the adult male labourer who alone visits these receptacles for everything that is wicked and degraded. Alas! no. The mother with her wailing child, the girl in company with her sweetheart, the mother in company with her daughter, the father with his son, the grey-haired grandsire with his half-clad grand-child, all ages come here—herding promiscuously with prostitutes, pickpockets, the very scum and refuse of society—all jumbled up together in an heterogeneous mass of evil . . .

The Abominable Irish. From some recent inquiries on the subject, it would appear, that upwards of 20,000 individuals live in cellars in Manchester alone. These are generally Irish families—handloom weavers, bricklayers' labourers, etc., etc., whose children are beggars or matchsellers in conjunction with their mothers. The crowds of beings that emerge from these dwellings every morning are truly astonishing, and present very little variety as to respectability of appearance; all are ragged, all are filthy, all are squalid . . . The domestic habits of these improvident creatures are vile in the extreme . . . The Irish cottier has brought with him his disgusting domestic companion the pig; for whenever he can scrape together a sufficient sum for the purchase of one of these animals, it becomes an inmate of his cellar . . .

Lodging-House Horrors. Another fertile source of the licentiousness in domestic manners, exists in the number of lodging-houses, which are very abundant in all the manufacturing districts. By a survey made in Manchester in 1832, there were found very near three hundred of these houses . . . The extraordinary sights presented by these lodging-houses during the night, are deplorable in the extreme. Five, six, seven beds are arranged on the floor—there being in the generality of cases, no bedsteads, or any substitutes for them; these are covered with clothing of the most scanty and filthy description. They are occupied indiscriminately by persons of both sexes, strangers perhaps to each other, except a few of the regular occupants. Young men and young women; men, wives, and their children—all lying in a noisome atmosphere, swarming with vermin, and often intoxicated . . .

P. GASKELL, *The Manufacturing Population of England* (1833), chs. 4, 5.

3

A Manchester Housewife's Weekly Budget

Mrs B., Manchester. This witness was accidentally met with, 13th May, 1844. She was waiting for Dr Hawkins, to consult him about her niece's health. I took her into a room, and examined her about the customs and comforts of operative families. I consider her evidence to be a specimen, somewhat under the average, of the way in which an operative family lives.

Her husband is a fine spinner, at Mr——, where he has been from 1816; has five children. Her eldest daughter, now going 14, has been her father's piecer for three years. At her present age, her labour is worth 4s 6d a week. At present her husband's earnings and her daughter's together amount to about 25s a week—at least she sees no more than 25s a week; and before her daughter could piece for him, and when he had to pay for a piecer in her stead, he only brought home 19s or 20s a week. (N.B. Whatever sum her husband may bring her home, his earnings as a fine spinner at Mr M's are certainly not less than 28s per week.)

Breakfast is generally porridge, bread and milk, lined with flour or oatmeal. On Sunday, a cup of tea and bread and butter.—*Dinner*, on week days, potatoes and bacon, and bread, which is generally white. On a Sunday, a little flesh meat; no butter, egg, or pudding.—*Tea-time* every day, tea, and bread and butter; nothing extra on Sunday at tea.—*Supper*, oatmeal porridge and milk; sometimes potatoes and milk. Sunday, sometimes a little bread and cheese for supper; never have this on week days. Now and then buys eggs when they are as low as a halfpenny apiece, and fries them to bacon.

*Consumption by the Week, of different Articles, by
her Husband, herself, and five Children*

	£	s	d
Butter, 1½ lb. at 10d		1	3
Tea, 1½ oz.			4½
Bread she makes herself; buys 24 lb. of flour, barm, salt, and baking, cost		4	6
Half a peck of oatmeal			6½
Bacon 1½ lb.			9
Potatoes, two score a week, at 8d a score		1	4
Milk, a quart a day, at 3d a quart		1	9
Flesh meat on Sunday, about a pound			7
Sugar, 1½ lb. a week at 6d			9
Pepper, mustard, salt, and extras, say			3
Soap and candles		1	0
Coals		1	6
Rent of house, per week		3	6
		18	1
Alleged total of weekly income	1	5	0
Deduct foregoing expenses		18	1
Leaves for clothing, sickness of seven persons, schooling, etc., a surplus of		6	11

They never taste any other vegetable than potatoes; never use any beer or spirits; now and then may take a gill of beer when ill, which costs a penny. Perhaps she and her husband may have two gills a week. Her husband never drinks any beer or spirits that she knows of beyond this.

The house consists of four rooms, two on each floor; the furniture consists of two beds in the same room, one for themselves and the other for the children; have four chairs, one table in the house, boxes to put clothes in, no chest of drawers, two pans and a tea-kettle for boiling, a gridiron and frying-pan, half-a-dozen large and small plates, four pair of knives and forks, several pewter spoons.

They subscribe a penny a week for each child to a funeral society for the children.

Two of the children go to school at 3d a week each; they are taught reading for this, but not writing. Have a few books, such as a Bible, hymn-book, and several small books that the children have got as prizes at the Sunday school.

*   *   *

Read over this account to S.L., an operative, and a respectable witness on their side. He thinks it somewhat below the average of comforts possessed by the working family. The generality, he thinks, have tea and coffee for breakfast, instead of porridge, and that their dinners are generally fresh meat; and he says, that factory families may be divided into two classes, in respect of living,—those in which the parents work in mills as well as the children, and those in which only the children work in mills. The first class live better than the second. (May 26, 1833.)

From the examinations taken by MR COWELL in the Lancashire District; Factory Commission Report; P.P. 1833, vol. XX, D 1, pp. 39–40.

4

A Clock in the Parlour

———

If we look back to the condition of the mass of the people as it existed in this country, even so recently as the beginning of the present century, and then look around us at the indications of greater comfort and respectability that meet us on every side, it is hardly possible to doubt that here, in England at least, the elements of social improvement have been successfully at work, and that they have been and are producing an increased amount of comfort to the great bulk of the people . . .

In nothing is the improvement more apparent than in the condition of the dwellings of the middle class . . . but it has not extended in an equal degree to those of the working classes. These, especially in large towns, are for the most part comfortless, and even unwholesome, ill furnished and ill kept, betraying a lamentable want of self-respect in their inmates, with a degree of recklessness that speaks unfavourably for their moral progress . . . It is worthy of remark, that this comfortless condition of the dwellings of the poor is not seen in all localities. In some places where no other appearances in the state of society would seem to indicate it, there is to be found an extraordinary degree of respectability in this particular. The town of Sheffield, for instance, contains a large manufacturing population, by no means remarkable for orderly conduct. The town itself is ill built and dirty, beyond the usual condition of English towns, but it is the custom for each family among the labouring population to occupy a separate dwelling, the rooms in which are furnished in a very comfortable manner, the floors are carpeted, and the tables are usually of mahogany; chests of drawers of the same material are commonly seen, and so in most cases is a clock also, the possession of which article of furniture has often been pointed out as the certain indication of prosperity and personal respectability on the part of the working man.

G. R. PORTER, *The Progress of the Nation* (1847), pp. 532–33.

5

Housing Conditions of the Factory Workers

On the early introduction of the cotton manufacture, the parties who entered into it were often men of limited capital, and anxious to invest the whole of it in mills and machinery, and therefore too much absorbed with the doubtful success of their own affairs to look after the necessities of their workpeople.

Families were attracted from all parts for the benefit of employment, and obliged as a temporary resort to crowd together into such dwellings as the neighbourhood afforded: often two families into one house; others into cellars or very small dwellings; eventually, as the works became established, either the proprietor or some neighbour would probably see it advantageous to build a few cottages; these were often of the worst description: in such case the prevailing consideration was not how to promote the health and comfort of the occupants, but how many cottages could be built upon the smallest space of ground and at the least possible cost.

Whatever the weekly income, the wife could never make such a house comfortable; she had only one room in which to do all her work;

55

it may be readily supposed the husband would not always find the comfort he wished in such a home. The public-house would then be his only resort. But here the evil does not end; the children brought up in such dwellings knew no better accommodation than such afforded, nor had they any opportunities of seeing better domestic arrangements.

Report on Sanitary Condition of the Labouring Population: Lords Sessional Reports, 1842, vol. 26, p. 239.

6

Mr Ashworth's Cottages

About twelve years ago we had occasion to introduce a considerable number of families into some new houses; in the course of a few months a most malignant fever broke out amongst them, and went from house to house, till we became seriously alarmed for the safety of the whole establishment. We instituted an inquiry into the state of the houses where the fever first appeared, and found that from the low habits of the occupants, and the ignorance of the proper decencies of life, the cottages were in so filthy a state that it was apparent that we should not long be free from a recurrence of the same evil unless we took some active means to effect a change in the habits of these people.

Although we felt very unwilling to do anything which appeared to interfere with the domestic management of our workpeople, still the urgency of the case at the time seemed to warrant such a step. We therefore ordered an examination of every cottage in our possession, both as regards cleanliness and ventilation, as well as bedding and furniture. The striking difference exhibited in the state of these cottages, the neatness and cleanness of some, the gross neglect of others, appearing to have no relation to the amount of income, convinced us that an occasional repetition of these visits would be essential in order to effect any permanent improvement amongst them.

These periodical visits have now been continued through a series of years; and as no evident distinction or selection was ever made, do not appear to have been viewed in the light of an intrusion; a week or two of notice being mostly given, a laudable degree of emulation has been excited as to whose bedding and furniture should be found in the best order; my brother or myself have occasionally joined in these visits.

Having had such opportunity of observing the great inconvenience arising from small dwellings where the families are large, both as regards bed-rooms and living-rooms, few cottages having more than two bed-rooms; and where there were children or young persons of both sexes, the indelicacy of this arrangement was apparent; we therefore concluded to build larger cottages, and make them with three bed-rooms each. These houses were sought after with great avidity, and families allowed to moved into them as an especial favour; the increase [in] rent of 1s to 1s 6d per week was a small consideration in regard to the additional comfort to a family where the income was from 24s to 50s or 60s per week, as is frequently the case with families employed in manufactures.

HENRY ASHWORTH, of Turton, near Bolton; P.P., Lords, 1842, vol. 26, p. 239.

(b) WORKING CONDITIONS

There can be no doubt that in the earlier phase of the Industrial Revolution the 'places of work', as the factories were generally called, were often abominable, and the only excuse that may be offered is, that the situation was a novel and altogether unprecedented one, and any improvements had to come out of hard and bitter experience.

Cobbett detested the factory system so much that he never set foot in a factory until near the end of his career. In his vigorous journalism he wrote of what others had told him, and his readers must have been disgusted and horrified by what he had to say (No. 1). If he wrote out of hearsay, James Leach did so out of his own experience. He was a factory worker before he became a printer and one of the leaders in Manchester of the Chartist agitation. His *Stubborn Facts* (No. 2) was not published until twenty years after Cobbett's indignant outburst, but it would seem that not much improvement had been effected in the interval.

The worst mills were undoubtedly those placed in remote parts, especially in Scotland. One of these was described, and not without reason, as resembling a 'receptacle of demons' (No. 3). The man responsible for the damning phrase was James Stuart (1775–1849), who is remembered for having killed in a duel Sir Alexander Boswell (eldest son of Dr Johnson's biographer) who had venomously assailed him in the press on account of his political views (he was a staunch Whig). He stood his trial in Edinburgh for murder—and was acquitted. After some years in America he returned to London, and did good work on the staff of the Factory Commission of 1833; another of his reports is quoted in No. 4, which makes much pleasanter reading. In 1836 he was appointed by Lord Melbourne, the Prime Minister, one of the new tribe of factory inspectors. Other Scottish mills are reported on in the medical reports made by Sir David Barry (1780–1835), an Irish surgeon who had seen service under Wellington in the Peninsular War and was of some note as a physiologist. The Factory Commission of 1833 employed him to investigate the sanitary conditions of some of the Scottish factories (No. 5).

On the whole, the English factories seem to have made the better showing, but it should be noted that most of the documents given here are of a fairly late date. Cobbett (No. 6) was agreeably surprised when he at length made his first visit to a factory, but then the mill he was taken to (Waterside Mills, Todmorden, West Riding) was one of the finest in the country. The Fielden Brothers were exemplary employers, and so was Mr Thomas Ashton, who received most favourable notice in Dr Kay's pamphlet, and also from Léon Faucher (No. 7), a distinguished French writer (and later statesman under Louis Napoleon), who visited England and wrote for a French newspaper a series of articles on industrial conditions that were translated into English under the title of *Manchester in 1844*. Mr Ashton's girls were provided with aprons to keep their clothes clean; Messrs. Greg's girls—apprentices drawn very largely from the Liverpool poor-house—had bacon every day for dinner. But there was even more to wonder at and to admire in the great mills at Saltaire, near Shipley, where Sir Titus Salt (1803–76), one of the first industrialists to be given the honour of knighthood, had built a splendid pile of buildings for the manufacture of alpaca and mohair, and alongside it a model town for his army of workpeople (No. 9).

These were among the businesses that attracted the public eye, but they were still the exceptions until well on into the century. The older mills, which were of course the great majority, left much to be desired. The arrangements for taking meals were generally most haphazard (No. 10), and nothing like sufficient attention was paid to the proper fencing of the machinery (No. 11), but even more reprehensible were the sanitary arrangements. In document after document we find mention of the deplorable condition of what were then usually described as privies, but also as necessaries, and even as bog-holes. Towards the end of our period the term water-closet is met with, but although a patent for a form of this convenience had been taken out by Joseph Bramah (better known for his locks) as early as 1778, they required for their functioning a proper water supply, and this was something that was still exceptional even in the middle of Victoria's reign. It was a frequent complaint of those who were concerned about public decency that in great numbers of factories there was no separation of the privy provision into what we should call 'Ladies' and 'Gents' (No. 12).

I

'Such Slavery, Such Cruelty'

Some of these lords of the loom have in their employ thousands of miserable creatures. In the cotton-spinning work, these creatures are kept, fourteen hours in each day, locked up, summer and winter, in a heat of from *eighty to eighty-four degrees*. The rules which they are subjected to are such as no negroes were ever subjected to . . .

Very seldom do we feel such a heat as this in England. The 31st of last August, and the 1st, 2nd, and 3rd of last September, were very hot days. The newspapers told us that men had dropped down dead in the harvest fields, and that many horses had fallen dead upon the road; and yet the heat during those days never exceeded eighty-four degrees in the *hottest part of the day*. We were retreating to the coolest rooms in our house; we were pulling off our coats, wiping the sweat off our faces, puffing, blowing, and panting, and yet we were living in a heat nothing like eighty degrees.

What, then, must be the situation of the poor creatures who are doomed to toil day after day, for three hundred and thirteen days in the year, fourteen hours in each day, in an average heat of eighty-two degrees? Can any man, with a heart in his body, and a tongue in his head, refrain from cursing a system that produces such slavery and such cruelty?

Observe, too, that these poor creatures have no cool room to retreat to, not a moment to wipe off the sweat, and not a breath of air to come and interpose itself between them and infection. The 'door of the place wherein they work, *is locked, except half an hour*, at tea-time, the workpeople are not allowed to send for water to drink, in the hot factory; even *the rain water is locked up*, by the master's order, otherwise they would be happy to drink even that. If any spinner be found with his *window open*, he is to pay a fine of a shilling! Mr Martin, of Galway, has procured acts of parliament to prevent *cruelty* to *animals*. If horses or dogs were shut up in a place like this, they would certainly be thought worthy of Mr Martin's attention.

Not only is there not a breath of sweet air in these truly infernal scenes, but, for a large part of the time, there is the abominable and pernicious stink of the *gas* to assist in the murderous effects of the heat. In addition to the noxious effluvia of the gas, mixed with the steam, there are the dust, and what is called cotton-flyings or fuz, which the unfortunate creatures have to inhale; and the fact is, the notorious fact is, that well constitutioned men are rendered old and past labour at forty years of age, and that children are rendered decrepit and deformed, and thousands upon thousands of them slaughtered by consumptions, before they arrive at the age of sixteen . . .

Nine hundred and ninety-nine thousandths of the people of England have not the most distant idea that such things are carried on, in a country calling itself free; in a country whose Minister for Foreign Affairs is everlastingly teasing and bothering other Powers to emulate England in 'her humanity', in abolishing the slave trade in the blacks. The blacks, when carried to the West Indies, are put into a paradise compared with the situation of these poor white creatures in Lancashire, and other factories of the North . . .

Then the immoralities engendered in these pestiferous scenes are notorious. . . . All experience proves, that the congregating of people together in great masses, is sure to be productive of impurity of thought and of manners. The country lad, who becomes a soldier, has a new soul in him by the time that he has passed a year in a barrack-room. Even in great schools, all experience tells us how difficult it is to prevent contagious immoralities. This is universally acknowledged. What, then, must be the consequences of heaping these poor creatures together in the cotton-factories? But, what more do we want; what other proof of the corrupting influence of these assemblages; what more than the following regulation, which I take from a list of fines, imposed at the factory of Tyldesley, in Lancashire? 'Any two spinners, *found together* in the *necessary*, each man . . . 1s.'

One is almost ashamed to put the thing on paper, though for the necessary purpose of exposing it to just indignation. To what a pitch must things have come; how familiar people must have become with infamy, before a master manufacturer could put such a thing into writing, and stick it up in his factory! . . .

WILLIAM COBBETT, *Political Register*, vol. LII, November 20, 1824.

2

Stubborn Facts from the Factories

In some factories none but women are allowed to labour, excepting a few men, such as managers . . . not because the women can perform the work better or turn off a greater quantity, but because they are considered to be more docile than men under the injustice that in some shape or form is daily practised upon them.

A great number of the females employed in factories are married, and not a small number of them are mothers. It frequently happens that the husband is refused work in the same mill with the wife; under these circumstances the poor creature is obliged to leave her husband in bed at five o'clock in the morning, while she hurries off to the mill to undergo her daily repetition of drudgery, in order to procure a scanty portion of food for her husband, herself, and her helpless children. We have repeatedly seen married females, in the last stage of pregnancy, slaving from morning till night beside these never-tiring machines, and when oppressed nature became so exhausted that they were obliged to sit down to take a moment's ease, and being seen by the manager, were fined *sixpence* for the offence. In some mills, the crime of sitting down to take a little rest is visited with a penalty of *one shilling*, but let the masters and their rules speak for themselves.

'1st. The door of the lodge will be closed ten minutes after the engine starts every morning, and no weaver will afterwards be admitted till breakfast-time. Any weaver who may be absent during that time shall forfeit three-pence per loom.

'2nd. Weavers absent at any other time when the engine is working, will be charged three-pence per hour each loom for such absence; and weavers leaving the room without the consent of the overlooker, shall forfeit three-pence . . .

'9th. All shuttles, brushes, oil-cans, wheels, windows, etc. if broken, shall be paid for by the weaver.

'11th. If any hand in the mill is seen *talking* to another, *whistling*, or *singing*, will be fined sixpence . . .

'12th. For every rod broken, one penny will be stopped . . .

16th. For every wheel that breaks, from one shilling to two and sixpence, according to size. Any weaver seen from his work during mill-hours, will be fined *sixpence*' . . .

It often happens that when the weaver goes to work in the morning, he finds the clock fifteen minutes forwarder than when he left in the evening. The hands on the factory clock do not always move from *internal wheels*, but very frequently from a little external aid; this always takes place after the hands have left the mill in the evening . . . The reader will best understand why this is done, when we inform him that *thirty* or *forty* people may be frequently seen at the lodge door locked out, in the morning, while the person with the *fine-book* has been through the rooms of the mill, taking down the numbers of the looms of those that were absent. On one occasion, we counted *ninety-five* persons that were thus locked out at half-past five o'clock in the morning. The way in which this method of *genteel robbery* was accomplished, was by putting the clock half an hour forward—that is, it was fifteen minutes later than the public clocks of the town in the evening, and fifteen minutes forwarder in the morning. These ninety-five persons were fined three-pence each . . .

At this mill, a short time ago, one of the cut-lookers was discharged, and another placed in his situation. When he had been there a fortnight, the master asked him, 'How it was that he had so little in his *bate book*'; the man replied, 'I think there's a great deal, I 'bate the weavers so much that I can't for shame look them in the face, when I meet them in the street'. The master answered, 'You be *d—d*, you are five pounds a week worse to *me* than the man that had this situation before you, and I'll kick you out of the place'. The man was discharged to make room for another *who knew his duty better*.

From *Stubborn Facts from the Factories by a Manchester Operative*, (James Leach), published and dedicated to the working classes by William Rashleigh, M.P. (1844), pp. 11–15.

3

'Receptacle of Demons'

It appears in evidence that in Scotland, and in the eastern part of England, where the harshest treatment of children has taken place, the greatest number of bad cases occur in the small obscure mills belonging to the smallest proprietors, and that the bad treatment is inflicted by violent and dissipated workmen, often the very men who raise the loudest outcry about the cruelties to which children are subject in factories.

A striking picture of a mill of this class, one of the very mills, indeed, in which various witnesses depose that the treatment is oftentimes harsh and brutal, is given by Mr Stuart [one of the Commissioners]:

'It seemed more to resemble a receptacle of demons than the workhouse of industrious human beings. We saw the workers, it must be admitted, at a moment not propitious for them, when they were only regaining their senses after the bacchanalian orgies of the previous evening and night, which had too obviously been spent in the riotous debauchery following a market or fair held at Bervie on the preceding day. The appearance and language of the workers, both men and women, proved the state of demoralization which exists here. The house of Gilchrist, the mill-owner, presented a picture of filth and want of comfort of every kind, such as I have rarely seen anywhere else. Those engaged in vicious courses . . . doubtless find a fit asylum here; but it was painful to find in the bothy, the eating and sleeping room of such a nest of profligates, two or three young females without a parent or relation there or in the neighbourhood to look after their conduct, or to make any attempt to rescue them.'

Report of the Central Board: Factories Commission, P.P. 1833, vol. XX, p. 20.

3. Factory Children going to work; from George Walker's *Costume of Yorkshire* (1814) (*photo*: The Mansell Collection)

4. Saltaire: the model alpaca mills and township built by Sir Titus Salt and opened in 1853; from a contemporary drawing by H. Warren

4

A Model Mill

Deanston Cotton-mill, near Doune, in Perthshire, is one of those beautifully situated and admirably regulated great manufacturing establishments which it is a pleasure to see, on account of the general arrangements of every department, as well as the happiness which a numerous population engaged in the pursuits of industry apparently enjoy.

The apartments in the mill are clean, well ventilated, and have the machinery well fenced . . . The windows, instead of being constructed in the usual way in many of the mills we have seen, so that only a single pane of glass in each window can be opened, are so hung that the whole of the upper pane of each window may be let down from the top, and a free current of air admitted. The general heat of the apartments is from 65° to 70°. There are forty spinners in an apartment 82 feet long by 52 in breadth.

There are here apartments for the females to dress and undress in, and a pipe of water in each story; sewering arrangement is adopted throughout the work that tends to the convenience and accommodation of the persons employed.

The workers live at the distance of about a mile from the works, with the exception of about a hundred of them, for whom the Company have built houses, let to them. There are bits of garden ground attached to each of the houses, and a drain has been constructed for carrying off every sort of filth. The whole arrangements about this extensive factory, at which cotton-spinning, power-weaving, iron-founding, and machine-making are carried on, are obviously made with a view as far as possible to the substantial comfort of the people, and a more cheerful, happy-looking set of industrious men and women, and of young people, is seldom, if I am not mistaken, to be found.

From MR JAMES STUART'S reports on Scottish factories; P.P. 1833, vol. XX, p. 16.

5

Scottish Contrasts

———————

At the Blantyre mills the spinners are all males. I visited the dwellings of nine of that class, without making any selection. Found that every one of them was married, and that the wife had been in every instance a mill girl, some of these women having begun factory work so early as at six and a half years of age. The number of children born to all these couples was 51; the number now living 46. As many of these children as are able, and can find vacancies, are employed in the mill. They all live in rooms rented from the owners, and are well lodged. I saw them at breakfast-time, and the meal was composed of porridge and milk for the children; coffee, eggs, bread, oaten cake, and butter, for the father.

*   *   *

New Lanark mills are particularly clean and carefully kept; there are even blinds to the southern windows; but they are deeply embosomed between two hills, approaching so closely, that the greater part of the village is built up against one of them, and must therefore be cold and damp on one side . . . A most extraordinary degree of attention is devoted to the education of the children of the workers here, candidates for admission to employment in the mills. They are taught reading, writing, with the elements of geography, music, dancing, natural history, etc., in fine spacious rooms. I witnessed considerable proficiency in some of these branches, and saw eight young persons, from ten to thirteen, dance a quadrille in the very best style, under their dancing-master. Employment in the mill is looked forward to by these children with much ambition, as the reward of diligence in their studies. It is quite clear that Mr Walker, the managing resident partner, devotes the kindest attention to his people: he is beloved by them all. About 300 of the eldest pupils pay 4d per month towards the expenses of their education; and there are 150 of the youngest, from three or four to eleven, who pay nothing.

The Catrine mills are in the very highest order. Several of the workers have built handsome houses in the village, and many are proprietors of houses and gardens which they have bought from the company . . .

*   *   *

The building (of Messrs Henry Monteith & Co.'s cotton-spinning and power-loom factory worked by water and steam power at Blantyre); charmingly situated on the left bank of the Clyde; planted, dry, and healthy. It is in part four stories, and in part five stories high, besides garret and cockloft. The height of the rooms is from 8 feet 5 inches to 6 feet 3 inches in the garret or cockloft. They are ventilated by means of sash windows, opening downwards. The night-soil falls into moveable receptacles, which are removed every day; there is one in each working-room, and the same privy is used by males and females. There are no washing, dressing, or eating rooms. The spinning-flats are close and hot, and there is an unpleasant smell about the privies. The rooms are whitewashed every year. There are no dust-fans in any of the rooms, nor have any improvements tending to promote health been effected in this mill since the year 1786.

SIR DAVID BARRY'S medical report; Factories Commission, 2nd Report, P.P. 1833, vol. XXI, A3, p. 53.

6

Cobbett's First Factory Visit

Here, at Todmorden, we are at the house, or, rather, houses of friends; friends whom we never knew before but who had the kindness to bespeak us at Manchester. I never was induced to go into a factory, in England before; but here is one for weaving by power-looms, belonging to the Messrs Fielding [Fielden], consisting of *one room* on a ground floor, which is of the surprising dimensions of a hundred and eighty feet square; and covering a statute acre of ground all but twenty-eight rods!

In this room, which is lighted from above, and in the most convenient and beautiful manner, there were five hundred pairs of looms at work, and five hundred persons attending those looms; and, owing to the goodness of the masters, the whole looking healthy and well-dressed.

WILLIAM COBBETT, *Political Register*, January 1830.

7

Aprons for Mr Ashton's Girls

The little town of Hyde was, at the commencement of the present century, a little hamlet, of only 800 souls, on the summit of a barren hill, the soil of which did not yield sufficient for the inhabitants. The brothers Ashton have peopled and enriched this desert. Ten thousand persons are now established in their five factories, and in which their daily wages are £1,000, or £300,000 per annum.

The head of this factory, Mr Thomas Ashton, has built himself a charming villa, in the midst of gardens and plantations; and on the other side of the road are two factories, situated between a torrent, which supplies the engines with water, and two coal mines, which furnish the fuel.

Mr T. Ashton employs 1500 work-people, of both sexes. One immense room, filled with looms, contains four hundred of them. The young women are well and decently clothed. A sort of large apron, extending from the shoulders to the feet, protects their outer garments from dirt . . .

The houses inhabited by the work-people form long and large streets. Mr Ashton has built three hundred of them, which he lets at 3s or 3s 6d per week. Each house contains upon the ground floor, a sitting-room, a kitchen, and a back yard, and above, are two or three bed-rooms. The proprietor furnishes, at his own charge, water to the houses, keeps them in good repair, and pays the local rates. As the value of a ton of coals is only eight or nine shillings, fuel is almost gratuitous. At all hours of the day there is warm water and a fire in each house. Everywhere is to be observed a cleanliness which bespeaks order and comfort. The furniture is simple, but sufficient; in some houses, a clock is to be seen; in others, a sofa; and in others again, a piano-forte. Books are plentiful, but I have seen few Bibles, and this seems to confirm that character for indifference in religious matters for which the work-people of Mr Ashton are celebrated . . .

LEON FAUCHER, *Manchester in 1844* (1844), pp. 105–107.

8

Bacon Every Day

At Quarry Bank, near Wilmslow, in Cheshire, is situated the oldest of the five establishments belonging to the great firm of Messrs Greg and Son, of Manchester, who work up the one-hundredth part of all the cotton consumed in Great Britain ...

At a little distance from the factory, on a sunny bank, stands a handsome house, two stories high, built for the accommodation of the female apprentices. Here are well fed, clothed, educated, and lodged, under kind superintendence, sixty young girls, who by their deportment in the mill, as well as in Wilmslow church on Sunday, evince a degree of comfort most creditable to the humane and intelligent proprietors ...

The female apprentices at Quarry Bank mill come partly from its own parish, but chiefly from the Liverpool poor-house ...Their ages vary from ten to twenty-one years. When they grow up they almost always marry some of the men belonging to the factory, often continue to work, and receive better wages than the other operatives, as they are obliged to take houses for themselves ...

The apprentices have milk-porridge for breakfast, potatoes and bacon for dinner, and butcher-meat on Sundays. They have bacon every day ...

ANDREW URE, M.D., *The Philosophy of Manufactures* (1835), pp. 346–348.

9

Saltaire Shows the World

About half a mile to the west of Shipley, in a delightful and salubrious part of Airedale, commanding an abundant supply of water from the river Aire, with the advantages of carriage upon the railway on one side of the buildings and the Leeds and Liverpool canal on the other, stands Saltaire, covering six acres of ground, with the well-planned town, built by Mr Salt, opposite . . .

The principal building, that appropriated to the spinning factory, includes six stories, and is intersected in the centre by the engine-house, containing four gigantic steam-engines, nominally of 400 horse-power, but really of the strength of 1200. The spinning-factory is constructed in the most massive style; the walls in thickness rivalling the Norman keeps of old, and supported by arches standing on iron pillars, and covered by a cast-iron roof, rendering the building consequently fire-proof.

Running at a right angle with the spinning establishment is the pile of buildings seven stories in height and 350 yards in length, devoted to the warehouses, and fitted with the most ingenious contrivances for conveying goods to and from various parts of the building . . . On each side of the warehouse, the ground is occupied with the preparing and weaving sheds, the latter containing upwards of one thousand looms of various descriptions . . . Under the floor of this shed the main shafting moving the machinery is placed, a plan which obviates any necessity for boxing or protecting it, to prevent accidents . . . Owing to the shafting and gearing working from under the floor, the room comprising an area of 8400 yards, is comparatively free from dust, and the giddy whirl of the shafting and gearing, and is certainly the most agreeable spot to work in that I have beheld in any factory.

The buildings constituting the west front are appropriated to counting-houses, dining rooms, warp-dressing rooms, and other suitable conveniences . . . The whole building is an example, that ornamental and graceful structures are not at all incompatible with the utilitarian purposes of a factory, but that both may be harmoniously combined . . .

A passing notice must be allotted to the manufacturing town raised for the accommodation of the workpeople, which number about 3000. The dwelling houses are built in a neat and convenient style, with especial attention to the health and comfort of the inmates, and well supplied with good water, and also with gas from the gasometer at Saltaire works, which is capable of yielding gas for 5000 lights.

Nor has the proprietor been unmindful of the improvement and recreation of the denizens of this new town, as mechanics' and other institutions to 'make the workman exult midst his toil', which have sprung up within its precincts, testify. Altogether, as the mill has been justly pronounced a 'model mill', this is a model town, and I hope that the operatives of Saltaire will become in sobriety, industry, and good conduct, a model to the whole of the manufacturing population of the world.

JOHN JAMES, *History of the Worsted Manufacture in England* (1857), p. 469.

10

'A bite and a run'

Occasionally, but not often, the work continues without intermission during the whole of the meal hours; the engine never stopping except about ten minutes to be oiled, and the workpeople 'eating how they can'. . . . 'Sometimes the breakfast would stand an hour and a half; sometimes we'd never touch it.' 'All in my room would rather stop, because the breakfast got covered with dust so.' 'No time for breakfast or tea; took it as they could; a bite and a run; sometimes not able to eat it from its being so covered with dust.' . . .

Where the practice of working during the whole of the meal hours prevails, the workpeople never leave the factory from the time they enter it in the morning until they have finished their work in the evening. What food they take is either prepared for them in the factory or brought to them already prepared by their friends. In some factories conveniences are gratuitously provided by the proprietors for cooking the food, and detached rooms are fitted up for the workpeople in which to wash, dress, and eat. Sometimes the school room in which the children are taught in the evening is appropriated as a dressing and eating room for the adults during the day. But in many cases there is no washing, dressing, or cooking rooms. There are no conveniences for cooking, except the steam-engine fires; and there is a deplorable want of comfort and cleanliness.

P.P. 1833, vol. XX, p. 10.

II

Dreadful Mutilations

The accidents which occur to the manufacturing population of Birmingham are very severe and numerous, as shown by the registers of the General Hospital. Many are the consequences of the want of proper attention to the fencing of machinery, which appears to be seldom thought of in the manufactories; and many are caused by loose portions of dress being caught by the machinery, so as to drag the unfortunate sufferers under its power. The shawls of the females, or their long hair, and the aprons and loose sleeves of the boys and men, are in this way frequent causes of dreadful mutilation.

Report on the Sanitary Condition of the Labouring Population; P.P. Lords, 1842, vol. 27, p. 208.

I2

Promiscuous Privies

Had the fact not been established by indubitable evidence, every one must have been slow to credit, that in this age and country the proprietors of extensive factories could have been indifferent to the well-being of their workpeople (for the matter is not one *merely* of convenience and comfort) to such a degree as is implied in the following statements:

'But one water-closet for both sexes, which children and men and women use indiscriminately.' 'Privies situated in view; common to males and females; this in his (witness's) opinion has a tendency to destroy shame, and conduces to immorality.' 'Workers complain of smells from water-closets.' 'Picking-rooms pretty well freed from dust by effective fanners; but there is a considerable annoyance to the workers from the effects of the water-closets; the effluvia must be unpleasant in warm weather; it made the walking through the apartments today very disagreeable in several places'; and yet this is the account given by one of the Commissioners of a factory stated to be 'remarkable as that at which the finest cotton is spun in Scotland . . .'

Factory Commission, 1st Report, P.P. 1833, vol. XX, p. 18.

* * *

A.B., employed in a pearl-button factory in Birmingham: In the manufactory, with 200 mechanics, there are only two privies, which were designed for the separate use of the men and women, but the fact is that they are promiscuously used by both sexes. Both these privies are in sight of three of the shops where men work. Has often seen, in consequence of the number of people, young girls and women, as many as half a dozen, waiting at the privies till the men come out. On these occasions it often happens that jesting takes place between the parties.

Children's Employment Commission, P.P. 1843, vol. XIV, page f 141.

CHILD LABOUR

(a) PARISH APPRENTICES

Child Labour was not an invention of the Industrial Revolution. From time immemorial children have been made to work for their living as soon as they were able, and the exploitation of children by their parents is no new thing either. But the Industrial Revolution did bring about great changes in the extent and character of juvenile labour.

For the first time in history children became important factors in the economic system. The manufacturers were crying out for hands to work in the new factories, and it was soon found that the nimble fingers of little children could be easily trained to perform a great variety of routine tasks. There was the further consideration that child labour was cheap.

To begin with, resort was had to the so-called free children, who had parents and homes to return to at night. But most of the factories were in sparsely populated districts, and the supply of child workers fell far short of the demand. So arose the iniquitous traffic in pauper children which John Fielden described with passionate resentment in his book, *The Curse of the Factory System*, from which the first extract is taken. Fielden (1784–1849) knew what he was writing about, since he was the son of a yeoman who about the time of his birth had embarked on cotton spinning on a very limited scale, and as a boy he worked for long hours in his father's mill (*see* Child Labour (*g*), No. 5). After his father's death in 1811 he joined with his brothers in the firm of Fielden Brothers, at the Waterside Mills at Todmorden, in the West Riding, which became one of the largest and most successful cotton manufacturing establishments in the country. But he never forgot his childish experiences, and especially after his election in 1833 as MP for Oldham he exerted himself in the cause of Factory Reform. 'Honest John Fielden' is what his friends called him, and he fully deserved the title.

In his book Fielden refers appreciatively to a recently published account of an apprentice boy, one Robert Blincoe: 'I wish every man and woman in England would see and read this pamphlet; it is published in Manchester, where the crippled subject of the memoir now lives to testify the truth of all that I have said . . .' The 'memoir' was written by one John Brown, and several pages from this sensational production are reproduced in No. 4. This is preceded by Blincoe's own account, given in evidence before a Government inquiry in 1833. (Incidentally, this document is the first of a very large number of extracts from the evidence given at committees, etc., in the shape of question-and-answer, and it should be understood that the questions are put by the chairman or other member of the committee, and the answers are made by the witness under examination.) From the report of an earlier Committee—known as Peel's Committee: see next section—have been taken the extraordinary accounts of Mr Moss the Apprentice Master and others connected with the mill at Backbarrow.

Not all parish apprentices were badly treated, however, if we may judge from the glowing account by Sir Thomas Bernard (No. 8), of Mr Dale's children at New Lanark (see also *Factory Life: Working Conditions* (No. 8) and *Woman's Place: Factory Wives* (No. 8). In most of the early factories, and especially those worked by small masters in out-of-the-way districts, the conditions seem to have been generally deplorable. In the outside world there were few who knew, or cared to know, of what went on behind the factory walls—until now and again the fevers that attacked the congregations of juvenile workers became a menace to the surrounding neighbourhoods. As early as 1784 an outbreak of fever in some cotton works at Radcliffe aroused the alarm of the county authorities in Lancashire, who requested some of the Manchester medical men to investigate its causes. This led to the emergence as a pioneer of public health of Dr Thomas Percival (1740–1804), who in 1796 drew up a Manifesto (No. 9) for the guidance of the Manchester Board of Health, in which it was urged that application should be made to Parliament for the regulation of cotton factories. Nothing was done, however, until 1802 when what is known as the First Factory Act was passed at the instigation of Sir Robert Peel; this is given in extenso in No. 10. As will be seen, this was quite ineffective in practice (No. 11) and for a number of years yet the parish apprentices continued their unprotected existence. Their condition is clearly disclosed in the report of a Committee that sat in 1814-15 to examine into the state of those coming from London (No. 12).

I

'Dismal solitudes of torture'

It may not be amiss to inquire how it came to pass originally, that, in England, always boasting of her humanity, laws were necessary in order to protect little children from the cruelties of the master manufacturers, and even of their own parents.

It is well known that Arkwright's (so called, at least) inventions took manufactures out of the cottages and farmhouses of England, where they had been carried on by mothers, or by daughters under the mother's eye, and assembled them in the counties of Derbyshire, Nottinghamshire, and, more particularly, in Lancashire, where the newly-invented machinery was used in large factories built on the side of streams capable of turning the water-wheel.

Thousands of hands were suddenly required in these places, remote from towns; and Lancashire in particular, being till then but comparatively thinly populated and barren, a population was all she now wanted. The small and nimble fingers of little children being by far the most in request, the custom instantly sprang up of procuring *apprentices* from the different parish workhouses of London, Birmingham, and elsewhere. Many, many thousands of these little hapless creatures were sent down into the North, being from the age of seven, to the age of thirteen or fourteen years old.

The custom was for the master to clothe his apprentices, and to feed and lodge them in an 'apprentice house' near the factory; overseers were appointed to see to the works, whose interest it was to work the children to the utmost, because their pay was in proportion to the quantity of work that they could exact. Cruelty was, of course, the consequence; and there is abundant evidence on record, and preserved in the recollections of some who still live, to show, that, in many of the manufacturing districts, but particularly, I am afraid, in the guilty county to which I belong, cruelties the most heart-rending were practised upon the unoffending and friendless creatures who were thus consigned to the charge of master-manufacturers; that they were harassed to the brink of death by excess of labour, that they were flogged, fettered, and tortured in the most exquisite refinement of cruelty; that they were, in many cases, starved to the bone while flogged to their work, and that even in some instances, they were driven to commit suicide to evade the cruelties of a world, in which, though born to it so recently, their happiest moments had been passed in the garb and coercion of a workhouse.

The beautiful and romantic valleys of Derbyshire, Nottinghamshire, and Lancashire, secluded from the public eye, became the dismal solitudes of torture, and of many a murder! . . .

The profits of manufacture were enormous; but this only whetted the appetite that it should have satisfied, and therefore the manufacturers had recourse to an expedient that seemed to secure to them those profits without any possibility of limit: they began the practice of what is termed 'night working', that is, having tired out one set of hands, by working them throughout the day, they had another set ready to go on working throughout the night; the day-set getting into the beds the night-set had just quitted, and, in their turn again, the night-set getting into the beds that the day-set quitted in the morning. It is a common tradition in Lancashire, that the beds *never got cold*!

JOHN FIELDEN, *The Curse of the Factory System* (1836), pp. 5–6.

2

One Idiot in Every Batch

These apprentice children were often sent one, two, or three hundred miles from their place of birth, separated for life from all relations, and deprived of the aid which even in their destitute situation they might derive from friends . . . It had been known that a gang, if he might use the term, of these children had been put up for sale with a bankrupt's effects, and were advertised publicly, *as a piece of the property*.

A most atrocious instance had come before the court of King's Bench two years ago, in which a number of these boys, apprenticed by a parish in London to one manufacturer, had been transferred to another, and had been found by some benevolent persons in a state of absolute famine. Another case, more horrible, had come to his knowledge while on a committee upstairs; that, not many years ago, an agreement had been made between a London parish and a Lancashire manufacturer, by which it was stipulated that with every *twenty sound* children, one *idiot* should be taken!

FRANCIS HORNER, MP, in the House of Commons, 6 June, 1815.

3

Robert Blincoe's Own Story

Robert Blincoe, a small manufacturer, once an apprentice to a cotton-mill, sworn, and examined by Dr Hawkins, 18th May, 1833:

Do you know where you were born?—No, I only know that I came out of St Pancras parish, London.

Do you know the names of your parents with certainty?—No. I used to be called, when young, Robert Saint; but when I received my indentures I was called in them Robert Blincoe, and I have gone by that name ever since.

What age are you?—Near upon forty, according to my indentures.

Have you no other means of knowing your age but what you find in your indentures?—No; I go by that.

Do you work at a cotton-mill?—Not now. I was bound apprentice to a cotton mill for fourteen years from St Pancras parish; then I got my indentures. I worked five or six years after at different mills, but now I have got a work of my own. I rent power from a mill in Stockport, and have a room to myself; my business is sheet wadding.

Why did you leave off working at the cotton mills?—I got tired of it, the system is so bad; and I had saved a few pounds. I got deformed there; my knees began to bend in when I was fifteen; you see how they are (*showing them*). There are many, many far worse than me in Manchester.

79

Can you exercise with ease?—A very little makes me sweat in walking; I have not the strength of those who are straight.

Have you ever been in a hospital, or under doctors, for your knees and legs?—Never in a hospital or under doctors for that, but for illness from overwork I have been; when I was near Nottingham there were about eighty of us together, boys and girls, all 'prenticed out from St Pancras parish, London, to cotton mills; many of us used to be ill, but the doctors said it was only for want of kitchen physic and of more rest.

Have you had any accidents from machinery?—No, nothing to signify much; I have not myself, but I saw, on the 6th of March last, a man killed by machinery at Stockport; he was smashed, and he died in four or five hours; I saw him while the accident took place; he was joking with me just before; it was in my own room. I employ a poor sore cripple under me, who could not easily get work any where else; a young man came good-naturedly from another room to help my cripple, and he was accidentally drawn up by the strap, and was killed. I have known many such accidents take place in the course of my life.

Recollect a few.—One was at Lytton Mill in Derbyshire; another was a master of a factory at Staley Bridge, of the name of Bailey. Many more I have known to receive injuries, such as the loss of a limb; there is plenty about Stockport that is going about now with one arm; they cannot work in the mills, but they go about with jackasses and such like. One girl, Mary Richards, was made a cripple, and remains so now, when I was in Lowdham mill near Nottingham; she was lapped up by a strap underneath the drawing frame.

Have you any children?—Three.

Do you send them to factories?—No; I would rather have them transported. In the first place, they are standing upon one leg, lifting up one knee, a great part of the day, keeping the ends up from the spindle; I consider that that employment makes many cripples; then there is the heat and the dust; then there are so many different forms of cruelty used upon them; then they are liable to have their fingers catched and to suffer other accidents from the machinery; then the hours is so long, that I have seen them tumble down asleep among the straps and machinery, and so get cruelly hurt; then I would not have a child of mine there because there is not good morals; there is such a lot of them together that they learn mischief.

What do you do with your children?—My eldest, of thirteen, has been to school, and can teach me. She now stays at home and helps her mother in the shop. She is as tall as me, and is very heavy; very different from what she would have been if she had worked in a factory. My two youngest go to school, and are both healthy. I send them every day two miles to school. I know from experience the ills of confinement.

What are the forms of cruelty that you spoke of just now as being practised upon children in factories?—I have seen the time when two hand-vices of a pound weight each, more or less, have been screwed to my ears, at Lytton mill in Derbyshire. There are the scars still remaining behind my ears. Then three or four of us have been hung at once on a cross-beam above the machinery, hanging by our hands, without shirts or stockings. Mind, we were apprentices, without father or mother to take care of us; I don't say that they often do that now. Then we used to stand up, in a skip, without our shirts, and be beat with straps or sticks; the skip was to prevent us from running away from the straps ... Then they used to tie up a 28-pounds weight (one or two at once), according to our size, to hang down our backs, with no shirt on. I have had them myself ... I have a book written about these things, describing my own life and sufferings. I will send it to you. (Enclosed for the inspection of the Central Board. It is entitled, 'A Memoir of Robert Blincoe ...')

Employment of Children in Manufactories, 2nd Report of the Central Board; P.P. 1833, vol. XXI, D 3, pp. 17-18.

4

The Boy from St Pancras Workhouse

[In 1796, when he was about four years old, Robert Blincoe was handed over to the parish authorities and placed in the workhouse of St Pancras, London.]

Blincoe declares, he was so weary of confinement, he would have gladly exchanged situations with the poorest of the poor children whom, from the upper windows of the workhouse, he had seen begging from door to door, or offering matches for sale ... From this state of early misanthropy, young Blincoe was suddenly diverted by a rumour, that filled many a heart among his comrades with terror, viz. that a day was appointed when the master-sweeps of the metropolis were to come and select such a number of boys as apprentices, till they attained the age of twenty-one years, as they might deign to take into their sable fraternity. These tidings . . . sounded like heavenly music to the ears of young Blincoe . . . who was often handled, examined, and rejected. He declared that his chagrin was inexpressible, when his failure was apparent . . .

From the period of Blincoe's disappointment, in being rejected by the sweeps, a sudden calm seems to have succeeded, which lasted till a rumour ran through the house, that a treaty was on foot between the Churchwardens and Overseers [of the Poor] of St Pancras, and the owner of a great cotton-factory in the vicinity of Nottingham, for the disposal of a large number of children, as apprentices, till they became twenty-one years of age. The rumour inspired Blincoe with new life and spirits—he dreamed not of the misery that impended, in the midst of which he would look back to St Pancras as to an Elysium . . .

Prior to the show-day of the pauper children to the purveyor or cotton master, the most illusive and artfully contrived falsehoods were spread, to fill the minds of these poor infants with the most absurd and ridiculous errors, as to the real nature of the servitude to which they were to be consigned. It was gravely stated to them, that they were all, when they arrived at the cotton-mill, to be transformed into ladies and gentlemen; that they would be fed on roast beef and plum-pudding —be allowed to ride their masters' horses, and have silver watches, and plenty of cash in their pockets . . . Their hopes being thus excited, and their imaginations inflamed, it was next stated, amongst the innocent victims of fraud and deception, that no one could be *compelled* to go, nor any but volunteers accepted . . .

This exhibition took place in August 1799, and eighty boys and girls as parish apprentices, and till they had respectively acquired the age of twenty-one years, were made over by the churchwardens and overseers of St Pancras parish, to Messrs Lamberts', cotton-spinners, hosiers, and lace-men, of St Mary's parish, Nottingham, the owners of Lowdham mill. The boys, during the latter part of their time, were to be instructed in the trade of stocking-weaving—the girls in lace-making . . .

Happy, no doubt, in the thought of transferring the burthen of the future support of fourscore young paupers to other parishes, the churchwardens and overseers distinguished the departure of this juvenile colony by acts of munificence. The children were completely new clothed, and each had two suits, one for their working and one for their holiday dress—a shilling in money was given to each—a new pocket handkerchief—and a large piece of gingerbread . . . The whole party seemed to start in very high spirits . . .

[They were conveyed in two large waggons, with clean straw for beds and the doors locked, to Nottingham; they were four days on the road.]

When the waggons drew up near the dwelling and warehouse of their future master, a crowd collected to see the *livestock* that was just imported from the metropolis, who were pitied, admired, and compared to lambs, led by butchers to slaughter! Care was taken that they should not hear or understand much of this sort of discourse. The boys and girls were distributed, some into the kitchen, others in a large ware-room, washed, combed, and supplied with refreshments; but there was no plum-pudding—no roast beef, no talk of horses they were to ride, nor of watches and fine clothing that they had been promised. Many looked very mournful . . .

After having been well refreshed, the whole of the boys and girls were drawn up in rows, to be *reviewed* by *their masters*, their friends and neighbours. In Blincoe's estimation, their masters, Messrs Lamberts, were 'stately sort of men'. They looked over the children, and finding them all right, according to the INVOICE, exhorted them to behave with proper humility and decorum. To pay the most prompt and submissive respects to the orders of those who would be appointed to instruct and superintend them at Lowdham Mill, and to be diligent and careful, each one to execute his or her task, and thereby avoid the punishment and disgrace which awaited idleness, insolence, or disobedience . . .

Lowdham Cotton-mills, situated near a village of that name, stood ten miles distant from Nottingham. Thither Blincoe and his associates were conveyed the next day in carts, and it was rather late when they arrived . . . When he came in view of the apprentice-house, which was half a mile distant from the mill, and was told that that *was to be his home for 14 years to come*, he was not greatly delighted, so closely did it resemble a workhouse. When the first cart, in which was young Blincoe, drove up to the door, a number of villagers flocked around, some of whom exclaimed, 'God help the poor wretches!'—'Eh!' said another, 'what a fine collection of children, little do they know to what a life of slavery they are doomed'. 'The Lord have mercy on them', said a third. 'They'll find little mercy here', said a fourth.

The young strangers were conducted into a spacious room, fitted up in the style of the dinner-room in Pancras old workhouse, viz. with long narrow deal tables, and wooden benches. Although the rooms seemed tolerably clean, there was a certain rank, oily smell which Blincoe did not very much admire. They were ordered to sit down at these tables—the boys and girls apart. The supper set before them consisted of milk-porridge, of a very blue complexion. The bread was partly made of rye—very black, and so soft, they could scarcely swallow it, as it stuck like bird-lime to their teeth. Poor Blincoe stared, recollecting this was not so good a fare as they had been used to at St Pancras. Where is our roast beef and plum-pudding, he said to himself . . .

The supper being devoured, the bell rang, that gave the signal to go to bed. The grim governor entered to take the charge of the newly arrived boys, and his wife, acting the same part by the girls, appeared every way suitable to so rough and unpolished a mate. In a surly, heart-chilling tone, she bade the girls follow her. Tremblingly and despondingly the little creatures obeyed, scarcely daring to cast a look at their fellow travellers, or bid them good night . . .

The room to which Blincoe and several of the boys were deposited was up two pair of stairs. The bed places was a sort of cribs, built in a double tier, all round the chamber. The apprentices slept two in a bed. The beds were of flock . . . The governor called the strangers to him and allotted to each his bed-place and bed-fellow, not allowing any two of the newly arrived inmates to sleep together. The boy, with whom Blincoe was to chum, sprang nimbly into his berth, and without saying a prayer, or anything else, fell asleep before Blincoe could undress himself. So completely was he cowed he could not restrain his tears . . .

From *A Memoir of Robert Blincoe, an Orphan Boy; sent from the workhouse at St Pancras, London, at seven years of age, to endure the* Horrors of a Cotton-Mill, *through his infancy and youth, with a minute detail of his sufferings, being the first memoir of the kind published.* By John Brown, Manchester, 1832.

5

Mr Moss the Apprentice-Master

Mr John Moss, called in and examined before the Select Committee of the House of Commons on the state of children employed in manufactories: May 24, 1816. Present occupation, that of governor of the workhouse at Preston, Lancs; from February 1814 to March 1815 was master of the apprentices, in charge of the apprentice-house, at Backbarrow.

Were any children employed in those mills?—There were 111 children employed when I went there at first, and as many as 150 when I left. All parish apprentices, chiefly from London—the parishes of Whitechapel, St James' and St Clement's, I think. There was a few from Liverpool workhouse. Those that came from London were from seven to eleven; those from Liverpool were from eight or ten to fifteen.

Was there any proportion of idiots among the children?—No, none. Up to what period were they apprenticed?—One and twenty.

What were the hours of work?—From 5 o'clock in the morning till 8 at night all the year through. What time was allowed for meals?— Half an hour for breakfast and half an hour for dinner. Had they any refreshment in the afternoon?—Yes, they had their drinking taken to the mill; their bagging, they call it. You mean luncheon?—Yes. Did they work whilst they ate their afternoon refreshment?—Yes. They had no cessation after dinner till 8 o'clock at night?—No.

At what hour was the breakfast?—at 7 in the morning; they came to their breakfast at 7 o'clock, and then the bell rang for them at half-past seven. Did they leave the mill at breakfast time?—Yes, they always left the mill and came to the house.

What was the dinner hour?—Twelve o'clock. They returned to the mill at half-past twelve.

Did they, beyond working those 15 hours, make up for any loss of time?—Yes, always. They continued working till 9 o'clock, sometimes later . . . Did the children actually work 14 hours in the day?— Yes. And one hour was allowed for the two meals, making 15 hours in the whole?—Yes.

Was this before the Apprentice Bill or after ? It was last year, and it is in practice now . . .

*   *   *

What time did they rise from bed ?—I always got them up at half-past four to get them ready for the mill by five. How far was their sleeping room from the mill ?—It might not be above a hundred yards; hardly so much. Did they rise at half-past four in the winter season ?—They were always to be at the mill by 5 o'clock winter and summer, and never later . . .

. Did any children work on the Sundays as cleaners of the machines ? —Yes; generally every Sunday; I do not know that ever they missed one Sunday while I was there. How many hours did they work on a Sunday ?—Their orders were from six to twelve. Did you remonstrate against this ?—Yes, I did frequently. It was never much better. Did the masters ever express any concern for such excessive labour ?—No.

*   *   *

Would the children sit or stand to work ?—Stand . . . The whole of their time ?—Yes. Were there any seats in the mill ?—None. Were they usually much fatigued at night ?—Yes, some of them were very much fatigued. Where did they sleep ?—In the apprentice-house. Did you inspect their beds ?—Yes, every night. For what purpose ?—Because there were always some of them missing, some sometimes might be run away, others sometimes I have found have been asleep in the mill, upon the mill-floor. Did the children frequently lie down upon the mill-floor at night when their work was done, and fall asleep before their supper ?—I have found them frequently upon the mill-floor after the time they should have been in bed.

At what hour did they go to bed ?—Nine o'clock was their hour, when they worked their usual time.

In summer time did you allow them to sit up a little later ?—Yes, sometimes till half-past nine.

*   *   *

Were any children injured by the machinery ?—Very frequently. Very often their fingers were crushed, and one had his arm broken.

Were any of the children deformed ?—Yes, several; there were two or three that were very crooked . . .

*   *   *

Did the parish officers of the parishes to which they belonged, ever come to the mills and inspect the children ?—No; there was one from

Liverpool; the overseer of Liverpool. Was there any other inspection by magistrates, or any other persons ?—No, there was no magistrates ever come into the children's house . . .

Is the mill in a healthy situation ?—Very. As the children grew up, did they in general appear to be healthy, or otherwise ?—There were some who were very healthy children, and there were others that were sickly looking.

How many died during the year you were at the mill ?—There was only one.

How were the children lodged ?—They had very good lodgings when we left them. Had they good lodgings when you first went there ?—No. Did you make any complaint of their bedding when you first went ? —Yes. When I first went there, their bedding was very bad; they had only a blanket to lie on, and a thin blanket to lie at top, and a horse cover, and some of them were very bad. Could they be preserved cleanly with sleeping only on blankets ?—They were not altogether clean.

Did you make complaint of that ?—Yes. Did the parish officer from Liverpool complain of it ?—Yes. Was it in consequence of his complaint and yours that the bedding was improved ?—Yes, it was; we got after that sheets and covers for every bed, and there never were sheets for any bed in the house, I believe, before . . .

*   *   *

Were the children fed well ?—Yes, very well.

Before your time at Backbarrow mill, were the children turned out on the high road to beg their way to their former parishes when the former proprietor stopped payment ? Were they taken from the mill in a cart, and then turned adrift near the sands on the Lancaster road ? —Yes, I was informed they were.

Did you hear that the gentlemen of Lancaster complained of this inhumanity ?—Yes. Were any fetched back in consequence of these complaints ?—Yes, I believe there were.

Were they then turned over to Messrs Ainsworth, the present proprietors ?—Yes. After they had served out their apprenticeship to Messrs Ainsworth, were they not compelled to serve extra time, under the pretence that so much time was lost by being turned out on the road, and obliged to go to Lancaster ?—Yes, there was one boy out of his time while I was there, and when the day came his master said that he had to serve six weeks, I think, longer, in consequence of his having run away; he said he never had run away, he was turned out, and he had worked at Caton factory, and they made him serve that time out . . .

*　　*　　*

Were the children bad in their morals ?—Yes, they were. They did not behave well one to another.

Who looked over them in the mill ?—Generally the older apprentices were overlookers over the younger ones.

Did the bigger boys beat the others ?—Yes, frequently.

What was the general character of the children? Very bad character.

Were they so confirmed in their bad behaviour you could not reform them ?—I could not reform them by any fair means, and to try foul ones I did not like.

From the Report on Children employed in Manufactories; P.P. 1816, vol. III, pp. 178–185.

6

'A parcel of bitches'

William Travers, employed until recently as an overlooker at Back-barrow Mill; he quitted the mill about a month after Mr Moss left: in examination before the Select Committee.

What was the general appearance of the children ?—Very good; they were very good looking; very few otherwise . . .

Was the house where the apprentices lodged properly calculated for their reception ?—It was a very good house.

Mr Moss was the person who had charge of the apprentices ? Yes, when out of the mill.

Is Mr Moss a man of good character ?—He seems a very decent man. I have never heard anything against him.

Had he a proper authority over the children—He had.

He had the power, but did he maintain the proper authority over the children ?—I do not think he did. I have seen him make too free with them myself.

What do you mean by making too free with them?—Take a stick and put it to a girl's petticoats, and heave them up a little, and say, let us see what sort of legs you have got; and I thought he was rather too loose there.

Was Mr Moss a married man?—He was a married man.

What was Mrs Moss's duty?—To look after them, as mistress of the house, to see that they were kept clean, and so on.

What was her general conduct towards the children?—She was too high for her situation; she did not look after them as she should do. I have heard her say on a sabbath day in the morning, when they were preparing to go to chapel, that she would not come amongst them for a parcel of bitches.

P.P. 1816, vol. III, p. 288.

7

Happy Backbarrow!

I do hereby certify that I have attended the apprentice house of Ainsworth, Catterall & Co. of Backbarrow, upwards of six years, and that during that time the children have been particularly healthy, and the number of deaths very few. I consider the treatment of the children very good in all respects. John Redhead, surgeon. Cartmel, May 25, 1816.

*   *   *

To all whom it may concern. These are to certify that the children or apprentices, belonging to the cotton factory of Messrs Ainsworth, Catterall and Co., at Backbarrow in the parish of Cartmel in the County of Lancaster, generally and regularly attend divine service in the chapel of Finsthwaite every Sunday when the weather will permit; that during the service they behave with great propriety; they appear neat and clean, and in all respects demean themselves in a decent and orderly manner. Given under my hand this 25th day of May 1816. Henry Seatle, Minister of Finsthwaite.

P.S. I beg leave to state that out of 150 children, the number employed, there have been only six deaths in the seven last years; and three of these came to the place in a very sickly state and one was drowned by accident.

*   *   *

Backbarrow Cotton Mills, May 25th, 1816

We the undersigned do hereby certify, That we attend every Sabbath-day at the apprentice-house of Ainsworth, Catterall & Company, and accompany the children to Finsthwaite Chapel for the morning's service; that in the afternoon we teach them to read the Bible, New Testament, or Spelling Book, according to their ability, and that every attention is paid to the strict observance of the Sabbath.—J. Slater. William Fennix. The above certified also by me, Thomas Coward, Governor of the Apprentice House at Backbarrow.

P.P. 1816, vol. III, p. 210.

8

Mr Dale's Apprentices

The cotton mills at New Lanark, in the county of Lanark in Scotland, are situated in a beautiful and romantic amphitheatre, near the high road between Carlisle and Glasgow. The rapid stream of the Clyde supplies that abundance of water which is the powerful operator of the machinery . . . The village contains about 1500 inhabitants, of whom all who are capable of work are employed in and about the mills. Of these there are about 500 children, who are entirely fed, clothed, and educated by Mr Dale. The others lodge with their parents in the village, and have a weekly allowance for their work.

The healthy and pleasurable appearance of these children has frequently attracted the attention of the traveller. Peculiar regulations, adopted by Mr Dale for the preservation of the health and morals of those under his protection, have made this striking difference between his manufactory and many other similar undertakings in this kingdom, so that while some other mills must be regarded as seminaries of vice and sources of disease, those at Lanark are so peculiarly exempt from these objections, that out of near 3000 children employed in these mills during a period of twelve years, from 1785 to 1797, only fourteen have died; and not one has been the object of judicial punishment.

In order to supply that first necessary of life—pure and fresh air—the windows of the manufactory are frequently opened; and in summer time there are air-holes left under every other window. Cleanliness is another great object of attention. The children wash themselves before they go to work, and also after it, before they appear in the schools. The floors and the machinery are washed once a week with hot water, and the ceilings and walls twice a year, with unslacked lime.

The children who reside in the house, and who have their maintenance in lieu of wages, are lodged in six large, airy apartments. The boys and girls are kept distinctly apart, not only in hours of rest and refreshment, but during the time of occupation. They sleep on cast-iron bedsteads, the bed-tick filled with straw, which is changed regularly every month. The bedrooms are swept, and the windows thrown open, every morning, and kept open all day. Many of the children have contrived to provide themselves with boxes with locks, in which they keep their books and their little property. Their upper clothing in summer is cotton, which is washed once a fortnight. In winter the boys are drest in woollen, and, as well as the girls, have dress suits for Sundays.

For dinner they have seven ounces each of fresh beef with barley broth, or alternately five ounces of cheese, and a plentiful allowance of potatoes or barley bread. This part of the table diet is seldom varied, except in winter by a dinner of fresh herrings as a change. Their breakfast and supper consists of oatmeal porridge, with the addition of milk in summer, and, during the winter, with a sauce made of molasses and beer.

Seven o'clock is the hour for supper; soon after work (for that pernicious practice, called night work, is entirely excluded from these mills) the schools commence, and continue till nine o'clock. Mr Dale has engaged three regular masters, who instruct the lesser children during the day. In the evening they are assisted by seven others, one of whom teaches writing. There is, likewise, a woman to teach the girls sewing, and another person who occasionally gives lessons in church music. The masters preside over the boys' dinner table. On Sundays they conduct them to the place of divine worship, and, in the evening of Sunday, attend to assist and improve them by religious and moral information.

From SIR THOMAS BERNARD'S *Society for Bettering the Condition and Increasing the Comforts of the Poor* (1797).

9

Dr Percival's Manifesto

It has already been stated that the objects of the present institution [the Manchester Board of Health, formed by Dr Percival and his associates in 1795] are to prevent the generation of diseases; to obviate the spreading of them by contagion, and to shorten the duration of those which exist, by affording the necessary aids and comforts to the sick. In the prosecution of this interesting undertaking, the Board have had their attention particularly directed to the large cotton factories established in the town and neighbourhood of Manchester; and they feel it a duty incumbent on them to lay before the public the result of heir inquiries:—

1. It appears that the children and others who work in the large factories, are peculiarly disposed to be affected by the contagion of fever, and that when such infection is received, it is rapidly propagated, not only amongst those who are crowded together in the same apartments, but in the families and neighbourhoods to which they belong.

2. The large factories are generally injurious to the constitution of those employed in them, even where no particular diseases prevail, from the close confinement which is enjoined, from the debilitating effects of hot or impure air, and from the want of the active exercises which nature points out as essential in childhood and youth, to invigorate the system, and to fit our species for the employments and for the duties of manhood.

3. The untimely labour of the night, and the protracted labour of the day, with respect to children, not only tends to diminish future expectations as to the general sum of life and industry, by impairing the strength and destroying the vital stamina of the rising generation, but it too often gives encouragement to idleness, extravagance and profligacy in the parents, who, contrary to the order of nature, subsist by the oppression of their offspring.

4. It appears that the children employed in factories are generally debarred from all opportunities of education, and from moral or religious instruction.

5. From the excellent regulations which subsist in several cotton factories, it appears that many of these evils may in a considerable degree, be obviated; we are therefore warranted by experience, and are assured we shall have the support of the liberal proprietors of these factories, in proposing an application for parliamentary aid (if other methods appear not likely to effect the purpose), to establish a general system of laws for the wise, humane and equal government of all such works.

Resolutions for the consideration of the Manchester Board of Health, drawn up by THOMAS PERCIVAL, MD, January 25, 1796; reprinted in P.P. 1816, vol. III, p. 377.

10

The First Factory Act

An Act for the Preservation of the Health and Morals of Apprentices and others, employed in Cotton and other Mills, and Cotton and other Factories.

Whereas it hath of late become a Practice in Cotton and Woollen Mills, and in Cotton and Woollen Factories, to employ a great Number of Male and Female Apprentices, and other Persons, in the same Building; in consequence of which certain Regulations are become necessary to preserve the Health and Morals of such Apprentices and other Persons; be it therefore enacted . . .

That, from and after the Second Day of December One thousand eight hundred and two, all such Mills and Factories within Great Britain and Ireland, wherein Three or more Apprentices, or Twenty or more other Persons, shall at any Time be employed, shall be subject to the Several Rules and Regulations contained in this Act . . .

II. And be it enacted, That all and every the Rooms and Apartments in or belonging to any such Mill or Factory shall, Twice at least in every Year, be well and sufficiently washed with Quick Lime and Water over every part of the Walls and Ceiling thereof; and that due Care and Attention shall be paid by the Master or Mistress of such Mills or Factories, to provide a sufficient Number of Windows and Openings in such Rooms and Apartments, to insure a proper Supply of fresh Air in and through the same.

III. And be it further enacted, That every such Master or Mistress shall constantly supply every Apprentice, during the Term of his or her Apprenticeship, with Two whole and complete Suits of Cloathing, with suitable Linen, Stockings, Hats, and Shoes; One new complete Suit being delivered to such Apprentice Once at least in every year.

IV. And be it further enacted, That no Apprentice that now is or hereafter shall be bound to any such Master or Mistress, shall be employed or compelled to work for more than Twelve Hours in any One Day, (reckoning from Six of the Clock in the morning to Nine of the Clock at Night), exclusive of the Time that may be occupied by such Apprentice in eating the necessary Meals . . .

VI. And be it further enacted, That every such Apprentice shall be instructed, in some Part of every working Day, for the First Four Years at least of his or her Apprenticeship . . . in the usual Hours of Work, in Reading, Writing, and Arithmetick, or either of them, according to the Age and Abilities of such Apprentice, by some discreet and proper Person, to be provided and paid by the Master or Mistress of such Apprentice, in some Room or Place in such Mill or Factory to be set apart for that Purpose . . .

VII. And be it further enacted, That the Room or Apartment in which any Male Apprentice shall sleep, shall be entirely separate and distinct from the Room or Apartment in which any Female Apprentice shall sleep; and that not more than Two Apprentices shall in any Case sleep in the same Bed.

VIII. And be it further enacted, That every Apprentice . . . shall, for the Space of One Hour at least every Sunday, be instructed and examined in the Principles of the Christian Religion, by some proper Person to be provided and paid by the Master or Mistress of such Apprentice . . .; and such Master or Mistress shall send all his or her Apprentices under the Care of some proper Person, Once in a Month at least, to attend during Divine Service in the Church of the Parish or Place in which the Mill or Factory shall be situated . . .

IX. And be it further enacted, That the Justices of the Peace for every County, Stewartry, Riding, Division, or Place, in which any such Mill or Factory shall be situated shall . . . at their annual Midsummer Sessions of the Peace, appoint Two Persons, not interested in, or in any way Connected with, any such Mills or Factories, to be Visitors of such Mills or Factories . . . One of whom shall be a Justice of the

Peace for such County . . . and the other shall be a Clergyman of the Established Church of England or Scotland, as the Case may be . . .; and the said Visitors, or either of them, shall have full Power and Authority from Time to Time throughout the Year, to enter into and inspect any such Mill or Factory, at any time of the Day, or during the Hours of Employment, as they shall think fit; and such Visitors shall report from Time to Time in Writing, to the Quarter Sessions of the Peace, the State or Condition of such Mills and Factories, and of the Apprentices therein, whether the same are or are not conducted and regulated according to the Directions of this Act, and the Laws of the Realm; and such Report shall be entered by the Clerk of the Peace among the Records of the Session in a Book kept for that purpose . . .

X. And be it further enacted, That in case the said Visitors or either of them shall find that any infectious Disorder appears to prevail in any Mill or Factory as aforesaid, it shall be lawful for them, or either of them, to require the Master or Mistress of any such Mill or Factory to call in forthwith some Physician, or other competent medical Person, for the purpose of ascertaining the Nature and probable Effects of such Disorder, and for applying such Remedies and recommending such Regulations as the said Physician, or other competent medical Person, shall think most proper for preventing the spreading of the Infection and for restoring the Health of the Sick; . . . and that any Expenses incurred in consequence of the Provisions aforesaid for medical Assistance, shall be discharged by the Master or Mistress of such Mill or Factory.

XIII. And be it further enacted, That every Master or Mistress of any such Mill or Factory who shall wilfully act contrary to or offend against any of the Provisions of this Act, shall for such Offence . . . forfeit and pay any Sum not exceeding Five Pounds nor less than Forty Shillings, at the Discretion of the Justices before whom such Offender shall be convicted . . .

Public General Statutes, 42nd Year of Geo. III, 87 (1802).

II

The Act that Never Was

William David Evans, barrister and Manchester magistrate, examined:
You have stated that you are the magistrate appointed under the 53rd
of the King, with a salary, to superintend the police (of Manchester):
what salary?—One thousand pounds a year.

Are you aware that the Act of Parliament, generally called by the
name of Sir Robert Peel's Act, directs the appointment of certain
inspectors by the magistrates, one of them to be a magistrate and the
other a clergyman?—Yes.

Has that provision been put in force in Manchester?—I have only
been aware of that provision since reading the Act yesterday.

Are the Committee to understand, that you were not aware of the
existence of this Act, so material to the interests of Manchester, till
you came to this Committee yesterday?—I certainly was aware of the
existence of an Act for the regulation of cotton mills; neither my
magisterial or professional functions have called upon me to look upon
particular occasions into that Act; and coming into the magistracy
long after the enactment itself, certainly I had not had the curiosity,
though I have read as many Acts of Parliament as most persons, to
read that till I came into this room.

Do you mean to assert, it would be a mere matter of curiosity to read
an Act of Parliament which has reference to the management of
Manchester, of which you are a magistrate?—I have certainly generally
found it the impression of our magistrates, in conversation, that that
Act was not of any efficient service, and why should any of us look into
it when not called upon to do so from any business coming before us?
There are a great many Acts of Parliament relating to particular trades,
which I have never read, although the magistrates have jurisdiction
given by them, and have an opportunity of applying them when an
occasion arises . . .

P.P. 1816, vol. III, p. 319.

12

The Parish Apprentices Report

In the populous districts of England, whether that Population is caused by Manufacturers or by other Employments, the same causes which produce it provide support for the Inhabitants of all ages, by various occupations adapted to their means. Thus in Manufacturing Districts the Children are early taught to gain their subsistence by the different branches of those manufactures. In Districts where Collieries or other Mines abound, they are accustomed almost from their infancy to employment under ground, which tend to train and inure them to the occupation of their ancestors. But in London the lower class of the Population is not of that nature, but is composed of many different descriptions, consisting of Servants in and out of place, Tradesmen, Artizans, Labourers, Widows, and Beggars, who being frequently destitute of the means of providing for themselves, are dependent on their Parishes for Relief, which is seldom bestowed without the Parish claiming the exclusive right of disposing, at their pleasure, of all the Children of the person receiving Relief.

The system of Apprenticeship is therefore resorted to of necessity, and with a view of getting rid of the burthen of supporting so many individuals; and as it is probably carried to a greater extent than any where else, for the reasons here stated, Your Committee has been enabled to form an opinion . . . whether it could be discontinued, without taking away from the Parishes the means of disposing of their Poor Children. It certainly does appear to Your Committee, that this purpose might be attained, without the violation of humanity, in separating Children forcibly, and conveying them to a distance from their Parents, whether those Parents be deserving or undeserving.

The peculiar circumstances of the Metropolis, already alluded to, may at first seem to furnish an argument in favour of a continuance of this practice; but it can hardly be a matter of doubt, that Apprentices, to the number of two hundred, which is the yearly number bound in the average of the ten years mentioned [1802-1811], might, with the most trifling possible exertion on the part of the Parish Officers, be annually

D   97

bound to trades and domestic employments, within such a distance as to admit of occasional intercourse with a Parent, and (what is perhaps of more consequence) the superintendence of the Officers of the Parish by which they were bound. That this is not attended with much difficulty seems evident, from the fact that many Parishes have never followed the practice of binding their Poor Children to a distance, though quite as numerous as those in which this practice has prevailed; and that some Parishes which had begun it have long discontinued it . . .

There are, without doubt, instances of Masters, who in some degree compensate to Children for the estrangement which frequently takes place at a very early age from their parents, and from the nurses and women in the Workhouses of London, and who pay due and proper attention to the health, education, and moral and religious conduct of their Apprentices; but these exceptions to the general rule by no means shake the Opinion of Your Committee as to the general impolicy of such a system.

The consideration of the inconvenience and expense brought on Parishes, by binding Apprentices from a distance, is of no weight, when compared with the more important one of the inhumanity of the practice. But it must not be kept out of sight, that the Magistrates of the West Riding of Yorkshire, or of Lancashire, who are of all others the most conversant with the subject, may in vain pass Resolutions, as they have done, declaring the impolicy of binding Parish Apprentices in the manner in which they are usually bound, and attempting to make regulations with a view to their better treatment, if these wholesome regulations can be entirely done away by the act of two Magistrates for Middlesex or Surrey, who can, without any previous notice or previous intimation, defeat these humane objects by binding scores or even hundreds of Children to Manufacturers in a distant county, and thus increase the very evil which it has been endeavoured to check or prevent.

Indeed, in so slovenly and careless a manner is this duty frequently performed, and with so little attention to the future condition of the Children bound, that in frequent instances the Magistrates have put their Signatures to Indentures not executed by the Parties. Two of these Indentures have been submitted to the inspection of Your Committee, purporting to bind a Boy and a Girl from a Parish in *Southwark* to a Cotton Manufacturer in *Lancashire*, and though signed by two Justices for the County of Surrey, neither dated nor executed by the Parish Officers, nor by the Master to whom the Children were bound. Under these Indentures, however, they served; and on the failure of their Master, about two years after their binding was supposed to have taken place, these Poor Children, with some hundreds more, were turned adrift on the world, one of them being at the age of nine, and the other of ten years.

The evils of the system of these distant removals, at all times severe, and aggravating the miseries of poverty, are yet felt more acutely and with a greater degree of aggravation, in the case of Children of six or seven years of age, who are removed from the care of their Parents and Relations at that tender time of life; and are in many cases prematurely subjected to a laborious employment, frequently very injurious to their health, and generally highly so to their morals, and from which they cannot hope to be set free under a period of fourteen or fifteen years, as, with the exception of two Parishes only in the Metropolis, they invariably are bound to the age of twenty-two years.

Without entering more at large into the Enquiry, Your Committee submit, That enough has been shown to call the attention of the House to the practicability of finding employment for Parish Apprentices, within a certain distance from their own homes, without the necessity of having recourse to a practice so much at variance with humanity.

Report of the Committee appointed to examine into the Number and State of Parish Apprentices, bound into the Country from the Parishes within the Bills of Mortality [i.e. London]; P.P. 1814–15, vol. V, pp. 5–7.

Parish Apprentices

The Churchwardens of Manchester have about 200 Apprentices of both sexes, to put out to respectable Manufacturers, Spinners, or others. They are in general very good Weavers, but their Master having become insolvent, they are now chargeable to the Town; their Indentures expire at various periods.

(Manchester newspaper, 5 Feb., 1812)

(b) PEEL'S COMMITTEE

Not surprisingly, it was Robert Owen who took the next step in proposing the legislative protection of the juvenile workers. In 1814 he had formed a new partnership at Lanark with men who gave him much more of a free hand in running it than his previous partners had done, and he was enabled to embark on a career of popular agitation. His first step was to call a meeting of prominent industrialists in Glasgow in 1815, at which he proposed that they should ask the Government to remit the duty on imported cotton, and secondly, to consider measures to improve the condition of the young children, and others, employed in textile mills of every kind. As might have been expected, the manufacturers carried the first proposal with acclamation, but jibbed at the second. Whereupon Owen went to London and set about interesting the leading members of Parliament in the cause of factory reform. Since he was not himself an MP he had to seek the help of someone who was, and the choice fell on Sir Robert Peel.

At this time the only child workers protected by law were the pauper apprentices employed in cotton mills, and, as we have seen, even in their case the protection was but nominal. As Owen pointed out, children were admitted into cotton, wool, flax, and silk mills at six, and sometimes even at five years of age, and their hours of work, unlimited by law, usually extended to fourteen hours a day but might be extended to fifteen, and even, 'by the most inhuman and avaricious', to sixteen. The Bill that Owen prepared and got Peel to sponsor, proposed that the employment of children under ten years of age should be prohibited, and that the hours of work of children in factories should be limited to ten hours a day. This was much more than Peel's fellow legislators could be induced to accept, and at length he agreed (much to Owen's disgust) to the appointment of a Committee to consider

the whole matter afresh. The Committee met under his chairmanship, whence the name by which it is generally referred to, and
it took evidence from a large number of witnesses, including
employers, doctors, magistrates, and other interested persons,
but no actual employees. Peel himself appeared before it as a
witness, and he made a statement (No. 1) in which he recalled
the situation as regards apprentice labour that had prevailed in
1802, when he secured the passing of the First Factory Act, and
explained how greatly it had changed. He expressed his own deep
sympathy with 'these little creatures', but much more represen-
tative of the employing class was the prominent Glasgow mill-
owner Archibald Buchanan (No. 2), who admitted to employing
little boys of eight or nine for twelve hours a day at a wage of a
shilling or so a week, and thought nothing much wrong with it;
and Josiah Wedgwood—called Josiah Wedgwood the Second, to
distinguish him from his famous father, the founder of the great
pottery establishment at Etruria, in Staffs; he was Charles
Darwin's uncle—declared his strong conviction, that the manufacturers were best left alone to manage their businesses in the
way that they found best. Some of the other witnesses were
equally refractory, but Owen spoke up manfully against his
fellow employers, and what added weight to his testimony was
that none could gainsay that he had been extraordinarily successful in running the great concern at New Lanark on his highly
personal but decidedly humanitarian principles.

While Peel managed to get his Bill through the House of
Commons it was summarily thrown out by the Lords, who
proceeded to set up a committee of their own, before which
appeared some most benighted medical gentlemen, e.g. Nos. 8
and 9. After this exhibition, Peel's friends in the Lords rallied
to his support; they got another committee appointed, and
procured a fresh set of medical witnesses who had no hesitation
in saying that their predecessors in the witness-chair had been
talking rubbish. Eventually an Act was passed in 1819 that
forbade the employment, in cotton mills only, of children under
the age of nine, and limited the hours of work of children between
nine and sixteen to twelve in the day, exclusive of meal-times.

Two documents are quoted from the report of the House of
Lords Committee appointed in 1819 to enquire into the state
and condition of the children employed in the Cotton Manu-

factories; No. 10 explains clearly enough why witnesses were sometimes reluctant to be called before such enquiries to give evidence, while No. 11 concerns a case of a father's brutal treatment of his child that so shocked their Lordships that they told him to leave the room.

I

Sir Robert's Fresh Appeal

The house in which I have a concern gave employment at one time to near one thousand children of this description. Having other pursuits, it was not often in my power to visit the factories, but whenever such visits were made, I was struck with the uniform appearance of bad health, and, in many cases, stinted growth of the children; the hours of labour were regulated by the interest of the overseer, whose remuneration depending on the quantity of the work done, he was often induced to make the poor children work excessive hours, and to stop their complaints by trifling bribes.

Finding our own factories under such management, and learning that the like practices prevailed in other parts of the kingdom where similar machinery was in use, the children being much over-worked, and often little or no regard paid to cleanliness and ventilation of the buildings; having the assistance of Dr Percival and other eminent medical gentlemen of Manchester, together with some distinguished characters both in and out of Parliament, I brought in a Bill in the 42nd year of the King, for the regulation of factories containing such parish apprentices. The hours of work allowed by that Bill being fewer in number than those formerly practised, a visible improvement in the health and general appearance of the children soon became evident, and since the complete operation of the Act contagious diseases have rarely occurred.

Diffident of my own abilities to originate legislative measures, I should have contented myself with the one alluded to, had I not perceived, that, owing to the present use of steam power in factories, the Forty-second of the King is likely to become a dead letter. Large buildings are now erected, not only as formerly on the banks of streams, but in the midst of populous towns, and instead of parish apprentices being sought after, the children of the surrounding poor are preferred, whose masters being free from the operation of the former Act of Parliament are subjected to no limitation of time in the prosecution of their business, though children are frequently admitted there to work thirteen or fourteen hours per day, at the tender age of seven years, and even in some cases still younger . . .

I most anxiously press upon the Committee, that unless some parliamentary interference takes place, the benefits of the Apprentice Bill will soon be entirely lost, the practice of employing parish apprentices will cease, their places will be wholly supplied by other children, between whom and their masters no permanent contract is likely to exist, and for whose good treatment there will not be the slightest security. Such indiscriminate and unlimited employment of the poor, consisting of a great proportion of the inhabitants of trading districts, will be attended with effects to the rising generation so serious and alarming, that I cannot contemplate them without dismay, and thus that great effort of British ingenuity, whereby the machinery of our manufactures has been brought to such perfection, instead of being a blessing to the nation, will be converted into the bitterest curse.

Gentlemen, if parish apprentices were formerly deemed worthy of the care of Parliament, I trust you will not withhold from the unprotected children of the present day an equal measure of mercy, as they have no masters who are obliged to support them in sickness or during unfavourable periods of trade.

Report on Children employed in Manufactories; P.P. 1816, vol. III, pp. 132–133.

2

Mr Buchanan Sees Nothing Much Wrong

Mr Archibald Buchanan called in and examined. Engaged in the management of the cotton mills in Scotland, the property of Messrs James Findlay and Company, merchants, of Glasgow, of which Company he is also a Partner. Been employed in the cotton-spinning business about 33 years, and was educated in it by Sir Richard Arkwright, at his mills at Cromford, Derbyshire. Now director of Catrine cotton mills, Ayrshire; Deanston works, Perthshire; and Ballindalloch cotton works in the county of Stirling.

What number of persons are employed in the different works?
—I can only speak to the works under my own particular management. At the Catrine works there are 875 persons employed, of whom 22 males and 37 females are under ten years of age. I suppose the youngest may be 8 or 9; we have no wish to employ them under ten years of age.

What are your hours of work?—Our working hours are twelve hours in the day. They begin at 6 o'clock in the morning, they stop at half-past seven at night, and they are allowed half an hour to breakfast, and an hour to dinner.

You have not observed that the twelve hours work has interfered with the health of the children?—I have not . . . I have seen many instances of children that were taken in the works as young as six, whose health did not appear at all to suffer; on the contrary, when they got to greater maturity, they appeared as healthy stout people as any in the country . . . They go to all trades, masons and joiners, and weavers, and so on.

Are they as tall?—Yes, I do not see any difference.

Do you conceive that the habits of regularity they are taught in the works, are advantageous to them in their pursuits afterwards?—I should think it was; that is the chief advantage tradesmen think they have in employing children from the factories.

That is, from their habits of industry?—Yes, and the ingenuity they acquire in the works.

Are the parents generally very desirous to send their children to you, or not?—Very desirous.

What are the weekly wages a child of nine years old, will acquire in your works?—The children of 9 years are generally learners, and receive 1s 6d to 2s per week, according to their ability.

In what manner are the children educated in your works?—We have three schools at present, I think, in the village: one of the schoolmasters we give a house to, with fire and candle, and £30 a year as a salary; he teaches one hour after the works stop on week days, and on Sundays he attends the Sunday schools; but I do not recollect the time the children attend.

You make the children's confinement fourteen hours, then?—They are not compelled to go to school in the evening.

P.P. 1816, vol. III, pp. 4–5.

3

Mr Wedgwood Wants to be Left Alone

Josiah Wedgwood called in and examined. Engaged in an extensive manufactory in the potteries; employs 387 persons, of whom 13 are under ten years and 103 between ten and eighteen.

What is the nature of the buildings of your manufactory?—They are very different from those of cotton works, and other manufactories in which machinery supplies the power; they are very irregular, and very much scattered, covering a great space of ground, and in general, of only two stories in height. The work-people are not at all crowded, but have ample space . . . The rooms are not close, the doors are generally open, and there are casements in the windows, which the work-people may open at their pleasure, as the temperature is of no importance in the process of the manufacture. The works are in general very healthy . . .

There is a part of the business which is unwholesome; it is that part that is connected with the applying the glaze upon the surface of the ware, called Dipping; that glaze is composed in part of white lead, and, like all other businesses in which the workmen have to do with lead, such as plumbers, house-painters, and a variety of others, they are, if careless in their method of living, and dirty, very subject to disease; but that depends very much upon the care the men take of themselves.

The hours of work for dippers in my manufactory are from 8 or 9 o'clock in the morning, to about 5 in the afternoon, with the interval of half an hour for breakfast and an hour for dinner . . . The hours of work for other persons in the manufactory are from half past six in the morning to six in the evening, with half an hour for breakfast and an hour for dinner, but during a part of the year when there is not sufficient day light, the hours are shortened to those hours in which they can see without candles, except from the 11th of November to the 3rd of February, in which period candles are burnt, and they work from half past seven in the morning to six. But we have a custom in our trade of working extra hours, called half nights or out of time, which is an extension of the hours of work to 9 o'clock in the evening; and this is a privilege which the men are generally very covetous of, and which the masters are generally inclined to grant in as small a degree as they can . . .

The children work the same time, because generally the young children are employed in attending on the men, and assisting them in carrying their moulds and other little services that they can perform for them, the men working by the piece, and paying the children themselves. The wages of the children are paid, I believe in all cases, to the parents. Much too often these additional wages are employed by the parents not in giving the children improved clothing and food but in procuring spirituous liquor for themselves . . .

Then the Committee is to understand from you, that although you think that the curtailment of labour to children would be extremely beneficial, you object to an Act of Parliament, not for containing these clauses which would be beneficial, but that you object to any Legislative interference with the manufactories?—I have a strong opinion that, from all I know at present of manufactories in general, and certainly from all I know of my own, we had better be left alone . . .

P.P. 1816, vol. III, pp. 60–64.

4

Too Busy for Crime

Then you admit that the employment of children in cotton manufactories is productive of benefit to their morals, in preventing the commission of crime?—Certainly; they have not the opportunity of committing overt acts as those have who are about the streets; in such a cotton mill as I saw [at Emscot, near Warwick] they could not commit any crime whatever that was of the nature of stealing, unless they took something from the mill into the house with them, for they could not go off the premises with it; they appeared as complete prisoners as they would be in gaol.

You were understood to say, that the occupation of so many hours had a favourable influence on morals, in preventing the commission of crimes?—Most assuredly; a person constantly under the eye of his master for twelve hours together, and not suffered to go out at night, cannot commit a crime of that nature; they may be bad in heart, but they cannot commit those acts.

THEODORE PRICE, JP; P.P. 1816, vol. III, p. 125.

5

Salutary Exercise

Is not these children being kept in a state of motion, by walking backwards and forwards, likely to be less prejudicial to health than if they were in a sedentary state?—Most assuredly; that exercise called loco-motive exercise is peculiarly salutary to young people.

Is the Committee to understand, that you consider the employment of children, under the age of ten years, to be wholly improper and inconvenient?—By no means wholly improper; I should think if it was limited to five or six hours, that would not only not be pernicious, but salutary.

SIR GILBERT BLANE, BART., MD, in evidence; P.P. 1816, vol. III, pp. 45–46.

6

Shilling Bargains

Mr George Gould, merchant in fustian goods, Manchester.

Will you state what you suppose to be the number employed in any of the manufactories under five years of age?—To enable me to get the best information I could, I had recourse to the town-officers, particularly the overseers of the poor; from the standing overseer of the poor of Salford, I learned (and that by a letter in his own hand-writing) that a woman living in such a street asserts, that two of her children . . . got employment in a factory when they were five years only, and they continued in that factory as long as the works were carried on.

Do you believe anything but a motive of humanity could have induced the individual you have spoken of to employ that woman's children?—I think that they employed them for their own interest.

Be so good as to explain that?—I think I can explain it. The spinning-men or women, whichever they are, have the privilege, I understand, generally to employ children of their own selecting; and if they can get a child to do their business for one shilling, or one shilling and six-pence, they will take that child before they will give three, four, five, six, or seven shillings, to an older one.

P.P. 1816, vol. III, pp. 99–100.

7

Robert Owen's Evidence

26 April, 1816, Sir Robert Peel, Bart., in the Chair: examination of Mr Robert Owen.

What is your situation in life?—I am principal proprietor and sole acting partner of the establishment of New Lanark, in Scotland.

How many persons, young and old, are immediately supported by the New Lanark manufactory and establishment?—About 2,300.

To how many out of that number do you give employment?—This number varies occasionally, but upon the average about sixteen or seventeen hundred.

The remainder of the 2,300 are the women and children?—Children too young, and persons too old, of the same families; some of the wives are employed.

At what age do you take children into your mills?—At ten and upwards.

What are the regular hours of labour per day, exclusive of meal times?—Ten hours and three quarters.

What time do you allow for meals?—Three quarters of an hour for dinner, and half an hour for breakfast.

Then your full time of work per day is twelve hours, out of which time you allow the mills to cease work for an hour and a quarter?—Yes.

Why do you not employ children at an earlier age?—Because I consider it would be injurious to the children, and not beneficial to the proprietors.

What reason have you to suppose it is injurious to the children to be employed in regular manufactories at an earlier age?—The evidence of very strong facts.

What are these facts?—Seventeen years ago, a number of individuals, with myself, purchased the New Lanark establishment from the late Mr Dale, of Glasgow. At that period I find that there were 500 children, who had been taken from poor-houses, chiefly in Edinburgh, and those children were generally from the age of five and six, to seven and eight; they were so taken because Mr Dale could not, I learned afterwards, obtain them at a more advanced period of life; if he did not take them at those ages, he could not obtain them at all. The hours of work at that time were thirteen, inclusive of meal times, and an hour and a half was allowed for meals. I very soon discovered that although those children were very well fed, well clothed, well lodged, and very great care taken of them when out of the mills, their growth and their minds were materially injured by being employed at those ages within the cotton mills for eleven hours and a half per day. It is true that those children, in consequence of being so well fed and clothed and lodged, looked fresh, and to a superficial observer, healthy in their countenances; yet their limbs were generally deformed, their growth was stunted, and although one of the best school-masters upon the old plan was engaged to instruct those children regularly every night, in general they made but a very slow progress, even in learning the common alphabet. . . .

In consequence, then, of your conviction that children are injured by being employed the usual daily hours in manufactories, when under ten years of age, you have for some time refused to receive children into your works till they are ten years of age?—Yes.

Do you think the age of ten the best period for the admission of children into full and constant employment for ten or eleven hours per day, within woollen, cotton, or other mills or manufactories?—I do not.

What other period would you recommend for their admission to full work?—Twelve years.

How, then, would you employ them from ten to the age of twelve?—

For the two years preceding, to be partially instructed; to be instructed one half the day, and the other half to be initiated into the manufactories by parties employing two sets of children in the day, on the same principle that two sets of children were employed when proprietors thought it their interest to work day and night.

Do you think ten hours and three quarters a day the proper time for children to be employed in manufactories ?—I do not.

What time do you recommend ?—About ten hours of actual employment, or, at the most, ten hours and a half.

Do you give instruction to any part of your population ?—Yes, to the children from three years old, upwards; and to every other part of the population that chuse to receive it.

P.P. 1816, vol. III, p. 20.

8

A Slight Expectoration ...

Thomas Wilson, surgeon and apothecary practising at Bingley, West Riding: employed also by the proprietors of a number of cotton mills in the vicinity.

There were 570 persons in the factories you examined, and there was only one found ill ? And that one got well in the extraordinary manner you have described, either charmed or frightened at the sight of the Doctor ?—She was almost well.

How long might the examination occupy you ?—About ten hours and a half the whole.

It was rather a rapid survey, I should think, you must have taken of the different factories, to have seen 570 people in ten hours. Did you ever examine the health of so many patients in so short a time before ? —No, I never examined so many in the same time before.

Then your examination must have been rather cursory and slight? —It was rather slight.

You found fifteen under the age of nine ?—Yes.

Should you not think that a lad of the age of fifteen years was sufficiently employed, if he was kept at work twelve hours out of the twenty-four, any where?—I never heard them complain of being over-worked.

Is it not, in your judgment as a medical man, necessary that young persons should have a little recreation or amusement during the day; is it not contributory to their general health?—I do not see it necessary.

Your opinion, as a medical man, is that a boy of fifteen years old might be kept under a constant course of attention, day after day throughout the year, with the intermission of Sunday, without injury to his health? —Yes.

Should you think it would be a beneficial thing for his health, if he were kept fifteen hours out of the twenty-four employed, without amusement, or recreation, or intermission?—No.

Then, in your judgment, twelve hours is the extent at which, in prudence, you think a person of fifteen ought to be so employed?—Yes.

Would you not allow, out of those twelve hours, an hour for his dinner?—No.

You would take the twelve hours, exclusive of hour for dinner?—Yes.

Probably, exclusive of any time for his breakfast?—Yes.

What is the earliest time, in your judgment, supposing he should be employed twelve hours, neither speaking of a very robust nor a very delicate boy, that a lad of fifteen years ought to begin his employment in winter?—About six.

An earlier hour, probably, in summer?—Yes, half past five . . .

In your judgment, as a medical man, is it not injurious to the health of a young person, of ten years, to keep him at work during the night, even though he has rest during the day?—I have never found it the case; at least, I have never noticed it.

Is it not highly injurious to the health of a young person, to come out of a temperature as high as 76°, after having been at work twelve hours, into a colder atmosphere?—I have never found it pernicious . . .

Should you not think it a dangerous thing to a young person to be from day to day inhaling the finer particles of the filaments of cotton? —No.

You think it would not be injurious to the lungs at all, to be receiving, day after day, those particles of cotton?—No.

Be so good as to state how the constitution would be safe under such circumstances, from receiving those things into the lungs?—Expectoration is occasioned, which brings it back again.

Would not a constant state of expectoration be injurious to the health of a very young person?—Not a slight expectoration . . .

Do you not think, the slighter the better, and better still if not at all ?—A degree of it is in that case beneficial.

Lords Committee, P.P. 1818, vol. 9, pp. 57–61.

9

The Doctor Who Couldn't (or Wouldn't) Say

Dr Thomas Turner, house surgeon and apothecary of the Manchester Poor House: cross-examined by Mr Sergeant Pell.

As a medical man . . . you represent to me, that unless you had a positive fact to guide your judgment by, you can form no judgment ? —I can form a judgment, but I do not choose to advance that judgment, being merely speculative.

The Chairman (Lord Kenyon) informs the Witness, that if he entertains an Opinion, he ought to state it.—I cannot give an opinion.

Mr Sergeant Pell: I am going to put an extreme case. Supposing you were asked, whether a man could take a pint of laudanum; do you think it would kill him ?—Then I should know from observation and facts that it would kill him.

From the quantity ?—Yes, from the quantity.

There is a time beyond which you would not, without knowing any precise fact, keep a young child standing upon his legs; as for instance, you would have no doubt that twenty-three hours would be too long ? —None whatever.

Then there is a limit ?—There is a limit; but I consider it difficult to define the line between that which would be salutary, and that which would injure the constitution.

Should you think a child of eight years old being kept fourteen hours upon his legs without any intermission; that that would or would not be dangerous if he was kept standing the whole time ?—I should think it might be fatiguing; whether the health would be materially injured by it, I am not prepared to say . . . I have no facts to guide me.

I ask you, as a medical man, whether you can form an opinion, either one way or another, that it would or would not be injurious to a child's health ?—I am not prepared to answer . . . I have no knowledge to guide me . . .

P.P. 1818, vol. 9, pp. 159–161.

10

'Be off now'

———————

Joshua Matley, 21-year-old spinner at Joseph Sykes' cotton factory at Ashton-under-Lyne:

When you received a summons to attend as a witness [at the House of Lords Committee], did your master make any observations upon the subject?—Yes, I received a summons on Friday last; I sent the over-looker to my master, with the summons on Saturday morning; he was not getting up, and he gave it to a little girl to take up stairs to him; so when he came to the mill, he came to the back of my wheel and said, that I must get my set off, and be off about my business. I said, must I be off now; and he asked me if there was ten pounds weight; I said no, there was not ten pounds. He said, if thou go, leaving that set on, he said, I will summons thee. I said, I must be at Stockport by 12 o'clock; he said, that is what I say to thee; and off he went out of the mill; and at breakfast time on Saturday I took the Head Constable to him; and the Constable told him, I was to come; and then he said, if he is like to go, he may go when he pleases; but when you come back, you shall have no work here; then he says to the Constable, his two brothers yonder, when they have done their work, may follow him if they please; they shall work here no longer.

House of Lords Committee . . . children employed in cotton manufactories; 1819, vol. 16, p. 49.

11

'It was me that pushed her'

———————

Titus Bryan, cotton-spinner at John Harrison and Bros.' mill at Manchester; age 33.

Have you a child of your own that scavenges for you?—Yes.

Was that child ever ill-used in the factory?—No.

Consider the question before you return an answer, and recollect you are upon your oath?—It never was, upon my oath.

Was the arm of that child ever broken?—Yes. How?—By a fall.

Not in consequence of being beaten?—No, it was not by beating, it was pushed down, and her arm went down under her.

Was not she pushed down in consequence of a beating and a kick; was it an accidental fall, or in consequence of her being beaten, and therefore falling?—It was me that pushed her down.

You pushed her down, and in consequence of your pushing her down her arm was broken?—Yes.

Where did you take her to?—A doctor.

Can you say the children are not unkindly treated, when you as a father were the cause of the arm of your own child being broken by ill usage?—It was my fault that the child's arm was broken.

How came you to push your child down?—It was for not just doing what I told her.

(Their Lordships decline, in consequence of the last answers of the witness, to ask him any further questions. The witness is directed to withdraw.)

House of Lords Committee . . . children employed in cotton manufactories, 1819; vol. 16, p. 448.

(c) SADLER'S COMMITTEE

Just as 'Peel's Committee' is commonly named after its chairman, so the Select Committee that was appointed by the House of Commons in 1832 to make a further enquiry into the condition of child factory workers is generally referred to by the name of the man who presided over all its sittings, and by his unremitting exertions was believed by his friends to have shortened his days.

Michael Thomas Sadler (1780–1835) was a staunch Churchman and in politics an enthusiastic Tory, who however was not afraid of striking out an original line for himself. He was in business in Leeds as partner in a firm importing Irish linens, and as early as 1823 he showed deep concern about the conditions of the children and young persons employed in the local factories. Unlike most of his class and station he could not get himself to believe that the pursuit of individual self-interest was bound to result in the greatest possible measure of public good, and he said as much in his speeches. In 1829 he was elected to Parliament as the Tory member for Newark, and in the House of Commons he soon made his mark as a supporter of further legislation to protect factory children. His sympathetic approach and dauntless vigour attracted the favourable notice of the leaders of the working class movements for factory reform, and they invited him to become their spokesman in Parliament. He accepted, and as such he introduced in 1831 a Bill prohibiting the employment in all factories of children under nine years of age and limiting the actual working hours of those children and young persons between nine and eighteen to ten hours a day from Monday to Friday, with two hours fewer on Saturdays. On March 16th, 1832, he moved the Bill's second reading (No. 1). As will be gathered from his peroration, the House was not prepared to pass the Bill as it stood but was intent upon the appointment of a Select Committee to enquire further into a matter which, in his opinion, had already been enquired into more than enough.

The Committee sat on 43 days between April and August, 1832, with Sadler in the chair, and it examined 89 witnesses, about half of whom were workpeople who could, and did, speak out of their own long, hard, and often bitter experience. In August he laid before the House a mass of evidence, constituting a most formidable indictment of factory conditions. It is this evidence which is referred to as the Report of Sadler's Committee. As printed it runs to several hundred pages, but the selections given here are fully typical. It is impossible not to be staggered by the revelations of human misery and cruelty and degradation—impossible not to be moved by the dreadful stories of children and young persons (and adults, too, for that matter) who were bullied and cursed and tormented, pushed around and knocked about by those placed in authority over them. Not that the picture is completely black. Now and again there shines through the gloom the little candle of a splendidly brave deed in a desperately wicked world, showing that even in the most degrading and demoralizing surroundings the spirit of comradeship and family affection managed to survive.

Critics have alleged that some of the evidence was biased, incomplete, sometimes inaccurate or even deliberately misleading, and it is true that a good deal of it referred to conditions that had long been ameliorated. But those who knew the system best were the most forthright in their condemnation of an abominable state of affairs—of a system which Richard Oastler (1789–1861; known for his untiring and self-sacrificing labours in behalf of factory reform as 'the factory king'), described in his evidence before the Committee as being of such a character as would have disgraced a West Indian plantation in the days of Negro slavery. When every allowance has been made for exaggerations and omissions and the rest, the 'report' stands as one of the classic documents of British social history.

To return to Sadler. With the passing of the great Reform Bill in 1832, the constituency for which he was then sitting was disfranchised as one of the 'rotten boroughs', and when he stood for Leeds as a Tory he had the misfortune to be opposed by the brilliant young Macaulay, who won the seat by 1984 votes to

Sadler's 1598. He tried to re-enter Parliament in 1834 but was again defeated, and in the following year he died, prematurely, at the age of fifty-five.

I

Sadler's Impassioned Oration

The Bill which I now implore the House to sanction with its authority, has for its object the liberation of children and other young persons employed in the mills and factories of the United Kingdom, from that over-exertion and long confinement which common sense, as well as experience, has shown to be utterly inconsistent with the improvement of their minds, the preservation of their morals, and the maintenance of their health—in a word, to rescue them from a state of suffering and degradation, which it is conceived the children of the industrious classes in hardly any other country has ever endured . . .

I apprehend, that the strongest objections that will be offered on this occasion, will be grounded upon the pretence that the very principle of the Bill is an improper interference between the employer and the employed, and an attempt to regulate by law the market of labour. Were the market supplied by free agents, properly so denominated, I should fully participate in these objections . . . but children, at all events, are not to be regarded as free labourers. The common-place objections that the parents are free agents, and that the children therefore ought to be regarded as such, I apprehend has but little force . . .

The parents who surrender their children to this infantile slavery may be separated into two classes. The first, and I trust by far the most numerous one, consists of those who are obliged, by extreme indigence, so to act, but who do it with great reluctance and bitter regret: themselves perhaps out of employment, or working at very low wages, and their families in a state of great destitution;—what can they do? The overseer refuses relief if they have children capable of working in factories whom they object to send thither. They choose therefore what they probably deem the lesser evil, and reluctantly resign their offspring to the captivity and pollution of the mill; they rouse them in the winter morning, which, as a poor father says before the Lords Committee, they 'feel very sorry to do'; they receive them fatigued and exhausted, many a weary hour after the day has closed; they see them droop and sicken, and in many cases become cripples and die, before they reach their prime: and they do all this, because they must otherwise suffer unrelieved, and starve amidst their starving children. It is a mockery to contend that these parents have a choice . . . Free agents! To suppose that parents are free agents while dooming their own flesh and blood to this fate, is to believe them monsters!

But, Sir, there are such monsters; unknown indeed in the brute creation, they belong to our own kind, and are found in our own country; and they are generated by the very system which I am attacking. Dead to the instincts of nature, and reversing the order of society; instead of providing for their offspring, they make their offspring provide for them: not only for their necessities, but for their intemperance and profligacy. They purchase idleness by the toil of their infants; the price of whose happiness, health, and existence, they spend in the haunts of dissipation and vice. Thus, at the very same hour of night that the father is at his guilty orgies, the child is panting in the factory. Such wretches count upon their children as upon their cattle;—nay, to so disgusting a state of degradation does the system lead, that they make the certainty of having offspring the indispensable condition of marriage, that they may breed a generation of slaves . . .

But I will proceed no further with these objections. The idea of treating children, and especially the children of the poor—above all, the children of the poor imprisoned in factories—as free agents, is too absurd . . . The protection of poor children and young persons from these hardships and cruelties to which their age and condition have always rendered them peculiarly liable, has ever been held one of the first and most important duties of every Christian legislature. Our own has not been unmindful in this respect; and it is mainly owing to the change of circumstances that many of its humane provisions have been rendered inoperative, and that the present measure has become most necessary . . .

The very same opposition that has so long and so often triumphed over justice and humanity, is again organized, and actively at work . . . Certificates and declarations will be obtained in abundance, from divines and doctors, as to the morality and health which the present system promotes and secures . . . They have said that the children who were worked without any regulation, and consequently according to their employer's sole will and pleasure, were not only equally, but more, healthy, and better instructed, than those not so occupied; that night labour was in no way prejudicial, but actually preferred; that the artificial heat of the rooms was really advantageous, and quite pleasant . . . That so far from being fatigued with, for example, twelve hours' labour the children performed even the last hour's work with greater intent and spirit than any of the rest! What a pity the term was not lengthened! In a few more hours they would have worked in a perfect ecstasy of delight! We had been indeed informed that the women and children often cried with fatigue, but their tears were doubtless tears of rapture . . .

Light labour! Is the labour of holding this pen and of writing with it strenuous? And yet, ask a clerk in any of the public offices, or in any private counting house, when he has been at his employment some half-dozen hours in the day less than any of these children, whether he does not think he has had enough of this light labour—to say nothing of holidays, of which he has many, and the child none . . . I might appeal to the Chair, whether the lingering hours which have to be endured here, though unaccompanied with any bodily exertion whatever, are not 'weariness of the flesh'. But what would be the feelings of the youngest and most active individual amongst us, if, for example, he were compelled to pass that time, engaged in some constant and anxious employment, stunned with the noise of revolving wheels, suffocated with the heat and stench of a low, crowded, and gas-lighted apartment, bathed in sweat, and stimulated by the scourge of an inexorable taskmaster? I say, what would be his idea of the light labour of twelve or fourteen hours in such a pursuit; and when, once or twice in every week, the night also was added to such a day? And how would he feel, if long years of such light labour lay before him? . . .

The overworking of these children occasions a weariness and lethargy which it is impossible always to resist: hence, drowsy and exhausted, the poor creatures fall too often among the machinery, which is not in many instances sufficiently sheathed; when their muscles are lacerated, their bones broken, or their limbs torn off, in which case they are constantly sent to the infirmaries to be cured, and if crippled for life, they are turned out and maintained at the public cost; or they are sometimes killed upon the spot . . .

Then, in order to keep the children awake, and to stimulate their exertions, means are made use of, to which I shall now advert . . . Sir, children are beaten with thongs prepared for the purpose. Yes, the females of this country, no matter whether children or grown up,—I hardly know which is the more disgusting outrage—are beaten upon the face, arms, and bosom—beaten in your 'free market of labour', as you term it, like slaves! These are the instruments.—(*Here the honourable member exhibited some black, heavy, leathern thongs,—one of them fixed in a sort of handle, the smack of which, when struck upon the table, resounded through the House.*)—They are quite equal to breaking an arm, but that the bones of the young are pliant. The marks, however, of the thong are long visible; and the poor wretch is flogged before its companions; flogged, I say, like a dog, by the tyrant overlooker. We speak with execration of the cart-whip of the West Indies—but let us see this night an equal feeling rise against the factory-thong of England . . .

I wish I could bring a group of these little ones to that bar—I am sure their silent appearance would plead more forcibly on their behalf than the loudest eloquence . . . At this late hour, while I am thus feebly, but earnestly, pleading the cause of these oppressed children, what numbers of them are still tethered to their toil, confined in heated rooms, bathed in perspiration, stunned with the roar of revolving wheels, poisoned with the noxious effluvia of grease and gas, till, at last, weary and exhausted, they turn out, almost naked, into the inclement air, and creep, shivering, to beds from which a relay of their young workfellows have just risen . . .

Sir, I have shown the suffering—the crime—the mortality, attendant upon this system . . . Earnestly do I wish that I could have prevailed upon this House and his Majesty's Government to adopt the proposed measure, without the delay which will attend it further . . . Would that we had at once decided, as we could wish others to decide concerning our own children, under like circumstances, or as we shall wish that we had done, when the Universal Parent shall call us to a strict account for our conduct to one of the least of these little ones! As the case, however, is otherwise . . . I will now move the second reading of this bill; and afterwards propose such a Committee as I hope, will assist in carrying into effect the principles of a measure so important to the prosperity, character, and happiness of the British people.

From the speech delivered by M. T. Sadler, M P, in the House of Commons, on March 16, 1832; *Memoirs of the Life and Writings of Michael Thomas Sadler* (1842), pp. 338–379.

2

The Trials of Elizabeth Bentley

Elizabeth Bentley, age 23, lives at Leeds, began work at the age of six in Mr Busk's flax-mill, as a little doffer. Hours 5 a.m. till 9 p.m. when they were 'thronged', otherwise 6 a.m. to 7 at night, with 40 minutes for meal at noon.

Do you consider doffing a laborious employment? Explain what you had to do.—When the frames are full, they have to stop the frames, and take the flyers off, and take the full bobbins off, and carry them to the roller; and then put empty ones on, and set the frame going again.

Does that keep you constantly on your feet?—Yes, there are so many frames, and they run so quick. Your labour is very excessive?—Yes; you have not time for anything. Suppose you flagged a little, or were too late, what would they do?—Strap us. Girls as well as boys?—Yes. Have you ever been strapped?—Yes. Severely?—Yes.

Were the girls so struck as to leave marks upon their skin?—Yes, they have had black marks many a time, and their parents dare not come to him about it, they were afraid of losing their work. If the parents were to complain of this excessive ill-usage, the probable consequence would be the loss of the situation of the child?—Yes.

In what part of the mill did you work?—In the card-room. It was exceedingly dusty?—Yes. Did it affect your health?—Yes; it was so dusty, the dust got upon my lungs, and the work was so hard: I was middling strong when I went there, but the work was so bad; I got so bad in health, that when I pulled the baskets down, I pulled my bones out of their places.

You dragged the baskets?—Yes, down the rooms to where they worked. And so you had been weakened by excessive labour, you could not stand that labour?—No. It has had the effect of pulling your shoulders out?—Yes, it was a great basket that stood higher than this table a good deal. It was a very large one, that was full of weights up-heaped, and pulling the basket pulled my shoulders out of its place, and my ribs have grown over it. You are considerably deformed in your person in consequence of this labour?—Yes, I am.

At what time did it arise?—I was about 13 years old when it began coming, and it has got worse since; it is five years since my mother died, and my mother was never able to get me a pair of good stays to hold me up, and when my mother died I had to do for myself, and got me a pair.

Were you perfectly straight and healthy before you worked in a mill? —Yes, I was as straight a little girl as ever went up and down to work . . . Where are you now?—In the poorhouse, at Hunslet.

Did you receive anything from your employers when you became afflicted?—When I was at home Mr Walker made me a present of 1s or 2s but since I have left my work and gone to the poorhouse, they have not come nigh me.

You are utterly incapable now of any exertion of that sort?—Yes. You were very willing to have worked as long as you were able, from your earliest age?—Yes. And to have supported your widowed mother as long as you could?—Yes. State what you think as to the circumstances in which you have been placed during all this time of labour, and what you have considered about it as to the hardship and cruelty of it.

(*The witness was too much affected to answer the question.*)

Committee on Factory Children's Labour, P.P. 1831–32; vol. XV, pp. 195–199.

3

What Made the Children Crooked

John Hall, overlooker at Mr John Wood's worsted mill at Bradford, was asked to describe to the Committee 'the position in which the children stand to piece in a worsted mill, as it may serve to explain the number and severity of those cases of distortion which occur'. At the top of the spindle there is a fly goes across, and the child takes hold of the fly by the ball of his left hand, and he throws the left shoulder up and the right knee inward; he has the thread to get with the right hand, and he has to stoop his head down to see what he is doing; they throw the right knee inward in that way, and all the children I have seen, that I could judge that are made cripples by the practice of piecening worsted, invariably bend in the right knee.

I knew a family, the whole of whom bent outwards as a family complaint, and one of those boys was sent to a worsted-mill, and first he became straight in his right knee, and then he became crooked in it the other way.

P.P. 1831–32, vol. XV, p. 115.

4

My Boy Edwin

Gillett Sharpe, aged 52, assistant Overseer of the Poor at Keighley, Yorks.

Have you any children, yourself, working at these mills?—My eldest daughter went when she was between six and seven; the next boy when he was just turned seven, perhaps a month or two; and my other daughter went at about the same age.

What effect had this labour upon your children?—With regard to my first daughter, it had no effect as to making her crooked in her limbs, but her health was impaired. She went to a worsted manufactory; but her stepmother dying, I took her away to manage the affairs of my house; she was very young, to be sure, but she did what I had to do, except what I hired out, and she is very healthy and strong. But with regard to my boy, Edwin, he was a proverb for being active and straight before he went . . . But when he had gone to the mill some time, perhaps about three years, he began to be weak in his knees; and it went on to that degree, that he could scarcely walk. I had three steps up into my house, and I have seen that boy get hold of the sides of the door to assist his getting up into the house. Many a one advised me to take him away; they said he would be ruined, and made quite a cripple; but I was a poor man, and could not afford to take him away, having a large family, six children, under my care . . . he still continued to go, but during the last six or seven months the factory has been short of work . . . and he is very much improved in that time with regard to the strength of his knees . . . but he is bent in one knee. I do not think he will ever recover, but I hope he will get strength, and I have no doubt that if I could take him away, and let him go to school, he would be a fine boy yet . . .

P.P. 1831–32, vol. XV, p. 209.

5

Why Mrs Hebergam Cried

Joseph Hebergam, aged 17, worked in worsted spinning factories at Huddersfield since he was seven:

When I had worked about half a year, a weakness fell into my knees and ankles; it continued, and it has got worse and worse. In the morning I could scarcely walk, and my brother and sister used out of kindness to take me under each arm, and run with me, a good mile, to the mill, and my legs dragged on the ground in consequence of the pain; I could not walk. If we were five minutes too late, the overlooker would take a strap, and beat us till we were black and blue . . .

Did the pain and weakness in your legs increase? Just show the Committee the situation in which your limbs are now. (*The witness accordingly stood up, and showed his limbs.*)

Were you originally a straight and healthy boy?—Yes, I was straight and healthful as any when I was seven years and a quarter old. . . .

Your mother being a widow and having but little, could not afford to take you away?—No.

Was she made very unhappy by seeing that you were getting crooked and deformed?—I have seen her weep sometimes, and I have asked her why she was weeping, but she would not tell me then, but she has told me since . . .

P.P. 1831–32, vol. XV, p. 159.

6

How They Kept the Children Awake

It is a very frequent thing at Mr Marshall's [at Shrewsbury] where the least children were employed (for there were plenty working at six years of age), for Mr Horscman to start the mill earlier in the morning than he formerly did; and provided a child should be drowsy, the overlooker walks round the room with a stick in his hand, and he touches that child on the shoulder, and says, 'Come here'. In a corner of the room there is an iron cistern; it is filled with water; he takes this boy, and takes him up by the legs, and dips him over head in the cistern, and sends him to work for the remainder of the day . . .

JONATHAN DOWNE, 25-year-old millworker at Leeds, who had worked at Marshall's at the age of seven; P.P. 1831–32, vol. XV, p. 205.

★   ★   ★

What means were taken to keep the children to their work?—Sometimes they would tap them over the head, or nip them over the nose, or give them a pinch of snuff, or throw water in their faces, or pull them off where they were, and job them about to keep them waking.

JAMES CARPENTER, Leeds millhand; P.P. 1831–32, vol. XV, 190.

7

Fines and Floggings

Mark Best, flax-mills overlooker, was asked to describe 'the sort of straps that are made use of' to keep the children at work:

They are about a foot and a half long, and there is a stick at the end; and that end they beat them with is cut in the direction of my fingers, thus, having five or six thongs, some of them. Some of them are set in a handle, some are not.

You say you had one of these delivered to you by a master, who urged you to make use of it, and to lay it on freely ?—Yes.

Do you think you could have got the quantity of work out of the children for so great a number of hours (from 6 a.m. to 7 p.m., or 5 a.m. to 9 p.m. when they were 'thronged') without that cruel treatment ?—For that number of hours, I could not, I think; it is a long time. The speed of the machinery is calculated, and they know how much work it will do; and unless they are driven and flogged up, they cannot get the quantity of work they want from them.

Were the children fined as well as beaten occasionally ?—Yes. For various things; if they were caught combing their hair before they went home, or washing themselves—if they caught them doing any other frivolous thing, such as cleaning their shoes or doing anything so as to go home decent at night.

Were the children allowed, when the work went well, to clean themselves at all in this manner ?—No, they did not allow them to do any such thing; they would not even allow them to speak to one another.

So there was profound silence enjoined ?—Yes.

Would they allow the girls to do a little sewing when the work was going on well ?—No; they would fine them for it, if they caught them at it.

Or any boy to read, if his work went well ?—No, they would not allow that.

P.P. 1831-32, vol. XV, p. 168.

8

Ann Coulson's Punishment

Samuel Coulson, tailor, at Stanningley, near Leeds, with three daughters working in the mills:

Have any of your children been strapped ?—Yes, every one; the eldest daughter; I was up in Lancashire a fortnight, and when I got home I saw her shoulders, and I said, 'Ann, what is the matter ?' She said, 'The overlooker has strapped me; but', she said, 'do not go to the overlooker, for if you do we shall lose our work.' I said I would not if she would tell me the truth as to what caused it. 'Well,' she said, 'I will tell you, father.' She says, 'I was fettling [tidying up] the waste, and the girl I had learning had got so perfect she could keep the side up till I could fettle the waste; the overlooker came round, and said, "What are you doing?" I said, "I am fettling while the other girl keeps the upper end up." ' He said, 'Drop it this minute'; she said, 'No, I must go on with this'; and because she did not do it, he took a strap, and beat her between the shoulders. My wife was out at the time, and when she came in she said her back was beat nearly to a jelly; and the rest of the girls encouraged her to go to Mrs Varley, and she went to her, and she rubbed it with a part of a glass of rum, and gave her an old silk handkerchief to cover the place with till it got well.

Did you observe those marks a fortnight afterwards?—Yes . . . We could not get the rum to dress it with, but we got some milk and water, and she told me that she bathed it with it till it was completely well.

You could not afford any medical person to visit your daughter when so cruelly used?—No; all I could get to take her to the Infirmary in Leeds was 2d, and I laid out 1d of it for an orange; I thought she would fall sick, and I bought one penny roll with the other . . .

P.P. 1831-32, vol. XV, p. 193.

9

The Sadistic Overlooker

Samuel Downe, age 29, factory worker living near Leeds; at the age of about ten began work at Mr Marshall's mill at Shrewsbury, where the customary hours when work was brisk were generally 5 a.m. to 8 p.m., sometimes from 5.30 a.m. to 8 or 9:

What means were taken to keep the children awake and vigilant, especially at the termination of such a day's labour as you have described?—There was generally a blow or a box, or a tap with a strap, or sometimes the hand.

Have you yourself been strapped?—Yes, most severely, till I could not bear to sit upon a chair without having pillows, and through that I left. I was strapped both on my own legs, and then I was put upon a man's back, and then strapped and buckled with two straps to an iron pillar, and flogged, and all by one overlooker; after that he took a piece of tow, and twisted it in the shape of a cord, and put it in my mouth, and tied it behind my head.

He gagged you?—Yes; and then he ordered me to run round a part of the machinery where he was overlooker, and he stood at one end, and every time I came there he struck me with a stick, which I believe was an ash plant, and which he generally carried in his hand, and sometimes he hit me, and sometimes he did not; and one of the men in the room came and begged me off, and that he let me go, and not beat me any more, and consequently he did.

You have been beaten with extraordinary severity?—Yes, I was beaten so that I had not power to cry at all, or hardly speak at one time. What age were you at that time?—Between 10 and 11.

P.P. 1831–32, vol. XV, p. 199.

10

They Had No Clock

Abraham Whitehead, clothier, residing near Holmfirth, 'nearly in the centre of 30 or 40 woollen mills'.

You say you have observed these children constantly for many years going there early in the morning to their work, and continuing at it till late at night?—Yes. I have seen children during this last winter coming from work on cold dark nights between 10 and 11 o'clock.

This requires that the cottagers should wake their children very early in the morning?—It cannot be expected they can go to their work asleep.

How early do you think that they leave their homes?—I can tell you what a neighbour told me six weeks ago; she is the wife of Jonas Barrowcliffe, near Scholes; her child works at a mill nearly two miles from home, and I have seen that child coming from its work this winter between 10 and 11 in the evening; and the mother told me that one morning this winter the child had been up by 2 o'clock in the morning,

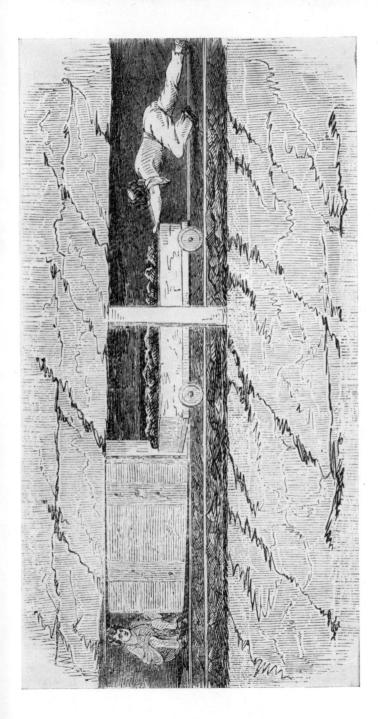

5. The Lonely Little Trapper: an illustration from the Report on the Employment of Children in Mines (P.P. 1842, vol. XV) (*photo*: British Museum)

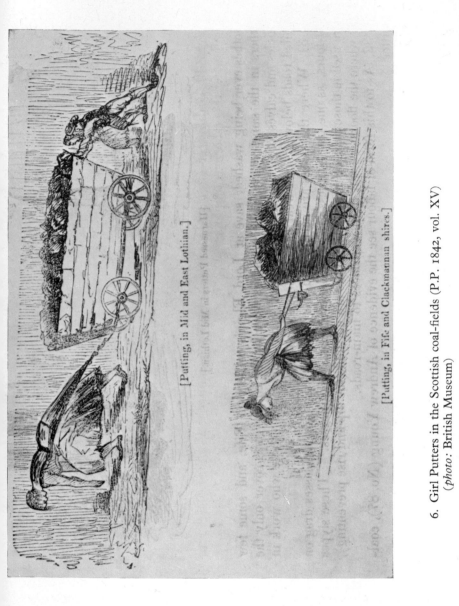

[Putting, in Mid and East Lothian.]

[Putting, in Fife and Clackmannan shires.]

6. Girl Putters in the Scottish coal-fields (P.P. 1842, vol. XV)
(*photo*: British Museum)

when it had only arrived from work at 11; it then had to go nearly two miles to the mill, where it had to stay at the door till the overlooker came to open it.

This family had no clock, I suppose?—They had no clock; and she believed, from what she afterwards learnt from the neighbours, that it was only 2 o'clock when the child was called up and went to work; but this has only generally happened when it has been moonlight, thinking the morning was approaching . . .

P.P. 1831–32, vol. XV, pp. 18–19.

II

Mother to the Rescue

William Kershaw, age 42, began work in a mill as a 'piecener' at the age of 8, at a wage of 2s 6d a week for twelve hours a day:

Yes, I have been ill-treated myself; and I have seen others that have been a good deal worse used. There is a difference in the disposition of the slubber or person under whom the child is placed; some have more humanity, and rather wish to encourage the children to attention, than to punish them for negligence. I have been employed under both. Some of them who are kind have some rewards, such as some fruit, and say that those who have the fewest number of ends in a given time shall have this fruit; and others will keep beating the children, whether they are in fault or not. I have been beat with a billy-roller [a roller running along the top of the machine, perhaps 2 or 3 yards long and 4 or 5 inches in circumference] towards night, when I have been particularly drowsy, till I repeatedly vomited blood . . .

I entreated my mother not to make a complaint, lest I should be further beaten. The next morning after I went to work, she followed me, and came to the slubber that had used me in that way, and gave him a sharp lecture; and when she had done she retired into the engine-feeder's house, and left me to my work; and as soon as she was gone, he beat me severely again for telling, when one of the young men that served the carder, went out and found my mother, and told her, and she came in again and inquired of me what instrument it was I was beaten with, but I durst not do it; some of the bystanders pointed out the instrument, the billy-roller, and she seized it immediately, and beat it about the fellow's head, and gave him one or two black eyes. How long ago was this?—About the year 1799.

PP. 1831-32, vol. XV, pp. 46-47.

12

The Girl Who Got Away

Alexander Dean, overlooker in a flax-mill at Dundee; age, going on for 27; having no parents to take care of him, he obtained his first job at the age of twelve in a flax mill in Dundee, where they worked not less than 17 hours a day, exclusive of meals, and for wages 'sometimes we got the clothes which were taken from others who had deserted the service'. Was beaten very often. His story continued:

One time I was struck by the master on the head with his clenched first, and kicked, when I was down. I saw one girl trailed by the hair of her head, and kicked by him, when she was down, till she roared 'Murder!' several times. The girl told me that the master had wished to use familiarities with her, and she had refused the night before; and he found a small deficiency in her work, and he took that opportunity of abusing her.

[Having run away, he eventually got work as an overlooker at Duntruin mill, where the hands were principally children, a great number of them below the age of twelve, and the poorest of the poor. Some were from the poorhouses of Edinburgh, the orphan-houses, and they were sent to the mill at six or seven, and some at the ages of three or four. From time to time there were attempts at escape.]

There were two girls that made their escape through the roof of the house, and left nearly all their clothes behind them. They finally escaped.

At the time I was in the mill, there was a young woman who had been kept seven months in the gaol at Dundee for deserting this mill; and she was brought back, after having been in the gaol for seven months, to make up for her lost time and the expenses incurred. One day I was alarmed by her cries. She was lying on the floor, and the master had her by the hair of her head, and was kicking her in the face till the blood was running down . . . After the master had retired from the flat [work-room], I opened the door and let her out, and told her to run; and the master came back and missing her out of the apartment, began cursing and swearing at me for letting her out, and ordered me to run after her, which I refused to do. I stated that owing to the ill-treatment she had received, I never would be the man that would run after her and bring her back to the torture. She was not brought back, and, not being in a situation to get any other employment, she became a prostitute. She was tried at the circuit of Perth for stealing, and transported to Van Dieman's Land.

P.P. 1831–32, vol. XV, pp. 369–374.

13

'Easing nature' to Order

Charles Burns, 'going of 14', who began work at the age of 8 at a flax mill in Leeds, was asked, 'Pray, how often were you allowed to make water?' and replied, Three times a day.

And were you allowed to make water at any time you wanted?—No; only when a boy came to tell you it was your turn, and whether you wanted to or no, that was the only time allowed us; if we did not go when he came round, we could not go at all. He started at one end and as soon as ever he came to the mill, and then went all round.

Could you hold your water all that time?—No; we were forced to let it go.

*   *   *

Peter Smart, overseer at a flax mill in Dundee, asked whether 'there are any improper restrictions of the children in regard to their easing nature', replied: In my flat, they go out when they please; when I was a boy at Mr Smith's mill, in Fife, the overseer gave us five minutes twice a day to go out of the factory, and we had a tub in the corner of the flat where we made water.

Both males and females ?—Yes.

P.P. 1831–32, vol. XV, pp. 165, 348.

14
High Marks for Mr Wood

William Sharp, surgeon at the Dispensary at Bradford, and also the medical man required by Mr Wood to pay particular attention to the children employed in his mills, was asked:

Has anything struck you as to the general management and arrangement of those mills ?—That they are particularly cleanly, and made as comfortable as they can be; that there is every attention paid to the comfort and cleanliness and health of those employed in them, as far as possible under the present system.

Are the mills well ventilated ?—Yes, I have endeavoured to direct my attention to that as much as possible. Kept as clean as possible? —Yes. Means adopted and opportunity given, for instance, to enable the children to keep themselves clean ?—Yes. And to wash themselves at their pleasure ?—Yes, I think there is. Has Mr Wood baths upon his premises ?—Yes. In which the hands may bathe as is thought advisable.

Do you happen to know whether seats are provided for them, so that they may in some measure abate the fatigue that too long standing and exertion occasion ?—There are; Mr Wood has taken pains to provide them all with seats, that they may sit down when they have opportunity, a minute or two at a time sometimes; but it is rarely for any length of time that they can do so.

Does it consist with your knowledge, that the hours in that mill are also quite as short as in any similar establishment, and shorter than in many ?—I believe shorter than in any at present.

Will you state the number of hours they are employed in Mr Wood's mill ?—From six to seven, with half an hour for breakfast and forty minutes for dinner. I think the present number of hours is too long a period of work.

P.P. 1831–32, vol. XV, p. 300.

15

Horses Preferred

—————

Thomas Bennett. When I was working at Mr Wood's mill at Dewsbury
. . . while we were taking our meals he used to come up and put the
machine agoing; and I used to say, 'You do not give us time to eat';
he used to reply, 'Chew it at your work'; and I often replied to him,
'I have not yet become debased like a brute, I do not chew my cud'.
   Once when Mr Wood was saying to the carrier who brought his
work in and out, 'How long has that horse of mine been at work?'
and the carrier told him the time, and he said, 'Loose him directly,
he has been at it too long', I made this reply to him, 'You have more
mercy and pity for your horse than you have for your men'.

P.P. 1831–2, vol. XV, p. 103.

16

Clothes Torn Off Her Back

—————

There was one orphan girl who spun at the same frame with me . . .
This girl was engaged at the mill for three years, for meat and clothes.
She one day got entangled in the machinery, till all her clothes were
torn off her back, and the overlooker was not at hand, but we got the
mill stopped, and when she was taken out she was very much abused
for her neglect in letting herself in.
   Do you imagine she was over-fatigued at her work?—Yes; she was
lying up against the box with an upright shaft, and the shaft got hold
of her clothes, and she was carried round the shaft.

ALEXANDER DEAN, flax-mill overlooker, in evidence; P.P. 1831–32, vol. XV,
   p. 371.

133

17

Richard Oastler on 'Yorkshire Slavery'

Richard Oastler, appearing before the Committee, when asked, 'Has your mind been latterly directed to the consideration of the condition of children and young persons engaged in the mills and factories', made answer:

The immediate circumstance which led my attention to the facts was a communication made to me by a very opulent spinner [Mr John Wood, of Horton Hall, Bradford], that it was the regular custom to work children in factories 13 hours a day, and only allow them half an hour for dinner, and that in many factories they were worked considerably more. . . . From that moment, which was the 29th of September 1830, I have never ceased to use every legal means, which I had it in my power to use, for the purpose of emancipating these innocent slaves. The very day on which the fact was communicated to me, I addressed a letter to the public, in the *Leeds Mercury*, upon the subject. I have since that had many opponents to contend against; but not one single fact which I have communicated has ever been contradicted, or ever can be . . .

The demoralizing effects of the system are as bad, I know it, as the demoralizing effects of slavery in the West Indies. I know that there are instances and scenes of the grossest prostitution amongst the poor creatures who are the victims of the system, and in some cases are the objects of the cruelty and rapacity and sensuality of their masters. These things I never dared to publish, but the cruelties which are inflicted personally upon the little children, not to mention the immensely long hours which they are subject to work, are such as I am very sure would disgrace a West Indian plantation.

On one occasion . . . I was in the company of a West India slave master and three Bradford spinners; they brought the two systems into fair comparison, and the spinners were obliged to be silent when the slave-owner said, 'Well, I have always thought myself disgraced by being the owner of black slaves, but we never, in the West Indies, thought it was possible for any human being to be so cruel as to require a child of nine years old to work twelve and a half hours a day; and that, you acknowledge, is your regular practice . . .'

In the West Riding of Yorkshire when I was a boy it was the custom for the children to mix learning their trades with other instruction and with amusement, and they learned their trades or their occupations, not by being put into places, to stop there from morning to night, but by having a little work to do, and then some time for instruction, and they were generally under the immediate care of their parents; the villages about Leeds and Huddersfield were occupied by respectable little clothiers, who could manufacture a piece of cloth or two in the week, or three or four or five pieces, and always had their family at home: and they could at that time make a good profit by what they sold; there were filial affection and parental feeling, and not over-labour.

But that race of manufacturers has been almost completely destroyed; there are scarcely any of the old-fashioned domestic manufacturers left, and the villages are composed of one or two, or in some cases of three or four, mill-owners, and the rest, poor creatures who are reduced and ground down to want, and in general are compelled to live upon the labour of their little ones. It is almost the general system for the little children in these manufacturing villages to know nothing of their parents at all excepting that in the morning very early, at 5 o'clock, very often before 4, they are awaked by a human being that they are told is their father, and are pulled out of bed (I have heard many a score of them give an account of it) when they are almost asleep, and lesser children are absolutely carried on the backs of the older children asleep to the mill, and they see no more of their parents, generally speaking, till they go home at night, and are sent to bed.

Now that system must necessarily prevent the growth of filial affection. It destroys the happiness in the cottage family, and leads both parents and children not to regard each other in the way that Providence designed they should . . . With regard to the fathers, I have heard many of them declare that it is such a pain to them to think that they are kept by their little children, and that their little children are subjected to so many inconveniences, that they scarcely know how to bear their lives; and I have heard many of them declare that they would much rather be transported than be compelled to submit to it. I have heard mothers, more than on ten or eleven occasions, absolutely say that they would rather that their lives were ended than that they should live to be subjected to such misery. The general effect of the system is this, and they know it, to place a bonus upon crimes; because their little children, and their parents too, know that if they only commit theft and break the laws, they will be taken up and put into the House of Correction, and there they will not have to work more than 6 or 7 hours a day . . .

P.P. 1831–32, vol. XV, pp. 445–455.

(*d*) CHILDREN IN FACTORIES (1833)

With Sadler out of the House of Commons, the factory reformers
had to look round for another spokesman in Parliament, and their
choice fell on Lord Ashley, who not until the death of his father in
1851 became the 7th Earl of Shaftesbury, the title under which he
is usually known. He had been an MP since 1826 and was like
Sadler a Tory, and yet he knew nothing of Sadler's Committee
until he read the reports of the evidence taken before it in the
columns of *The Times*. He was profoundly shocked by what he
read, and since he had not the slightest acquaintance with the
factory world it was only after much heart-searching and delibera-
tion that he accepted the invitation brought him by the Rev.
George Stringer Bull (1799–1865), vicar of Brierley, near Leeds,
who was known throughout the West Riding as 'Parson Bull' and
honoured as a true friend of the factory workers.

There could not have been a better choice than Ashley. He was
deeply religious of the Evangelical persuasion, a tremendously
hard worker, highly conscientious, and experienced in parliamentary business. His humanitarian sympathies were beyond dispute,
and his aristocratic connections made him *persona grata* with the
rising middle class. His first reactions to the invitation were of
'astonishment and doubt and terror', but once he had convinced
himself that the call was of God he never drew back or spared
himself.

Early in 1833 Ashley reintroduced Sadler's Bill; it was given
a first reading, but then the manufacturing interest persuaded the
Government that more facts were needed before reaching a
decision, since so much of the evidence given to Sadler's Committee had been (so it was alleged) so very one-sided. A Commission was forthwith appointed 'to collect information in the
manufacturing districts with respect to the employment of

children in factories, and to devise the best means for the curtail-
ment of their labour'. Three commissioners were nominated, and
all three became eminent in their respective spheres: Thomas
Tooke, economist; Edwin Chadwick, Civil Servant; and Dr
Southwood Smith, London doctor. Chadwick and Southwood
Smith we shall meet again in later pages.

The Commissioners had a far from friendly reception in the
manufacturing districts, since the operatives looked upon them as
tools of the employers. But when their report was published it was
found that on the whole it supported the case for reform (Nos.
1–3). The selections from the evidence speak for themselves; it
will be seen that they very largely confirm the statements made to
Sadler's Committee. A case of alleged cruelty that aroused much
public interest was that of the 'Little girl who was "weighted"'
(No. 6). Rowland Detrosier (1800?–1834), the witness in No. 7,
was a remarkable character. The illegitimate son of a Manchester
man and a French woman who abandoned him when he was a
month old, he was brought up by a benevolent fustian-cutter,
who apprenticed him to his own trade when he was twelve. He
married early, and was often in want. In the spells of unemploy-
ment he taught himself French, Latin, etc., and after some years
as a book-keeper and salesman with a firm of cotton-spinners
found his niche as a public lecturer on social and political subjects.
Also of special interest is No. 9, in which Mr Tufnell (Edward
Carleton Tufnell, 1806–1886; an assistant Poor Law Commissioner 1835–74, and of some importance in the development of
popular education in England) described conditions in the 'best'
mines in Lancashire as being far worse than in the worst-conducted factory.

The Commission's Report was on the whole well received; but
when Ashley's Bill came before the House for a third reading,
thirteen was substituted for eighteen as the age below which
juvenile workers should be given legislative protection. Ashley
protested, and also Cobbett, in a speech in which he referred
caustically to the 'great discovery' about Lancashire's little mill-
girls (No. 10).

The Bill became law as the Factory Act 1833, and on the whole
it was a great improvement on previous legislation. The hours of
labour of children between 9 and 13 years of age were not to
exceed forty-eight, and of young persons up to the age of 18,

sixty-nine. Children were to attend school during working hours for not less than two hours a day. What was of most importance, however, was the appointment of four factory inspectors to see that the Act was complied with. Thus was born the Factory Inspector, one of the most beneficial British innovations of the nineteenth century. The men appointed were mostly of high quality, notably Leonard Horner (1785–1864), from whose early reports are quoted Nos. 11 and 12. In both there is reference to the certificates of age that were required before children might be employed, and it is worth remembering that there was no official registration of births until 1837.

I

The Child Beaters

It will appear from the evidence annexed to this Report that the Commissioners have everywhere investigated with the utmost care the treatment to which children are subjected while engaged in the labour of the factory. These inquiries have obtained from the children themselves, from their parents, from operatives, overlookers, proprietors, medical practitioners, and magistrates, such statements amongst others as the following:—

'When she was a child too little to put on her ain claithes, the overlooker used to beat her till she screamed again.'

'Gets many a good beating and swearing. They are very ill-used. The overseer carries a strap.'

'Has been licked four or five times.'

'The boys are often severely strapped; the girls sometimes get a clout. The mothers often complain of this. Has seen the boys have black and blue marks after strapping.'

'Three weeks ago the overseer struck him in the eye with his clenched fist so as to force him to be absent two days; another overseer used to beat him with his fist, striking him so that his arm was black and blue.

'Has often seen the workers beat cruelly. Has seen the girls strapped;

but the boys were beat so that they fell to the floor in the course of the beating, with a rope with four tails, called a cat. Has seen the boys black and blue, crying for mercy.'

'The other night a little girl came home cruelly beaten; wished to go before a magistrate, but was advised not. That man is always strapping the children.'

'The boys are badly used. They are whipped with a strap till they cry out and shed tears; has seen the manager kick and strike them. Has suffered much from the slubbers' ill-treatment. It is the practice of the slubbers to go out and amuse themselves for an hour or so, and then make up their work in the same time, which is a great fatigue to the pieceners, keeping them "on the run" for an hour and a half together, besides kicking and beating them for doing it badly, when they are so much tired.'

'The slubbers are all brutes to the children; they get intoxicated, and then kick them about; they are all alike.'

'There is an overlooker in the room, who is a man; the doffer always scolds her when she is idle, not the overlooker; the doffer is a girl; sometimes sees her hit the little hands; always hits them with her hand; sometimes the overlooker hits the little hands; always with her hand when she does; the overseer scolds the little hands; says he'll bag 'em; sometimes swears at 'em; sometimes overseer beats a "little hand"; when he does it is always with his open hand; it is not so very hard; sometimes on the face, sometimes on the back; he never beats her; some on 'em cries when they are beat, some doesn't; he beats very seldom; didn't beat any yesterday, nor last week, nor week before; doesn't know how long it is ago since she has seen him strike a girl. If our little helper gets careless we may have occasion to correct her a bit; some uses 'em very bad; beats 'em; but only with the hand, and pulls their ears; some cry, but not often; ours is a good overlooker, but has heard overlookers curse very bad; the women themselves curse; has never cursed herself; can say so honestly from her heart.'

Factory Commission, 1st Report; P.P. 1833, vol. XX, pp. 18–20.

2

Lament for the Tired Little Ones

The statements of the children, and more especially of the younger children, as to their own feeling of fatigue, may be said to be uniform . . . The expressions of fatigue are the strongest and the most constant on the part of the young children employed in the factories in Scotland, because there the ordinary hours of work are in general longer by an hour or an hour and a quarter than in the factories of England. We have been struck with the perfect uniformity of the answers returned to the Commissioners by the young workers in this country, in the largest and best regulated factories as well as in the smaller and less advantageously conducted. In fact, whether the factory be in the pure air of the country, or in the large town; under the best or the worst management; and whatever be the nature of the work, whether light or laborious; or the kind of treatment, whether considerate and gentle or strict and harsh; the account of the child, when questioned as to its feelings of fatigue is always the same. The answer always being, 'sick-tired, especially in the winter nights'. 'So tired when she leaves the mill that she can do nothing.' 'Feels so tired, she throws herself down when she gangs hame, no caring what she does.' 'Often much tired, feels sore, standing so long on her legs.' 'Often so tired she could not eat her supper.'

Young persons of more advanced age, speaking of their own feelings when younger, give to the Commissioners such representations as the following:—'Many a time has been so fatigued that she could hardly take off her clothes at night, or put them on in the morning; her mother would be raging at her, because when she sat down she could not get up again . . .' 'Looks on the long hours as a great bondage.' 'Thinks they are not much better than the Israelites in Egypt, and their life is no pleasure to them.' 'When a child, was so tired that she could seldom eat her supper, and never awoke of herself.'

'Are the hours to be shortened?' earnestly demanded one of these girls of the Commissioner who was examining her, 'for they are too long . . .'

These statements are confirmed by the evidence of the adult operatives. The depositions of witnesses of this class are to the effect that 'the younger workers are greatly fatigued'; that 'children are often very swere (unwilling) in the mornings'; that 'children are quite tired out'; that 'the long hours exhaust the workers, especially the younger ones, to such a degree that they can hardly walk home'; that 'young workers are absolutely oppressed, and so tired as to be unable to sit down or rise up'; that 'young workers are so tired they often cannot raise their hands to their head'; that 'all children are very keen on shorter hours, thinking them now such bondage that they might well be in a prison...'

P.P. 1833, vol. XX, pp. 25-27.

3

A Case is Made Out . . .

From the whole of the evidence laid before us . . . We find—

1st. That the children employed in all the principal branches of manufacture throughout the kingdom work during the same number of hours as the adults.

2d. That the effects of labour during such hours are, in a great number of cases,

Permanent deterioration of the physical constitution:

The production of disease often wholly irremediable: and

The partial or entire exclusion (by reason of excessive fatigue) from the means of obtaining adequate education and acquiring useful habits, or of profiting by those means when afforded.

3d. That at the age when children suffer these injuries from the labour they undergo, they are not free agents, but are let out to hire, the wages they earn being received and appropriated by their parents and guardians.

We are therefore of the opinion that a case is made out for the interference of the Legislature in behalf of the children employed in factories ...

P.P. 1833, vol. XX, pp. 31-32.

4

Fast Asleep

I have frequently had complaints against myself by the parents of children for beating them. I used to beat them. I am sure that no man can do without it who works long hours; I am sure he cannot. I told them I was very sorry after I had done it, but I was forced to it. The master expected me to do my work, and I could not do mine unless they did theirs. I used to joke with them to keep up their spirits.

I have seen them fall asleep, and they have been performing their work with their hands while they were asleep, after the billy had stopped, when their work was over. I have stopped and looked at them for two minutes, going through the motions of piecening fast asleep, when there was really no work to do, and they were really doing nothing . . .

JOSEPH BADDER, a spinner at Mr Bradley's, Leicester: evidence collected by Mr Drinkwater; Factory Commission, 1833; P.P. vol. XX, page C 1, 19.

* * *

James Gillespie, grocer, of John Street, Aberdeen, formerly an over-looker at a spinning-mill: He remembers one instance of a young female child being brought to the mill of Messrs Richards and Company; that she was so young that the general remark was, she was fitter for her cradle than for the work; that she used frequently to fall asleep, and he felt so much for her that he allowed her to remain undisturbed, and the rest of the girls, who felt in a similar way, did her work for her in the mean time . . .

P.P. 1833, vol. XX, A 1, 58.

5

'All the masters licked me'

W—W—, a girl of 17 (who was allowed to remain anonymous), began working in mills at Manchester 'before I was eight'. In evidence said:

Have had pains in my feet since 10 years of age. Began to be bad about twelve. My hours in work at M'Connell's mill were from a few minutes before half-past five in the morning till seven at night. Half an hour for breakfast; an hour for dinner; no bagging (tea).

Were you ever too late of a morning at M'Connell's?—Yes, sir.

Did they scold you?—The spinners always licked me; they always lick the piecers when they are too late of a morning. Generally with a strap, either a strap or a rope; very seldom with the hand.

How many blows did they give you when they kicked you?—Well, sir, I never took particular notice. I have been licked for five minutes together as hard as he could lick me. I was seldom too late, for mother was asthmatical, and began being very bad of a morning, that waked us up. That, and the watchman together. We had a watchman, too, to wake us.

Did he ever lick you for anything else?—Sometimes when I've gone for his meat, and I have been longer than I should have been.

Did all the masters lick you?—I never worked with a master yet but what he licked me when I was late in the morning. One master used to lick me of all colours if I was two minutes too late. I've gone off from home half dressed, he used to be so very savage. Mother has held me to put on my clothes, but I would be off first.

Where did he get the straps?—Some was old straps; he used to turn the wheel; and some he fetched 'em from home.

How long were they?—About half a yard long. How thick?—About this thick (measuring more than a quarter of an inch on her nail). The rope, was it knotted?—Some had 'em knotted, and some they hadn't.

Was this beating pretty much the case in all the mills where you have been?—Yes, the spinners all beat the piecers. You see it throws 'em behind of their work if the piecers a'nt there.

From the evidence taken by Mr Cowell, Manchester; P.P. 1833, vol. XX, D 1, pp. 76–77.

6

The Strange Tale of the Little Girl Who Was 'Weighted'

Extract from a speech made by Mr Grant, a Manchester spinner, at a meeting held at Chorlton upon Medlock; reported in the *Manchester Courier* of April 20, 1833:

'Much was said of black slaves and their chains; no doubt they were entitled to freedom, but were there no slaves except those of sable hue?... He would name an instance of this kind of slavery which took place at Wigan. A child, not ten years of age, having been late at the factory one morning, had, as a punishment, a rope put round its neck, to which a weight of twenty pounds was attached; and thus burthened like a galley-slave, it was compelled to labour for a length of time in the midst of an impure atmosphere and a heated room. (Loud cries of shame.) The truth of this had been denied by Mr Richard Potter, the member for Wigan; but he (the speaker) reiterated its correctness. He had seen the child, and its mother's eyes were filled with tears whilst she had told him this shocking tale of infant suffering.'

*　　*　　*

Ellen Hootton examined 15th June, 1833.

How old are you?—I shall be ten on the 4th August.

How old were you when you began to work in Eccles' factory [at Wigan]?—I wasn't quite eight. Worked there above a year.

Were you beaten and scolded at Eccles'?—Yes. Who by?—William Swanton. What for?—For having my ends down. How often were you beaten by him?—Twice a week. What with?—His hands. Did he hurt you much?—No; but it made my head sore with his hands.

Did Mr Swanton ever tie a weight to you?—Yes, to my back. What was it tied with, a string?—Yes, it was tied with one string round my neck, one round my shoulders, and one round my middle. How heavy was it?—I don't know. It was a great piece of iron, and two more beside. How big were they?—One was as big as this book (pointing to the Lords' Report of 1818). Was it as thick?—No; it was thicker. (Pointing to an unbound octavo book of 419 pages.) As thick as that.

What time of the day was it?—It was after breakfast. How long was it kept on you?—About half an hour. What did you do?—I walked up and down the room. What did you walk up and down the room for?—He made me. Was it that other children might see you with it?—Yes.

Did you ever see such weights tied to other children?—Yes; there was one other that had them tied to his legs. Was there more than one? —Yes, there was two beside him. How long did they wear it?—About an hour. Did they walk up and down the room too?—Yes.

*   *   *

Now mind and don't tell a lie; what had you done?—I did nothing but run away because he beat me. Had you stolen any thing?—No. Did you tell your mother of it?—Yes. She said nothing.

Is your father dead?—I have no father.

Mary Hootton (the girl's mother). Age 41 last Christmas-day.

How many children have you?—None but yon young girl. (N.B. 'Yon' is a provincialism; the girl was not in the room.) What was your husband?—I have no husband, sir. Is she a natural child?—Yes.

What do you do for a living?—I am a weaver. At a dandy-shop. It is not good getting money at a dandy-shop. It is as much as I can do to earn 3s.

Did you ever put your little girl to Eccles'?—Yes. Did you have her wages?—Yes, sir; but not at that time. She was a good time a learning before she had wages; I dare say twenty weeks. She had 10½d a week for tenting half a side at first; then she had a side at 1s 9d; then she had another half side; and that would be 2s 7½d.

Was she sent away from there, or did you take her away?—I neither took her away, nor he didn't send her away. She left her place; she run away; she was missing a whole day, and didn't come home till 9 o'clock at night.

Had she ever run away before?—Yes, many a time. Did she ever tell you it was because she was beaten and ill-treated?—Yes, she has told me that.

Who did she say beat and ill-treated her?—Her looker-over, William Swanton. Did you ever speak to him about beating and ill-treating her? —I axed him what it was for, and he told me she wouldn't mind her work and keep her ends up.

Why did you not take her away?—Because she were a very stupid girl . . . How often did she run away?—I dare say it were ten. How many times do you think she was weighted?—I cannot tell exact; it's about five, I think, but to tell true I really cannot.

Had she stolen any thing?—Not at that time she hadn't; but she did steal 6d and 4d, and a little brass box to carry silver. I went to the mill the next morning, and I met Betty Chapman; she asked me whether my Ellen had got some money; I said yes; when Betty said she had taken 6d in silver and 4d in copper after. I told her that I would stop it out of her wages that week, and I took it to her, and gave it to her, and likewise thanked her. Was she weighted for this?—No, sir.

Did she often steal little things of other people, and at home?—She stole 6½d from me. I left a box open, and she took it out. It was all I had to make my breakfast on, and I was forced to borrow.

Have you beaten her much yourself?—Yes, I have beaten her many a time. For being stupid, and not heeding what I said to her . . .

William Swanton, overlooker, age 31, in Mr Eccles' mill, at 22s 6d a week.

Do you know Ellen Hootton?—Yes. She was a throstle-spinner at Eccles' mill. Her mother came down and axed me if she might learn.

Did you ever beat her?—Yes; by persuading by her parents. What did you beat her with?—A strap. For neglect of work and stealing. How often?—A few times; not so oft; not as oft as I was told by her parents for to lick her.

What do you mean by her parents?—I mean her mother; I don't know her father; I never saw him. Her mother has often told me to lick her; often; and to kill her, once, she told me.

What did her mother tell you this for?—For the naughtiness of the girl; she couldn't manage her herself, so she turned her over to me . . . She has told me to take her to myself, and have her earnings, and keep her on bread and water, and put a lock of straw in one corner of the room for her to lie on. Did you ever do this?—No; I told her I would have nothing at all to do with it.

Did you ever put a weight upon her?—Yes. Two or three times. How long did it remain on each time?—Half an hour. How heavy was it?—Betwixt eight and ten pounds. What was it of?—Cast iron. Where was it put?—A top of her back. What was its shape?—Square.

Did you ever put more than one piece on her?—Yes. Two small pieces besides. Betwixt two and four pounds each. About 14 or 16 pounds altogether. The two small ones were fixed a top of the big one. How were they fixed to her?—Tied by two bands over her shoulders and across the waist.

Was any thing else put upon her?—No. Nothing like a cap, to expose her?—Oh, a cap; I thought you meant a weight. She had a cap on her head, and a stick in her hand.

Did she stoop much with it?—Well, she fell down several times with fighting with the other hands. She fought them with the stick. Did the other hands teaze her, or hoot at her?—Yes, they plucked as she went by; then she turned round and struck them with the stick. That's what I gave her the stick for, and I told her to do it if they plucked her. Did the weight appear to give her pain?—No; she laughed at them, and made fun of the joke . . .

Then I understand your story to be, that this was a lazy, idle, good-for-nothing runaway girl, whom you couldn't manage by any means?—Well, I can say nothing more than that she is a very bad girl, and I have had a good deal of pains with her; I have put myself out of my way for the sake of her mother; it has cost me a deal of trouble and uneasiness. I have often sent her away, and her mother has brought her back again, and requested me to let her work on . . .

P.S. by Mr Cowell, the Commissioner who enquired into the case: I have to remark on the foregoing set of examinations, that the girl is certainly a very bad, lying girl. I hardly know what to say of the mother. Swanton, I believe, meant no harm, and the weighting the girl gave her no pain. It was an ignorant, stupid device of his to cure the girl of running away, but not cruelly intended. The story of her being compelled to work is not only a gross exaggeration, but any man who is a spinner must have known the absolute impossibility of a girl working at throstle-spinning with a weight on her back. Neither could any person who has ever been in a throstle-room believe it for a moment. I think it right to say that all the parties . . . spoke such broad dialect, that I was often compelled to make them repeat their answers once or twice before I could seize their meaning. Neither did they always understand me at first . . .

P.P. 1833, vol. XX, D 1, pp. 103–111.

7

Why Children Leave Home

Rowland Detrosier, having stated 'that in many instances where the parents live upon the labours of the children, the children fare very poorly', was asked to give any instances that had come under his immediate observation:

A man and his wife, living in a cellar in Silver Street, Hulme, had three children, the eldest of which at that time did not exceed twelve years of age, and the youngest seven or eight. The parents were most dissipated characters, living in a state of almost constant idleness, working only at intervals, and that not very long at a time. The children worked in the factory, and regularly brought home their weekly earnings. These parents have been frequently known to lock up the three children on a Saturday night, after having given to them a miserable pittance of what they called tea and bread, and go to the public-house together, and spend a considerable portion of that money in drink, and to return home, perhaps about midnight, in a state of beastly intoxication, and some times to abuse the poor children whose hard-earned money they had been so profligately spending. On the following morning (Sunday) they sent the children out to beg bread, or anything they could obtain, for their breakfast, and I have frequently supplied those children on a Sunday morning from my own table. The starved appearance of the children, and the vile conduct of the parents, led to an inquiry in the neighbourhood; the overseers were applied to, and I believe the parents were at last summoned before the magistrates, but comparatively little change took place for the better.

This may have been an extreme case, and I am disposed to believe it was; but I very much fear that there are hundreds of cases at the present time that differ from it only in degree; indeed, hundreds of the children employed in our cotton manufactures are kept in a most miserable way. The consequence of this state of things is, that as the parents spend the money principally upon themselves and that portion of the family that cannot get work, dissatisfaction arises as the working children grow up, and they refuse to contribute the whole amount of their wages; they want better clothes, and they demand them as a right; and a state of dissatisfaction and bickering is carried on for some time, and is at last settled by the parents' agreeing to take a certain stipulated sum per week for the meat, drink, washing, lodging, and cooking, the boy or girl retaining the remainder of his or her wages for the purchase of clothes, or for any other purpose to which they may think proper to apply it.

This gives rise to a sort of independence of the parent, and in most cases completely destroys that feeling of mutual affection which ought to subsist between parent and child; the one always thinks he pays too much, the other that too little is paid . . . At last he leaves the house of his parents, takes a lodging somewhere else, finishes with the folly of an early marriage, becomes a parent before he is a man, and in the end goes through the same routine of circumstances with his own children to which he has himself previously been a victim . . .

P.P. 1833, vol. XX, E 17–19.

8

Dragged Naked from Their Beds

Robert Arnot, aged 44, now working at a spinning-mill at Monteith, was in 1826 overseer at Baxters mill at Dundee, where he saw 'the boys, when too late of a morning, dragged naked from their beds by the overseers, and even by the master, with their clothes in their hands to the mill, where they put them on'. He had seen this done 'oftener than he can tell, and the boys were strapped naked as they got out of bed'.

This was confirmed by Barbara Watson, who worked with Arnot at the same mill. She went on to state that 'she remembers William Edwards, an overseer in the spinning-flat of this mill, coming to the bothy [the hut where the girl workers slept] when one of the girls was too late and in bed, that he turned her round and took her out of bed naked; that he took her out of the bothy in this state, but she prigged sair (pleaded earnestly), and he at last let her come back to put on her claithes before going into the mill; that the man was in an awfu' passion that morning . . .'

P.P. 1833, vol. XX, A 1, p. 40.

9

The Black Holes of Worsley

Examination of Thomas Gibson and George Bryan, witnesses from the coal mines at Worsley:

Have you worked from a boy in a coal mine?—(Both) Yes.

What had you to do then?—Thrutching the basket and drawing. It is done by little boys; one draws the basket and the other pushes it behind. Is that hard labour?—Yes, very hard labour.

For how many hours a day did you work?—Nearly nine hours regularly; sometimes twelve; I have worked above thirteen. We used to go in at six in the morning, and took a bit of bread and cheese in our pocket, and stopped two or three minutes; and some days nothing at all to eat.

How was it that sometimes you had nothing to eat?—We were over-burdened. I had only a mother, and she had nothing to give me. I was sometimes half starved . . .

Do they work in the same way now exactly?—Yes, they do; they have nothing more than a bit of bread and cheese in their pocket, and sometimes can't eat it all, owing to the dust and damp and badness of air; and sometimes it is as hot as an oven; sometimes I have seen it so hot as to melt a candle.

What are the usual wages of a boy of eight?—They used to get 3d or 4d a day. Now a man's wages is divided into eight eighths; and when a boy is eight years old he gets one of those eighths; at eleven, two eighths; at thirteen, three eighths; at fifteen, four eighths; at twenty, man's wages.

What are the wages of a man?—About 15s if he is in full employment, but often not more than 10s, and out of that he has to get his tools and candles. He consumes about four candles in nine hours' work, in some places six; 6d per pound, and twenty-four candles to the pound.

Were you ever beaten as a child?—Yes, many a score of times; both purs (a Lancashire term for a kick) and kicks and thumps.

Are many girls employed in the pits?—Yes, a vast of those. They do the same kind of work as the boys till they get above 14 years of age, when they get the wages of half a man, and never get more, and continue at the same work for many years.

Did they ever fight together?—Yes, many days together. Both boys and girls; sometimes they are very loving with one another . . .

Note by Mr Tufnell: After the examination of the preceding witnesses, I descended into one of the mines. The mode of entrance was by means of a bucket, in which I was let down to a depth of 70 yards, when we came to a canal, which runs for a considerable distance in a subterranean channel . . . At this canal I got into a barge . . . which was made to advance by the boatmen pushing against small staples fastened into the roof . . . In this way I travelled more than half a mile. The first mine we arrived at was approached by a small tunnel, in which it was impossible to stand upright, the height not exceeding 3 or 4 feet. The place where the working was going on was nothing more than a continuation of this tunnel . . . Having returned to the barge I was landed about half a mile further on at another mine, which was described to me as the best and largest in the district. The approach to it was rather higher than in the other, and led to an excavation about 18 feet square, where the mining processes were carried on. The hole was said to be 7 feet high, but there were only a few square feet in the centre in which I could stand upright; and as the coal was extracted from the sides, it was obviously impossible for the miners to work in any other position than in one constantly bent. This mine was very damp, and a great part of it wet under foot . . .

As this was said to be the best mine in the place, I cannot much err in coming to the conclusion, that the hardest labour in the worst room in the worst-conducted factory is less hard, less cruel, and less demoralizing than the labour in the best of coal-mines.

From Mr Tufnell's report on the mines in Lancashire; P.P. 1833, vol. XX, pp. D 2, 79–82.

10

Lancashire's Little Girls

———————

At about one o'clock this morning, the House of Commons divided on the Factory Bill of Lord Ashley, and defeated his bill, in fact, by 238 votes against 93 . . . It is now six o'clock, and I did not get to bed till half after two; and this must be printed and published this afternoon. I think it right, to prevent misrepresentation, to report what I said upon the subject, especially as it was so very little.

What I said was that which here follows, as near as I can recollect, word for word. 'Sir, I will make but one observation upon this subject, and that is this: that this *reformed* House has, this night, made a *discovery* greater than all the discoveries that all former Houses of Commons have ever made, even if all their discoveries could have been put into one. Heretofore, we have been sometimes told that our ships, our mercantile traffic with foreign nations by the means of those ships, together with our body of rich merchants; we have sometimes been told that these form the source of our wealth, power, and security. At other times, the land has stepped forward, and bid us look to it, and its yeomanry, as the sure and solid foundation of our greatness and our safety. At other times, the Bank has pushed forward with her claims, and has told us, that great as the others were, they were nothing without "public credit", upon which, not only the prosperity and happiness, but the very independence of the country depended. But, Sir, we have this night discovered, that the shipping, the land, and the Bank and its credit, are all nothing compared with the labour of three hundred thousand little girls in Lancashire! Aye, when compared with only an eighth part of the labour of these three hundred thousand little girls, from whose labour, if we only deduct two hours a day, away goes the wealth, away goes the capital, away go the resources, the power, and the glory of England!'

WILLIAM COBBBETT, *Political Register*, LXXXI, July 20, 1833.

11

Avaricious Parents

In a visit to a mill near Bury, on the 23rd of November last, I noticed a girl who was working, as I was informed, 12 hours a day, and had been doing so for more than two years, who appeared to me to be too young to have a certificate of thirteen; and on examining her father, by whom she was employed as his piecer, he admitted that she was between eleven and twelve years of age. On calling for her certificate, I found that it was dated the 17th of August 1836. Here, then, was a father, in the receipt of good wages and in regular employment, who had been knowingly working his own child twelve hours a day, and that too, from the time when she was little more than nine years old. It is not at all improbable that he was one of those who sent up petitions on Parliament to interfere for the protection of the poor factory children, 'the white slaves', who were so cruelly over-worked by 'the hard-hearted avaricious masters . . .'

LEONARD HORNER, an Inspector of Factories: Reports of H.M. Inspectors of Factories, P.P. 1839, vol. XIX, p. 15.

12

The Anonymous Letter

On the 4th of May I visited with Mr Sub-Inspector Jones, the factory of Messrs Christopher Bracewell and Brothers at Earby, between Colne and Skipton. It stands apart from the village, in an open field, and as we came near, one of the brothers was seen running with considerable speed from his house to the mill. This looked very suspicious, but we did not discover anything wrong.

A few days afterwards I received an anonymous letter dated the 11th of May, stating, that when the Inspector was at the mill on the 4th, so soon as Mr Bracewell saw him he went to the mill, and got those under age and those without certificates [of age], about twenty in number, into the privies; that several of those employed as young persons were children; that the times for meals were considerably less than the time required by law; and that the mill worked from 13 to 14 hours a-day.

I immediately conferred with Mr Jones as to the steps to be taken, in order to discover how far the allegations contained in this letter were well founded. In a few days Mr Jones went again to the mill, taking the superintendent of police at Colne along with him. As the mill could then be at work in daylight only, it was not possible for any stranger to approach it without being seen; and, as it afterwards appeared, a watch must have been set to give the necessary alarm in such an event. Mr Jones directed the constable to go at once to the alleged places of concealment; but he found that none such could be entered from the outside of the mill. He was placed at the door to prevent any one from coming out, while Mr Jones went through the factory, which is a large weaving-shed.

After having made his first examination, he directed the constable to search the privies, and there were found in them thirteen children and young persons, male and female, packed as close together as they could lie one upon another. I need scarcely add that all of them were found to have been illegally employed in the mill . . .

To bring up such shameless offenders before the magistrates . . . was an obvious and imperative duty . . . The case was heard at Colne on the 29th of May . . . when by the unanimous decision of the bench, the defendants were convicted on all the informations, and penalties to the amount of £136 were imposed . . .

LEONARD HORNER, Inspector of Factories; report for the half-year ended 30th April, 1850; P.P. 1850, vol. XXIII, pp. 8–9.

(e) CHILDREN IN COAL MINES

Children and young persons employed in textile mills had now been given some measure of protection in their working lives, but there were great numbers of juvenile workers—nobody could say for sure just how many, or even make a plausible guess—employed in all sorts of other jobs, in all sorts of conditions. Over the years their numbers had grown, but practically nothing was known of their working lives. Now public attention was directed towards them.

In 1840 it was decided to set up a Commission to inquire into the state of children in mines and manufactories. The Commissioners were Thomas Tooke and Dr Southwood Smith, who had been Commissioners in the Factory Commission of 1833, and two factory inspectors, Leonard Horner and R. J. Saunders. Some twenty sub-commissioners were appointed to make the necessary inquiries, collect evidence, etc.

The first report appeared in May 1842, and covered the employment of children and young persons (and also women) in mines. The Conclusions of the Commissioners are given in full in No. 1, and there follows a number of selections from the evidence appended thereto. Altogether the Report was a masterly document, clear in expression, sober in presentation, and most comprehensive. There was also one striking innovation. Dr Southwood Smith had impressed on his colleagues that Members of Parliament were busy people and could not be expected to read through the mass of evidence, and he suggested, therefore, that the text should be accompanied by illustrations of the working conditions that had been found. As he had shrewdly anticipated, these were strikingly successful in arousing public interest.

Probably it was the plight of the little 'trappers' that evoked most concern, and the various aspects of their employment are fully displayed in the documents given here.

Bringing up the rear is a report (No. 21) from *Hansard*, of remarks made by Lord Londonderry, one of the largest and most influential coal-owners, when presenting a petition to the House of Lords against legislative action. His Lordship scoffed at the way in which evidence had been taken from 'artful boys and ignorant young girls', but what most aroused his indignation was the pictures . . .

A month after the publication of the Report, Lord Ashley introduced a Bill into the House of Commons that would have greatly improved the condition of children, young persons, and women employed in the mines. The Bill passed the Commons, but was greatly modified in the Upper House; although it did prohibit the employment of children in coal-mines under the age of ten.

I

Children in Coal Mines: The 1842 Report

From the whole of the evidence which has been collected, and of which we have thus endeavoured to give a digest, we find—In regard to COAL MINES—

1. That instances occur in which Children are taken into these mines to work as early as four years of age, sometimes at five, and between five and six, not unfrequently between six and seven, and often from seven to eight, while from eight to nine is the ordinary age at which employment in these mines commences.

2. That a very large proportion of the persons employed in carrying on the work of these mines is under thirteen years of age; and a still larger proportion between thirteen and eighteen.

3. That in several districts female Children begin to work in these mines at the same early ages as the males.

4. That a great body of the Children and Young Persons employed in these mines are of the families of the adult workpeople engaged in

the pits, or belong to the poorest population in the neighbourhood, and are hired and paid in some districts by the workpeople, but in others by the proprietors or contractors.

5. That there are in some districts also a small number of parish apprentices, who are bound to serve their masters until twenty-one years of age, in an employment in which there is nothing deserving the name of skill to be acquired, under circumstances of frequent ill-treatment, and under the oppressive condition that they shall receive only food and clothing, while their free companions may be obtaining a man's wages.

6. That in many instances much that skill and capital can effect to render the place of work unoppressive, healthy, and safe, is done, often with complete success, as far as regards the healthfulness and comfort of the mines; but that to render them perfectly safe does not appear to be practicable by any means yet known; while in great numbers of instances their condition in regard both to ventilation and drainage is lamentably defective.

7. That the nature of the employment which is assigned to the youngest Children, generally that of 'trapping', requires that they should be in the pit as soon as the work of the day commences, and, according to the present system, that they should not leave the pit before the work of the day is at an end.

8. That although this employment scarcely deserves the name of labour, yet, as the Children engaged in it are commonly excluded from light and are always without companions, it would, were it not for the passing and repassing of the coal carriages, amount to solitary confinement of the worst order.

9. That in those districts in which the seams of coal are so thick that horses go direct to the workings, or in which the side passages from the workings to the horseways are not of any great length, the lights in the main ways render the situation of these Children comparatively less cheerless, dull, and stupefying; but that in some districts they remain in solitude and darkness during the whole time they are in the pit, and, according to their own account, many of them never see the light of day for weeks together during the greater part of the winter season, excepting on those days in the week when work is not going on, and on the Sundays.

10. That at different ages, from six years old and upwards, the hard work of pushing and dragging the carriages of coal from the workings to the main ways, or to the foot of the shaft, begins; a labour which all

classes of witnesses concur in stating requires the unremitting exertion of all the physical power which the young workers possess.

11. That, in the districts in which females are taken down into the coal mines, both sexes are employed together in precisely the same kind of labour, and work for the same number of hours; that the girls and boys, and the young men and women, and even married women and women with child, commonly work almost naked, and the men, in many mines, quite naked; and that all classes of witnesses bear testimony to the demoralizing influence of the employment of females underground.

12. That, in the East of Scotland, a much larger proportion of Children and Young Persons are employed in these mines than in other districts, many of whom are girls; and that the chief part of their labour consists in carrying the coals on their backs up steep ladders.

13. That when the workpeople are in full employment, the regular hours of work for Children and Young Persons are rarely less than eleven; more often they are twelve; in some districts they are thirteen; and in one district they are generally fourteen and upwards.

14. That in the great majority of these mines night-work is a part of the ordinary system of labour, more or less regularly carried on according to the demand for coals, and one which the whole body of evidence shows to act most injuriously both on the physical and moral condition of the workpeople, and more especially on that of the Children and Young Persons.

15. That the labour performed daily for this number of hours, though it cannot strictly be said to be continuous, because, from the nature of the employment, intervals of a few minutes necessarily occur during which the muscles are not in active exertion, is nevertheless generally uninterrupted by any regular time set apart for rest and refreshment; what food is taken in the pit being eaten as best it may while labour continues.

16. That in well-regulated mines, in which in general the hours of work are the shortest, and in some few of which from half an hour to an hour is regularly set apart for meals, little or no fatigue is complained of after an ordinary day's work, when the Children are ten years old and upwards; but in other instances great complaint is made of the feeling of fatigue, and the workpeople are never without this feeling, often in an extremely painful degree.

17. That in many cases the Children and Young Persons have little cause of complaint in regard to the treatment they receive from the persons in authority in the mine, or from the colliers; but that in general

the younger Children are roughly used by their older companions; whilst in many mines the conduct of the adult colliers to the Children and Young Persons who assist them is harsh and cruel; the persons in authority in these mines, who must be cognizant of this ill-usage, never interfering to prevent it, and some of them distinctly stating that that they do not conceive that they have any right to do so.

18. That, with some exceptions, little interest is taken by the coal owners in the Children and Young Persons employed in their works after the daily labour is over; at least little is done to afford them the means of enjoying innocent amusement and healthful recreation.

19. That in all the coal-fields accidents of a fearful nature are extremely frequent; and that the returns made to our own queries, as well as the registry tables, prove that of the workpeople who perish by such accidents, the proportion of Children and Young Persons sometimes equals and rarely falls much below that of adults.

20. That one of the most frequent causes of accidents in these mines is the want of superintendence by overlookers or otherwise to see to the security of the machinery for letting down and bringing up the workpeople, the restriction of the number of persons who ascend and descend at a time, the state of the mine as to the quantity of noxious gas in it, the efficiency of the ventilation, the exactness with which the air-door keepers perform their duty, the places into which it is safe or unsafe to go with a naked lighted candle, and the security of the proppings to uphold the roof, etc.

21. That another frequent cause of fatal accidents in coal mines is the almost universal practice of intrusting the closing of the air-doors to very young Children.

22. That there are many mines in which the most ordinary precautions to guard against accidents are neglected, and in which no money appears to be expended with a view to secure the safety, much less the comfort, of the workpeople.

23. That there are moreover two practices peculiar to a few districts which deserve the highest reprobation, namely,—first, the practice not unknown in some of the smaller mines in Yorkshire, and common in Lancashire, of employing ropes that are unsafe for letting down and drawing up the workpeople; and second, the practice, occasionally met with in Yorkshire, and common in Derbyshire and Lancashire, of employing boys at the steam-engines for letting down and drawing up the workpeople.

24. That in general the Children and Young Persons who work in

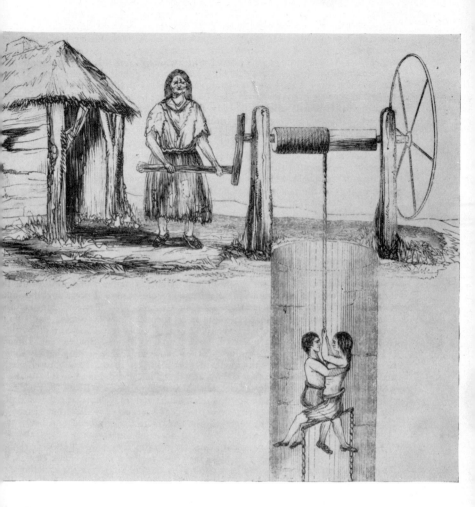

Ann Ambler and Will Dyson being drawn up the pit-shaft crosslapped
(P.P. 1842, vol. XV) (*photo:* British Museum)

8. Little Girls making buttons in a Birmingham workshop (from Chas. Knight's *Cyclopaedia of Industry of All Nations* (1851)) (*photo:* Mansell Collection)

these mines have sufficient food, and, when above ground, decent and comfortable clothing, their usually high rate of wages securing to them these advantages; but in many cases, particularly in some parts of Yorkshire, in Derbyshire, in South Gloucestershire, and very generally in the East of Scotland, the food is poor in quality, and insufficient in quantity; the Children themselves say that they have not enough to eat; and the Sub-Commissioners describe them as covered with rags, and state that the common excuse they make for confining themselves to their homes on the Sundays, instead of taking recreation in the fresh air, or attending a place of worship, is that they have no clothes to go in; so that in these cases, notwithstanding the intense labour performed by these Children, they do not procure even sufficient food and raiment: in general, however, the Children who are in this unhappy case are the Children of idle and dissolute parents, who spend the hard-earned wages of their offspring at the public-house.

25. That the employment in these mines commonly produces in the first instance an extraordinary degree of muscular development accompanied by a corresponding degree of muscular strength; this preternatural development and strength being acquired at the expense of the other organs, as is shown by the general stunted growth of the body.

26. That partly by the severity of the labour and the long hours of work, and partly through the unhealthy state of the place of work, this employment, as at present carried on in all the districts, deteriorates the physical constitution; in the thin-seam mines, more especially, the limbs become crippled and the body distorted; and in general the muscular powers give way, and the workpeople are incapable of following their occupation, at an earlier period of life than is common in other branches of industry.

27. That by the same causes the seeds of painful and mortal diseases are very often sown in childhood and youth; these, slowly but steadily developing themselves, assume a formidable character between the ages of thirty and forty; and each generation of this class of the population is commonly extinct soon after fifty.

When we consider the extent of this branch of industry, the vast amount of capital embarked in it, and the intimate connexion in which it stands with almost all other great branches of trade and manufacture, as a main source of our national wealth and greatness, it is satisfactory to have established, by indubitable evidence, the two following conclusions:—

1. That the coal mine, when properly ventilated and drained, and when both the main and the side passages are of tolerable height, is not only not unhealthy, but, the temperature being moderate and very uniform, it is, considered as a place of work, more salubrious and even agreeable than that in which many kinds of labour are carried on above ground.

2. That the labour in which Children and Young Persons are chiefly employed in coal mines, namely, in pushing the loaded carriages of coals from the workings to the mainways or to the foot of the shaft, so far from being in itself an unhealthy employment, is a description of exercise which, while it greatly develops the muscles of the arms, shoulders, chest, back, and legs, without confining any part of the body in an unnatural and constrained posture, might, but for the abuse of it, afford an equally healthful excitement to all the other organs; the physical injuries produced by it, as it is at present carried on, independently of those which are caused by imperfect ventilation and drainage, being chiefly attributable to the early age at which it commences, and to the length of time during which it is continued.

There is, however, one case of peculiar difficulty, viz., that in which all the subterranean roadways, and especially the side passages, are below a certain height; by the Evidence collected under this Commission, it is proved that there are coal mines at present in work in which these passages are so small, that even the youngest Children cannot move along them without crawling on their hands and feet, in which unnatural and constrained posture they drag the loaded carriages after them; and yet, as it is impossible, by any outlay compatible with a profitable return, to render such coal mines, happily not numerous nor of great extent, fit for human beings to work in, they never will be placed in such a condition, and consequently they never can be worked without inflicting great and irreparable injury on the health of the Children.

[Then follow conclusions in regard to Ironstone mines, blast furnaces, underground labour in tin, copper, lead, and zinc mines, etc.]

THOS TOOKE, T. SOUTHWOOD SMITH,
LEONARD HORNER, ROBERT J. SAUNDERS.

Children's Employment Commission (Mines); P.P. 1842, vol. XV, pp. 255–259.

2

Lonely Little Trappers

It is almost superfluous to state, that on the proper ventilation of air the lives of the miners depend. The ventilation again depends entirely on the trap-doors being kept shut and on their being properly closed immediately after the carriages conveying the coal have passed them.

The youngest children in the mines are intrusted with this important office! They are called trappers. Their duty consists in sitting in a little hole, scooped out for them in the side of the gates behind each door, where they sit with a string in their hands attached to the door, and pull it the moment they hear the corves (i.e. the carriages for conveying the coal) at hand, and the moment it has passed they let the door fall to, which it does of its own weight. If anything impedes the shutting of the door they remove it, or, if unable to do so, run to the nearest man to do it for them. They have nothing else to do; but, as their office must be performed from the repassing of the first to the passing of the last corve during the day, they are in the pit the whole time it is worked, frequently about 12 hours a day. They sit, moreover, in the dark, often with a damp floor to stand on, and exposed necessarily to drafts, though I have seldom found the temperature lower at their posts than 58°, and often higher.

The ages of these children vary from 5½ to 10 years old; few come before they are nearly seven, and few remain longer than 9 or 10. There is no hard work for these children to do,—nothing can be easier; but it is a most painful thing to contemplate the dull dungeon-like life these little creatures are doomed to spend; a life, for the most part, passed in solitude, damp, and darkness. They are allowed no light; but sometimes a good-natured collier will bestow a little bit of candle on them as a treat.

P.P. 1842, vol. XVI, p. 174.

3

'I daren't sing in the dark'

Sarah Gooder, age 8: I'm a trapper in the Gawber pit. It does not tire me, but I have to trap without a light, and I'm scared. Sometimes I sing when I have a light, but not in the dark; I dare not sing then. I don't like being in the pit.

I go to Sunday-schools and read Reading made Easy. (She knows her letters and can read little words.) They teach me to pray. (She repeated the Lord's Prayer, not very perfectly, and ran on with the following addition:—'God bless my father and mother, and sister and brother, uncles and aunts and cousins, and everybody else, and God bless me and make me a good servant. Amen.'). I have heard tell of Jesus many a time. I don't know why he came to earth, I'm sure, and I don't know why he died, but he had stones for his head to rest on. I would like to be at school far better than in the pit.

P.P. 1842, vol. XVI, pp. 252–253.

4

Her Lamp Had Gone Out

Mary Davis, near seven years old, keeper of an air-door in a pit in South Wales, was described by Sub-Commissioner Franks as, 'A very pretty little girl, who was fast asleep under a piece of rock near the air-door below ground. Her lamp had gone out for want of oil; and upon waking her, she said the rats or some one had run away with her bread and cheese, so she went to sleep. The oversman, who was with me, thought she was not so old, though he felt sure she had been below near 18 months.'

P.P. 1842, vol. XVII, p. 513.

5

Little Boy Lost

I imagine one of the first questions an anxious mother would ask would be, 'Is there not a great danger of little boys of ten years of age being lost in the passages of the dark mine?'

Formerly there was great danger of this kind, with very little boys, under ten, or even eight years old. But, on the whole, very few cases of this kind have occurred in the northern pits. The trappers are stationary, and if found away from their doors are thumped and threatened . . . Many sit there, too, in fear of the hobgoblins to be met with in the pit; and the reputation of hobgoblins is sustained for their good behaviour. Some friend, if not the father, takes them to the door, and probably comes for them at 'kenner' or 'lose' time.

Very recently a little boy was lost in one of the Welsh pits. His name was William Withers, and on a Friday morning he went to work with his father as usual. On arriving at the pit, he found that he had forgotten his lamp, and returned for the purpose of getting it, intending to follow his father into the mine. As he, however, proceeded along the sub-terranean road, he lost his light, and as a consequence his way, and wandered into some old works. From that time till Monday morning he was not seen or heard of. He was then found by the hauliers in a very weak state, and taken home . . . His own account is as follows:—

'After I lost my light, I found that I was lost, and in a strange road. I could hear my father at work all Friday, I knocked the side, and made as much noise as I possibly could, but no one answered me. They all went out that night, leaving me there; I cried very much. I thought I saw the stars two or three times, although I was 100 yards under ground. I saved my dinner as much as I could, only eating a bit at a time, not knowing whether I should ever be found. The pit broke (work) on Saturday morning, so there was no work until Monday morning. The whole time I had been wandering about in the dark, when I heard the hauliers, and I made my way to them.

When asked what day it was, the poor little fellow did not know, but thought he had been lost seven or eight days.

J. R. LEIFCHILD, *Our Coal Fields and Our Coal Pits* (1853), pp. 162–163.

6

The Boy Who Stole a Dinner

There have been cases of the maltreatment of children in collieries brought before the magistrates—perhaps one or two a year. The maltreatment was always according to barbarous rules among the workers themselves, inflicting punishment on supposed delinquents, generally by holding the head fast between the legs of another, and inflicting each a certain number of blows on the bare posteriors with pieces of wood, called 'cuts', about a foot long and an inch in diameter, used as tokens to distinguish one man's tubs from another. However the one punished may cry, they stick to him; and in the last case, where a hungry lad had stolen a pit-dinner, they mangled his body seriously. In other cases the injured parties could not work at all for some time. In the case mentioned, the offenders were made to placard the town with an apology, to render some compensation in money to the party, and promise not to follow any such course in future.

JOSEPH WILD, chief constable of Oldham; P.P. 1842, vol. XVII, p. 857.

7

Vicious-tempered Colliers

The treatment [of children employed in coal mines] varies, not only in different pits, but according to the disposition of the men under whom each drawer works. That any harsh usage is contrary to the wish, and even the peremptory orders, of the proprietors and undertakers, is certainly the case in almost every pit; but the colliers are uneducated people, and are usually vicious in temper ... What passes under ground in the dark tunnels in which the people work is not known even to the under-ground overlooker; for the Children dare not complain, and he (the overlooker) can only be in one of the many burrows of which a coal-mine consists, and cannot hear what passes in the others.

A. AUSTIN'S report on the Lancashire coal-mines; P.P. 1842, vol. XV, p. 131.

8

They Soon Got Used to It

When a child first goes into the pits [in North Wales] he is taken down by his father, or some friend who has employment in the work; he is usually put to keep an air-door, or to some light work. In examining the boys, few would own that they felt much fear or distress on entering the pits, and all say they very soon became used and reconciled to their work. They are for the most part children of colliers, and from infancy familiar with the idea of under-ground work, and anxious to go below and begin to work.

This wish of course meets with no opposition from the parents, who, lured by the wages, are never backward in sending their children to the pits as soon as they can get them into employ, so that no sooner is a collier's son able to exert a little muscular force than he becomes an under-ground machine, destitute of the slightest mental cultivation.

P.P. 1842, vol. XV, p. 97.

9

Four-year-old Miner

There is evidence that some Children begin to work in the pits of the Coalbrook Dale district . . . as early as six years of age. One instance, indeed, came under the observation of the Sub-Commissioner, in which a Child two years younger, that is, four years of age, was regularly taken into the pit by his father. 'This remarkable instance became known to me', says Dr Mitchell, 'when exploring the Hill's Lane Pit, belonging to the Madeley Wood Company; the ground-bailiff, two charter-masters (the persons who contract to work the mines), and a labouring collier accompanied me. "I say, Jonas," said the ground-bailiff to one of the charter-masters, "there are very few Children working in this mine; I think we have none under ten or eleven." The collier immediately said, "Sir, my boy is only a little more than four." This was a very unseasonable interruption; and all that the ground-bailiff said was, "Well, I suppose that you take good care of him: you take him down and up when you go yourself".'

P.P. 1842, vol. XV, p. 9.

10

Quite a Catch!

Families of *boys* are, amongst pit-people, valuable property, on account of their earnings in the pits. A widow with a family of boys is considered a *catch*. I was told that such a widow was accosted by a suitor even at her husband's grave. Her reply was, 'You are too late: I am engaged. I accepted B—before starting for the funeral!'

J. R. LEIFCHILD, *Our Coal Fields and Our Coal Pits*, vol. I, p. 197.

11

The Price of a Drink

Many a collier spends in drink what he has shut up a young child the whole week to earn in a dark corner as a trapper.

GEORGE ARMITAGE, school-teacher and ex-collier at Silkstone pit; P.P. 1842, vol. XVI, p. 261.

12

'A very ignorant child'

Susan Pitchforth, aged 11, living at Elland: I have worked at this pit going two years. Come to work at eight or before, but I set off from home at seven. I walk a mile and a half to my work, both in winter and summer. I get porridge for breakfast before I come, and bring my dinner with me—a muffin. When I have done about twelve loads I eat it while at work; I run 24 corves a day; I cannot come up till I have done them all. If I want to relieve myself I go into any part of the pit. Sometimes the boys see me when they go by. My father slaps me sometimes upon the head, or upon the back, so as to make me cry . . .

A very ignorant child (commented Mr Scriven, the Sub-Commissioner). She stood shivering before me from cold. The rag that hung about her waist was once called a shift, which is as black as the coal she thrusts, and saturated with water, from the dripping of the roof and shaft. During my examination of her the banksman whom I had left in the pit came to the public-house and wanted to take her away, because, as he expressed himself, it was not *decent* that she should be (her person) *exposed* to us; oh no! it was criminal above ground; and, like the two or three other colliers in the cabin, he became evidently mortified that these deeds of darkness should be brought to light.

P.P. 1842, vol. XVII, p. 104.

13

Higher than St Paul's

Ellison Jack, 11-years-old girl coal-bearer at Loanhead colliery, Scotland:
I have been working below three years on my father's account; he takes me down at two in the morning, and I come up at one and two

next afternoon. I go to bed at six at night to be ready for work next morning: the part of the pit I bear in the seams are much on the edge. I have to bear my burthen up four traps, or ladders, before I get to the main road which leads to the pit bottom. My task is four or five tubs: each tub holds $4\frac{1}{4}$ cwt. I fill five tubs in twenty journeys.

I have had the strap when I did not do my bidding. Am very glad when my task is wrought, as it sore fatigues. I can read, and was learning the writing; can do a little; not been at school for two years; go to kirk occasionally, over to Lasswade: don't know much about the Bible, so long since read.

R. H. Franks, Esq., the sub-commissioner: A brief description of this child's place of work will illustrate her evidence. She has first to descend a nine-ladder pit to the first rest, even to which a shaft is sunk, to draw up the baskets or tubs of coals filled by the bearers; she then takes her creel (a basket formed to the back, not unlike a cockle-shell flattened towards the neck, so as to allow lumps of coal to rest on the back of the neck and shoulders), and pursues her journey to the wall-face, or as it is called here, the room of work. She then lays down her basket, into which the coal is rolled, and it is frequently more than one man can do to lift the burden on her back. The tugs or straps are placed over the forehead, and the body bent in a semicircular form, in order to stiffen the arch.

Large lumps of coal are then placed on the neck, and she then commences her journey with her burden to the pit bottom, first hanging her lamp to the cloth crossing her head. In this girl's case she has first to travel about 14 fathoms (84 feet) from wall-face to the first ladder, which is 18 feet high: leaving the first ladder she proceeds along the main road, probably 3 feet 6 inches to 4 feet 6 inches high, to the second ladder, 18 feet high, so on to the third and fourth ladders, till she reaches the pit-bottom, where she casts her load, varying from 1 cwt to $1\frac{1}{2}$ cwt., into the tub.

This one journey is designated a rake; the height ascended, and the distance along the roads added together, exceed the height of St Paul's Cathedral; and it not unfrequently happens that the tugs break, and the load falls upon those females who are following. However incredible it may be, yet I have taken the evidence of fathers who have ruptured themselves from straining to lift coal on their Children's backs.

P.P. 1842, vol. XV, pp. 91–92.

14

'Perfectly Beautiful'

Margaret Leveston, 6 years old, coal-bearer in the East of Scotland coal-field; described by Mr Franks, the Sub-Commissioner, as 'a most interesting child, and perfectly beautiful'. She said: 'Been down at coal-carrying six weeks; makes ten to fourteen rakes [journeys] a day; carries full 56 lbs. of coal in a wooden backit [Scots for a shallow wooden trough]. The work is na guid; it is so very sair. I work with sister Jesse and mother; dinna ken the time we gang; it is gai dark.'

P.P. 1842, vol. XV, p. 91.

15

'Father Makes Me Like It'

Janet Cumming, 11-years-old coal-bearer, East of Scotland coalfield: Works with father; has done so for two years:

Father gangs at 2 in the morning: I gang with the women at 5, and come up at 5 at night; work all night on Fridays, and come away at 12 in the day. I carry the large bits of coal from the wall-face to the pit-bottom, and the small pieces called chows, in a creel; the weight is usually a hundred-weight; does not know how many pounds there are in the hundred-weight, but it is some work to carry; it takes three journeys to fill a tub of 4 cwt . . . The roof is very low; I have to bend my back and legs, and the water comes frequently up to the calves of my legs; has no likening for the work; father makes me like it . . . Never got hurt, but often obliged to scramble out when bad air was in the pit.

I am learning to read at the night-school; am in the twopenny book; sometimes to Sabbath-school. Jesus was God; David wrote the Bible; has a slight knowledge of the first six questions in the Shorter Catechism.

P.P. 1842, vol. XVI, p. 436.

16

Little Ann Ambler

We have but one girl working with us, by name Ann Ambler, who goes down with us on the clatch harness; she wears her breeches when she goes down, and while at work, and comes up the pit cross-lapped with us in the clatch harness; when she is down she hurries with us in the same way as we do, without shoes or stockings.

William Dyson, aged 14, employed in Messrs Ditchforth & Clay's colliery, Elland, Yorks; the sketch is intended to represent Ann Ambler and Will Dyson being drawn up cross-lapped upon the clatch-iron by a woman. As soon as they arrived at the top the handle was made fast ... the woman grasped a hand of both and by main force brought them to land.

P.P. 1842, vol. XV, pp. 61, 80.

17

'A pick in my bottom'

Thomas Moorhouse, a collier boy: I don't know how old I am; father is dead; I am a chance child; mother is dead also; I don't know how long she has been dead; 'tis better na three years.

I began to hurry when I was 9 years old for William Greenwood; I was apprenticed to him till I should be 21 ... The overseers gave him a sovereign to buy clothes with, but he never laid it out; I ran away from him because he lost my indentures, for he served me very bad; he struck a pick into me twice in my bottom. (Here I made the boy strip, and I found a large cicatrix likely to have been occasioned by such an instrument ... There were twenty other wounds, occasioned by hurrying in low workings . . .) He used to hit me with the belt, and mawl or sledge, and fling coals at me; he served me so bad that I left him, and went about to see if I could get a job.

I used to sleep in the cabins upon the pit's bank, and in the old pits that had done working; I laid upon the shale all night; I used to get what I could to eat; I eat for a long time the candles that I found in the pits that the colliers left over night; I had nothing else to eat . . . When I got out next morning, I looked about for work, and begged of the people a bit. I got to Bradford after a while . . . I work now here for John Cawtherly; he took me into his house, and is serving me well; I hurry for him now, and he finds me in victuals and drink.

MR SCRIVEN's report; P.P. 1842, vol. XV, p. 43.

18

The Miner's Apprentice

Besides my husband I have a boy who works on the band [i.e. breaking up the coal and loading it to meet the band or chain drawing up the shaft] with my husband, a dirt carrier, at 2s a day. We have also an apprentice, but we don't know his age nor he himself 'except what we guessen'. He came from Manchester; a boatman picked him up upon the canal side and brought him with him to drive his horse, and he could not find his way back. He was 10 or 11 years old, named William Butler, and he used to lie about and get burnt at the coke hearths. A woman brought him to me and asked if I would have him; and I pieced a pair of trousers and waistcoat for him, and a pair of shoes that were too small for one of my wenches I had tipped and put on his feet. He bound himself apprentice.

A miner's wife at Bilston, S. Staffs; Midland Mining Report, P.P. 1843, vol. XIII, p. 92.

19

A Minor Disaster

No rewards excepting the stick, that's all the rewards in pits for little lads. Has within three months seen a boy 9 years old beaten by a butty until he wetted his breeches, because he had not come the day before. He has often seen them beat so that they were black and blue, and if the parents were by they dare not say anything or they would be turned off the ground directly.

SAMUEL RICHARDS, aged 40, employed in Awsworth colliery, Derbyshire; P.P. 1842, vol. XVII, p. 307.

20

Young Lump

James Taylor, alias Lump Lad, going on 11; works in colliery near Oldham.

The old colliers call his father Old Lump, so they call him Young Lump. Is going on eleven, and working in Messrs Evans's pit, up Royton Road, at Robin Hill Pit . . . Now thrutches the waggons with his head and hands, as is the common practice. The waggons hold three baskets (6 cwt.) and are filled by the biggest waggoner . . . The big lad goes to the front with his 'yead' to the waggon, and walking backwards, to keep it coming down too fast. They work only in their clogs, stockings, trousers, and cap . . .

Father lives in Lord-street, Oldham; there are two rooms i' th' house —the chamber and th' house. The chamber is above th' house. They all sleep in the chamber, which has one bed, in which all four children sleep with their father and mother. There is one chair in the room besides, but nothing else.

Mother does naught for him when he gets home but gives him something to eat if she has it. Washes his hands and face every day, and his whole body once a week. Has only one shirt, one pair of stockings, and the ragged and dirty coat, waistcoat, and trousers he has on. When he has had something to eat, runs into the street and plays; always finds someone to play wi', and can play at aught as they can: plays at 'trinnill' and 'th'hammer and block'—these oftener than aught else.

MR FLETCHER's collection of evidence; P.P. 1842, vol. XVII, p. 849.

21

Lord Londonderry's Rejoinder

The Marquess of Londonderry, presenting a petition to the House of Lords from owners of collieries in Durham and Northumberland, said that it appeared that the Commissioners had come to this inquiry fresh from the Factory Commission, with all the prejudices which that commission was likely to excite, and with an expectation and desire of finding similar oppressions amongst the miners to those which they had found amongst the manufacturing population. Their instructions were to examine the children themselves, and the mode in which they collected their evidence—communicating with artful boys and ignorant young girls, and putting questions in a manner which in many cases seemed to suggest the answer, was anything but a fair and impartial mode ... Again he thought the manner in which the Report had been accompanied by pictures of an extravagant and disgusting, and in some cases of a scandalous and obscene character, was not such as should have been adopted in a grave publication, and was more calculated to excite the feelings than to enlighten the judgment ...

[The document presented to the House by his Lordship contained the following]: The trapper's employment is neither cheerless, dull, nor stupefying; nor is he, nor can he be, kept in solitude and darkness all the time he is in the pit. The working trap-doors are all placed in the principal passages, leading from the bottom of the pit to the various works, so that an interval of seldom more than five minutes, but generally much less, passes without some person passing through his door, and having a word with the trapper. Neither is the trapper deprived of light by any means general, as the stationary lights on the rolly and tram ways are frequently placed near to the trapper's seat.

The trapper is generally cheerful and contented, and to be found, like other children of his age, occupied with some childish amusement —as cutting sticks, making models of windmills, waggons, etc., and frequently in drawing figures with chalk on his door, modelling figures of men and animals in clay, etc.

Hansard, House of Lords, June 24, 1842.

(f) CHILDREN IN TRADES AND MANUFACTURES

A second Report of the Children's Employment Commission was published early in 1843. It was concerned with children and young persons employed in Trades and Manufactures, and because of its scope and the thoroughness with which the sub-commissioners had gone about their work it is one of the most illuminating of our social documents. For the first time the immense part played by young workers in the development of British industry received full recognition, and at the same time it was made clear that the conditions under which they were made to work were such as no nation venturing to call itself civilized could continue to tolerate.

The conclusions of the Commissioners, summarizing the contents of the Report as a whole, are given in No. 1, and the final document in this section is the companion summary of the conclusions concerning the Moral Condition (which also covers Education, etc.) of the young workers—not only in Trades and Manufactures, it should be noticed, but also in Mines, the subject of the Report of 1842. In between these two comprehensive documents appear selections from the reports on the trades in which juveniles were largely employed. Where such a wealth of material is available, the work of selection becomes more than ever difficult, but it may be claimed that the documents quoted give a fair indication of the nature and quality of the whole.

The Report proved a powerful weapon in the hands of Ashley, Fielden, and the rest of the factory reformers; but it was not until 1847 that a ten hours' day for all workers under eighteen was enacted.

I

Child Workers: The 1843 Report in Outline

From the whole of the evidence which has been collected under the present Commission . . . relative to the *Employment* and the *Physical Condition* of the Children and Young Persons included within its terms, who are engaged in *Trades and Manufactures*, we find—

1. That instances occur in which Children begin to work as early as three and four years of age; not unfrequently at five, and between five and six; while, in general, regular employment commences between seven and eight; the great majority of the Children having begun to work before they are nine years old, although in some few occupations no Children are employed until they are ten and even twelve years old and upwards.

2. That in all cases the persons that employ mere Infants and the very youngest Children are the parents themselves, who put their Children to work at some processes of manufacture under their own eye, in their own houses; but Children begin to work together in numbers, in larger or smaller manufactories, at all ages, from five years old and upwards.

3. That of the whole number of persons employed in carrying on these Trades and Manufactures, a large portion are under thirteen years of age, and a still larger portion between thirteen and eighteen, although in some cases the numbers under thirteen nearly equal those between thirteen and eighteen; and there are instances in which the numbers below thirteen even exceed those between thirteen and eighteen.

4. That in a very large proportion of these Trades and Manufactures female Children are employed equally with boys, and at the same tender ages: in some indeed the number of girls exceeds that of boys; and in a few cases the work, as far as it is performed by those under adult age, is carried on almost entirely by girls and young women.

5. That in some branches of Manufacture of large extent, such as pillow-lace making, straw plaiting, and card setting, the greater part

of the Children of the youngest ages, excepting those who are employed at home under the eye of their own parents, are engaged by mistresses, and work in what are termed schools, but which are rather workshops.

6. That in the great majority of the Trades and Manufactures the youngest Children as well as the Young Persons are hired and paid by the workmen, and are entirely under their control; the employers exercising no sort of superintendence over them, and apparently knowing nothing whatever about them.

7. That in some of these Trades and Manufactures, though comparatively few, the Children and Young Persons are employed directly by the proprietors.

8. That in by far the majority of these Trades and Manufactures it is the practice to employ apprentices to a great extent.

9. That in some Trades, those especially requiring skilled workmen, these apprentices are bound by legal indentures, usually at the age of fourteen, and for a term of seven years, the age being rarely younger, and the period of servitude very seldom longer; but by far the greater number are bound without any prescribed legal forms, and in almost all these cases they are required to serve their masters, at whatever age they may commence their apprenticeship, until they reach the age of twenty-one, in some instances in employments in which there is nothing deserving the name of skill to be acquired, and in other instances in employments in which they are taught to make only one particular part of the article manufactured; so that at the end of their servitude they are altogether unable to make any one article of their trade in a complete state.

10. That a large proportion of these apprentices consist of orphans, or are the children of widows, or belong to the very poorest families, and frequently are apprenticed by boards of guardians.

11. That the term of servitude of these apprentices may, and sometimes does commence as early as seven years of age, and is often passed under circumstances of great hardship and ill-usage, and under the condition that, during the greater part, if not the whole, of their term, they receive nothing for their labour beyond food and clothing.

12. That this system of apprenticeship is most prevalent in the districts round Wolverhampton, and is most abused by what are called 'small masters', persons who are either themselves journeymen, or who, if working on their own account, work with their apprentices.

13. That in these districts it is the practice among some of the employers to engage the services of Children by a simple written

agreement, on the breach of which the defaulter is liable to be committed to gaol, and in fact often is so without regard to age.

14. That in these districts it is common for parents to borrow money of the employers, and to stipulate by express agreement to repay it from their Children's wages; a practice which prevails likewise in Birmingham and Warrington: in most other places no evidence was discovered of its existence.

15. That in some few Trades and Manufactures, but these of large extent, care is taken to render the place of work convenient, healthy, and safe; but in the great majority of instances the places of work are very defective in drainage, ventilation, and the due regulation of temperature, while little or no attention is paid to cleanliness.

16. That even in those Trades and Manufactures in which deleterious substances are used, there is in general no accommodation for the workpeople to change their clothes on leaving the place of work, or to wash themselves if they remain at meal-times; and it is very uncommon for any means to be provided for the workpeople to dress and warm their food.

17. That in all the districts the privies are very commonly in a disgusting state of filth, and in great numbers of instances there is no separate accommodation for the males and females; but in almost all the buildings recently constructed a greater attention has been paid to the health and the decent comfort of the workpeople than in those of older date.

18. That the work in which Children and Young Persons are employed is seldom in itself oppressive, or even laborious; and very few indeed of the processes in the care and management of which Children take any part are in their own nature injurious; but to this there are some lamentable exceptions in certain processes connected with the Manufacture of metal wares, of earthenware, and of glass.

19. That in some few instances the regular hours of work do not exceed ten, exclusive of the time allowed for meals; sometimes they are eleven, but more commonly twelve; and in great numbers of instances the employment is continued for fifteen, sixteen, and even eighteen hours consecutively.

20. That in almost every instance the Children work as long as the adults; being sometimes kept at work sixteen, and even eighteen hours without any intermission.

21. That in the case of young women employed in the millinery and dressmaking business in the metropolis, and in some of the large

provincial cities, even in what are considered the best regulated establishments, during the busy season, occupying in London about four months of the year, the regular hours of work are fifteen; but on emergencies, which frequently recur, these hours are extended to eighteen; and in many establishments the hours of work during the season are unlimited, the young women never getting more than six, often not more than four, sometimes only three, and occasionally not more than two hours for rest and sleep out of the twenty-four, and very frequently they work all night; there being in fact no other limit to the duration of their labour than their physical inability to work longer.

22. That in the Trades and Manufactures (and these constituting the great majority) in which the master is considered to be exonerated from all care and charge of the Children, because they are hired and paid by the workmen, the hours of work for the Children are almost always the longest, and their labour is performed under the most oppressive circumstances; it being the common practice with many of these workmen to work most irregularly; remaining idle during the early part of the week, and then working excessively at the latter end of it; and by their hours of work, whatever they may be, those of the Children must be regulated.

23. That in some processes of Manufacture, as in winding for lace machines, the Children have no regular and certain time whatever for sleep or recreation, being liable to be called upon at any period during sixteen, twenty, or twenty-two hours out of the twenty-four, while they have frequently to go from one place of work to another, often at considerable distances, at all hours of the night, and in all seasons.

24. That in many Trades and Manufactures of great extent and importance there is no night-work; but in others it is so general and constant that it may be regarded as part of the regular system of carrying on these branches of industry; while all classes of witnesses, in all the districts in which this practice is prevalent, concur in stating that its effect is most injurious, physically and morally, on the workpeople in general, and on the Children in particular; and a large body of evidence is presented by them to show that no countervailing advantage is ultimately obtained from it even by the employers.

25. That in the great majority of these Trades and Manufactures, from one hour and a half to two hours are regularly set apart for meals, during which period the work is commonly suspended, and often the machinery is stopped; but that there are in many of the districts large branches of manufacture in which, though a nominal time is allowed

for rest and refreshment, there is really little or no interruption to the labour, and the food is taken very irregularly.

26. That, although in general little or nothing is done to afford the Children and Young Persons the means of enjoying innocent amusement and healthful recreation in the intervals of their labour, they have often a good deal of idle time; seldom working on the usual national holidays and festivals; and being frequently allowed holidays at the fairs and races of the neighbourhood; while it is a common practice for them to leave off work at an early hour on the afternoon of Saturday.

27. That in the cases in which the Children are the servants of the workmen, and under their sole control, the master apparently knowing nothing about their treatment, and certainly taking no charge of it, they are almost always roughly, very often harshly, and sometimes cruelly used; and in the districts around Wolverhampton, in particular, the treatment of them is oppressive and brutal to the last degree.

28. That in the comparatively few large establishments in which the Children are employed and paid directly by the master, and in which, either by his own personal inspection, or by that of an intelligent and vigilant agent, he exercises a superintendence over the Children, there is not only a great increase in their happiness, but uniformly a striking improvement in their general conduct; and that in every trade and district there are some establishments in which corporal punishment is neither allowed nor practised, and from which any workman who ill-uses a Child is dismissed; while the general tenor of the evidence shows that, in almost all the Trades and Manufactures in all the districts, the treatment of the Children in later years is less inconsiderate, harsh, and oppressive than it was in former times.

29. That, although in some few Trades and Manufactures machinery of a dangerous character is employed, and accidents of a serious character occasionally occur, yet in general Children are but little exposed to danger from this cause; that accidents—such as hands contused, fingers cut off, jammed between cog-wheels, or drawn in between rollers, and arms caught in straps—are, however, in some establishments, by no means uncommon; that sometimes the straps, wheels, etc. are so crowded and exposed that the utmost care is required on the part of the workpeople to escape injury; and that, in by far the greater number of instances, accidents might be prevented, if proper attention were paid to the disposition and fencing of the machinery.

30. That in many of these Trades and Manufactures, and especially

in pin-making, nail-making, lace-making, the hosiery trades, calico-printing, the earthenware trades, and tobacco-making, the Children have not good and sufficient food, nor warm and decent clothing; great numbers of them when questioned stating that they have seldom or never enough to eat, and many of them being clothed in rags; and it is a general complaint that they are prevented by want of proper clothing from going to the Sunday-school, or to a place of public worship.

31. That in all these occupations, in all the districts, some of the Children are robust, active, and healthy, although in general even these are undersized; but that, from the early ages at which the great majority commence work, from their long hours of work, and from the insufficiency of their food and clothing, their 'bodily health' is seriously and generally injured; they are for the most part stunted in growth, their aspect being pale, delicate, and sickly, and they present altogether the appearance of a race which has suffered general physical deterioration.

32. That the diseases which are prevalent amongst them, and to which they are more subject than Children of their age and station unemployed in labour, are disordered states of the nutritive organs, curvature and distortion of the spine, deformity of the limbs, and diseases of the lungs, ending in atrophy and consumption.

Second Report of the Commissioners on the Employment of Children (Trades & Manufactures), 1843; P.P. vol. XIII, pp. 195–199.

2

The Little Pin-Makers

November 30th, 1840. Visit to Messrs Phipson's Pin Manufactory, Broad-street, Birmingham, by Mr R. Grainger, sub-commissioner:—

The workshops, with the exception of those in which the children who head the pins, who are called 'headers', are employed, are in general, well-lighted and airy. There are two shops for the 'headers'; one of these, where 48 children work, is 24 feet 9 inches by 20 feet, and 9 feet 1 inch high; it is lighted by two opposite rows of windows. This room is too small and too low for the number of workers, and is very close at night, especially in the winter, when lights are required. The second shop contains forty-nine machines . . . it is 41 feet by 12 feet; there is only one row of windows, and it is like the other, much too crowded and close, particularly at night and at this time of the year.

It is impossible to pass over the state of the privies. There are two privies for the workpeople, excepting the headers; these are kept locked. For the use of 90 to 100 headers, boys and girls, there is one privy; this, at the period of my first visit, was loaded with excrement on the floor and elsewhere, and utterly unfit for the use of human beings. On my last visit I found this place had been emptied and the floor washed; it was still, however, in a filthy state.

December 8th. Visited the manufactory at a quarter to 8 p.m.; all the children at work in both shops. In Jay's shop the woman was walking about with the cane in her hand, watching the children, and her whole business evidently being to catch them relaxing in their work. Saw her through the window go and strike a child. On a former visit in the other shop, I heard all the machines suddenly greatly increased in their activity, and on looking round I saw the female overlooker with a cane in her hand, which I have no doubt had either been used or held up in terrorem. All the adults had left at 7, except one man who stopped for some purpose till about 8.

As most of these poor children looked very young, I was anxious to obtain some of their ages, and indiscriminately took down the following: Joseph Norwood, seven years old; John Bridgewater, 7; John Feay, 7; Edward Burnett, 9; H. Bearman, 7; Elizabeth Cannon, 10; Jane Cannon, younger.

P.P. 1843, vol. XIV, p. f 119.

3

'I dolly and I blow'

The chain trade is extensively carried on in the neighbourhood of Stourbridge. It is only the chain cables that require large works, the chief articles of manufacture being the smaller kinds of chains used for gardens, enclosures, traces, etc., and these are made by different families working at home. These small chains are commonly known by the name of *swimmers*, on account of the continual demand for them across the water, particularly in America.

The process of making them is by the forge and hammer, with the help of a tool which they call a *dolly*. This is a kind of hammer, the head of which is a little arched, or concave, at the face or under part; and this being laid upon the iron, is then struck upon the upper part of its head by hammers. By this means the rounded shape of the link is rapidly formed without many blows, or much turning about of the links.

A man with a heavy hammer, and holding the links by a pair of tongs in the other hand, is assisted by a boy with a lighter hammer, who manages the dolly with his left hand. A man often works with two boys in this way; and when the chains are large, he frequently has three or four boys (sometimes as many as six) to assist in the work.

When the children are too little to be efficient, on account of their stature, blocks are placed half round the anvil, upon which the little creatures have to stand. Children are also employed in blowing the bellows. On asking them what work they usually did, the answer was generally, 'I dolly, and I blow'. The children are put to this work at 7 or 8 years of age, or as soon as they can use the hammer. I met with one little boy, more than usually strong for his years, who had been put to chain-making at four years of age.

P.P. 1843, vol. XV, p. Q 88, para. 838.

4

'Little black dens' of Sedgeley

The nature of the occupation of the children and young persons in the parish of Sedgeley is almost entirely that of nail-making at the forge. Many of the forges (i.e. workshops) are at the back of the hovels in which the working classes reside ... The best kind are little brick shops of about 15 feet long by 12 feet wide, in which seven or eight individuals constantly work together, with no ventilation except the door and two slits, or loop-holes, in the wall; but the great majority . . . are very much smaller, filthily dirty, and in looking in upon one of them when the fire is not lighted, it presents the appearance of a dilapidated coal-hole or little black den . . . In this dirty den there are commonly at work a man and his wife and daughter, with a boy and girl hired by the year. Sometimes there is an elder son with his sister, and two girls hired; sometimes the wife (the husband being a collier, too old to work, has taken to drinking, or is perhaps dead) carries on a forge with the aid of her children.

These little work-places have the forge placed in the centre generally, round which they each have barely standing room at an anvil; and in some instances there are two forges erected in one of these shops. There is scarcely ever room for anyone to pass round to his or her stand while others are at work, so that men and women, and boys and girls, are almost continually obliged to clamber over each other's bodies, or else step upon the hot cinders to get over the forge, in order to reach the door.

The effluvia of these little work-dens, from the filthiness of the ground, from the half-ragged, half-naked unwashed persons at work, and from the hot smoke, ashes, water, and clouds of dust (besides the frequent smell of tobacco) are really dreadful.

R. H. HORNE's report; P.P. 1843, vol. XV, Q 76.

5

'Infant slaves' in Stirlingshire Nail-Works

The manufacture of nails in the East of Scotland is principally confined to the neighbourhood of Camelon and St Ninian's, Stirlingshire, where a great number of boys are employed, especially at the former place, where they are taken to labour at a very early age . . .

The child in the first place squares the rod of heated iron of which the nails are formed, i.e. flattens the rod equally on four sides; the hammer in striking off the required lengths of rod by a little ingenuity at the same time points the nail, which, being received into, and firmly held by, a small pair of block pincers, is shanked or headed to the required form by repeated blows of the hammer on a small portion of the rod left exposed for that purpose; this process is executed with great rapidity, and I was informed by several of the nail-masters that three months' teaching was sufficient to enable an infant to accomplish the manufacture of 1000 nails per day—provided they were (as it is termed) tasked,—of which 'tasking' it may be necessary here to give some explanation. The first task is up to 'porridge time' (general name for their first meal), during which time they have to complete never less than 250, frequently 300 nails. The second task is up to 'taturs and herring', from 300 to 500 nails; and the third task up to broth or tea-time, the number required to complete the entire 1000 or 1250 nails, as is required of boys who have been two or three years at the work. But even this last meal does not put a close to their labours, as the men frequently work till 10 or 11 o'clock at night, assisted by their infant apprentices, who recommence their toil at 5 or 6 the next morning.

Such is a plain and unexaggerated account of the extraordinary labour of these infant slaves, who strongly evidence the nature of their toil from their emaciated looks and stunted growth; clothed, too, in apparel which few paupers would be found begging in; of these rags they have rarely any change.

Report by R. H. FRANKS; P.P. 1843, vol. XV, K 3, paras. 17–20.

6

Lancashire Nailers

There are a considerable number of children employed in nail-making in the neighbourhoods of Atherton and Leigh, and also at Billinge and Upholland, near Wigan, though, with few exceptions, the number of children in any one smithy rarely exceeds two or three.

The nailers' smithies are little, low sheds attached to the houses. Children are put to work between 8 and 9 years old; the hours of work are not very long for the children, and from the sheds being open to the air, the work is not so oppressive as in a close room. The masters and their children are swarthy and dirty in appearance, and have the reputation of being ill-educated, drunken, and profligate.

J. L. KENNEDY, P.P. 1843, vol. XIV, p. B 40, para. 276.

7

'A flash of lightning'

The district which requires special notice on account of the general and almost incredible abuse of the children is that of Wolverhampton and the neighbourhood. In the town of Wolverhampton itself among the large masters, children are not punished with severity, and in some of the trades, as among the japanners, they are not beaten at all; but in the nail and tip manufactories, in some of the foundries, and among the very numerous class of small manufacturers generally, the punishments are harsh and cruel; and in some cases they may be designated as ferocious.

In Willenhall the children are shamefully and most cruelly beaten with a horsewhip, strap, stick, hammer handle, file, or whatever tool is nearest at hand, or are struck with the clenched fist or kicked.

In Sedgley they are sometimes struck with a red-hot iron, and burnt and bruised simultaneously. Sometimes they have 'a flash of lightning' sent at them. 'When a bar of iron is drawn white-hot from the forge it emits fiery particles, which the man commonly flings in a shower upon the ground by a swing of his arm before placing the bar upon the anvil. This shower is sometimes directed at the boy. It may come over his hand and face, his naked arms, or on his breast. If his shirt be open in front, which is usually the case, the red-hot particles are lodged therein, and he has to shake them out as fast as he can.'

The punishment of nailing the ear to the counter, and of 'winding up', is stated on the authority of one witness only, a child of twelve years old [see below].

In Darlaston the children appear to be very little beaten, and in Bilston there were only a few instances of cruel treatment. In

Wednesbury the treatment is better than in any other town in the district. The boys are not generally subject to any severe corporal chastisement, though a few cases of ill-treatment occasionally occur. 'A few months ago an adult workman broke a boy's arm by a blow with a piece of iron; the boy went to school till his arm got well; his father and mother thought it a good opportunity to give him some schooling.'

P.P. 1843, vol. XIII, p. 80.

8

'Nailed to the Counter'

Boy, aged 12: works at nails; has worked at it above a year and a half, and gets from 3s 6d to 4s a week. His mother takes the nails he makes into the warehouse, and gets the money . . . Some of the boys are not well treated by their masters; they don't get enough victuals, and some are beat.

Knows a boy that makes scraps (bad nails), and somebody in the warehouse took him and put his head down on an iron counter and hammered a nail through one ear, and the boy made good nails ever since.

They don't hammer nails through boys' ears now: they wind 'em up sometimes. There's a hook used to wind up the nail-boys, and they put the hook on the boys' trousers, and wind 'em up from the floor below through a trap in the ceiling into the room above, with their heads downwards; but it an't high . . . He never saw anybody wound up; his mother did, and told him on it . . .

P.P. 1843, vol. XV, p. q 57.

9

Sheer Carelessness !

Amidst the numerous manufactories and foundries, and the almost innumerable workshops of the town of Wolverhampton there are comparatively few accidents . . . But there is one manufactory at which it is probable that as many accidents have occurred in the last two or three years as in all the others collectively. I allude to the nail and tip manufactory of Hemingsley & Co.

On Friday evening, March 19th, a part of the upper floor of Hemingsley's manufactory fell, and killed one little boy on the spot by the descent of a heap of iron tips upon him, and another boy had both his thighs broke and one arm. Three other boys were also injured . . . The ordinary run of accidents occur to children and young persons, of whom there are as many as 60 to 70 employed under 18 years of age; their ages are from 9 upwards.

The rooms are all crowded with dangerous machinery; so close that you can hardly pass; indeed, some operations have to be stopped in order that you may pass at all, so that there shall be room for the body to effect its passage, a safe distance being out of the question. Not any of this machinery is boxed off, or guarded in any way.

It is a frightful place, turn which way you will. There is a constant hammering roar of wheels, so that you could not possibly hear any warning voice. You have but once to stumble on your passage from one place to another; or to be thinking of something else, and you are certain to be punished with the loss of a limb.

Little boys and girls are here seen at work at the tip-punching machines (all acting by steam power) with their fingers in constant danger of being punched off once in every second, while at the same time they have their heads between the whirling wheels a few inches distant from each ear. 'They seldom lose the hand,' said one of the proprietors to me, in explanation; 'it only takes off a finger at the first or second joint. Sheer carelessness—looking about them—sheer carelessness!'

From MR HORNE's report; P.P. 1943, vol. XIII, pp. 90–91.

10

'A kick o' the rump'

Witness No. 96, a boy aged 16 'as near as he can guess', works at Messrs Hemingsley's nail and tip manufactory at Wolverhampton. Accidents happen there every week, very near; finger ends are continually pinched, sometimes pinched off, or cut off . . . Often seen boys and girls beaten at Hemingsley's, with a belt of leather, and sometimes the men they work under beat them with their fist; they cry out, but nobody can hear it for the noise of the machines; they often slap the girls about the jaws, or catch them with a kick o' the rump; it's the safest place; but it's the most regular thing to slap them on the jaws, or beat them with the fist, the best way they can get the opportunity at them.

P.P. 1843, vol. XV, Q 21.

11

'Make the place stink'

January 4, 1841. Mr Wallis's Mill, Dartmouth-street, Birmingham—a mill let out to three spoon-polishers, a nail-maker, and a snuffer-polisher.

The windows are very much broken; the shops are extremely close, crowded and confined; they are full of dust, and no attempt is made to get rid of it. There is a most noxious smell, and the dust makes the eyes smart in a very short time. The people are quite black with dirt and filth; some work with handkerchiefs muffled around the mouth; they are 'huddled' together, men, women, boys, and girls, all in the same shop. Altogether I never saw a shop in a more filthy or wretched condition . . .

The people in the neighbourhood complain of these works as a nuisance. Mr Wallis objected to my examining the children in his counting-house, because, as he stated, 'it would make the place stink so, that his customers would not stay in it'.

R. D. GRAINGER; P.P. 1843, vol. XIV, p. f 158.

12

Horrible Prospect for Sheffield's Young Grinders

It is a peculiar feature of the Sheffield trades that children are both apprenticed to and hired by the journeymen with whom they work, and who teach them their trades . . . It requires but little capital to start as a small cutler; and it is by these persons, and the men they employ, that the children are for the most part over-worked and ill-used. Some make knives even on a smaller scale. For 6d or 1s a week a vice and bench may be hired. Some of the rougher work, such as cast-metal scissors, forks, etc., requiring filing, is often given out to be done by children and girls at home, where a little bench and rough vice is put up; and this often in the poorest houses . . .

Dr Knight, a physician of eminence residing in Sheffield states: Those who are to be brought up as grinders usually begin to work when they are about 14 years old . . . Grinders who have good constitutions seldom experience much inconvenience from their trade until they arrive at about 20 years of age; about that time the symptoms of their peculiar complaint begin to steal upon them; their breathing becomes more than usually embarrassed on slight exertions, particularly in going up stairs or ascending a hill; their shoulders are elevated . . . they stoop forward, and appear to breathe most comfortably in that position in which they are accustomed to sit at their work, viz. with their elbows resting on their knee. Their complexion assumes a dirty, muddy appearance. Their countenance indicates anxiety; they complain of a sense of tightness across the chest; their voice is rough and hoarse, their cough loud, and as if the air were driven through wooden tubes. They occasionally expectorate considerable quantities of dust,

9. The Girl Brick-maker; from W. H. Pyne's *Costume of Great Britain* (1808)
   (*photo*: Mansell Collection)

10. The Picture that shocked Victorian England: Girl with belt-and-chain dragging coal tubs underground (P.P. 1842, vol. XV) (*photo:* British Museum)

sometimes mixed up with mucus . . . Inability to lie down, night sweats . . . diarrhoea, extreme emaciation, together with all the usual symptoms of pulmonary consumption, at length carry them off, but not until they have lingered through months and even years of suffering, incapable of working so as to support either themselves or their families.

Report by J. C. SYMONS; P.P. 1843, vol. XIV, E 3–5.

13

Infant Lace-workers

In all the districts in which machine-lace manufacture is carried on extensively, instances are found in which mere infants are put to employment; but in this district [Notts.] the Sub-Commissioner found an instance in which an infant under two years was thus regularly employed by its mother. 'Unless I had obtained personal knowledge of the fact,' says Mr Grainger, 'I should have hesitated to have reported that, in this country, a child was placed at work by its parents before it was two years old.'

The children of this family, and the mother, who reside in Walker Street, New Sneinton, give the following evidence: Mary Houghton, four years old, 'Has drawn lace two years; her mother gives her a penny a week'. Anne Houghton, six years old: 'Has been a drawer three years.' Mrs Houghton, the mother of these children: 'Is a lace-drawer and has four children: Harriet 8 years, Anne 6, Mary 4, and Eliza 2 years old; of these the three elder are employed as lace drawers. Harriet was not quite three when she began to work. Anne was about the same, and Mary was not quite two years old.' 'Eliza has drawn a few threads out.'

All this (says the Sub-Commissioner) was interrupted with, 'Mind your work', 'Take care', 'Make haste', 'Now, Anne, get on', 'Mind your work'.

Begins generally at 6 a.m. in the summer and 7 a.m. in the winter; in the former goes on till dark, in the latter till 10 p.m. The two biggest children work with witness these hours; Mary begins at the same time in the morning, but she leaves off about 6 p.m. The children have no time to go out to play: 'they go out very seldom'. Have breakfast whilst they have time to get it; the same with dinner and tea. Have about a quarter of an hour for each meal.

The children are obliged to sit at their work; they sit all day. ('Mind your work.') The work tries the eye; the black is the worst; 'it is dree work'. ('Now mind your work.')

Sub-Commissioner: The children are very fine and pretty girls, and appear healthy; the two younger sit perched on chairs, their legs being too short to reach the ground.

P.P. 1843, vol. XIII, p. 10.

14

Dangerous Busks

All accounts agree in representing the occupation of lace-making in these districts [Northants, Oxon, Beds, and Bucks] as highly injurious to those engaged in it . . . The health of the majority of the children is impaired, says one of the surgeons, by the practice of working together in small, crowded, and ill-ventilated apartments, and the evil is increased by the habit the which the young girls have contracted, of wearing a strong wooden busk in their stays to support them when stooping over their pillow-laces; this, being worn when young, while the bones are yet soft, acts very injuriously to the sternum and ribs, causing great contraction of the chest. Mr Collier, surgeon, states that he measured several of these girls, and found the chest so much narrowed, that they were considerably broader across the shoulders than across the breast; that they cannot be induced to leave off the busk and elevate the cushion, and that great numbers of them ultimately die of consumption . . .

P.P. 1843, vol. XIII, p. 111.

15

'Early slavery' in the Kidderminster Carpet Factories

In Kidderminster, the workshops are generally well built, and, if kept clean, may be considered not unhealthy; but owing to the dirt, the size used in the carpets, and above all, the want of common care in sweeping on the part of the workmen, and lime washing on the part of the masters, they are noisome holes . . .

The weaver, in most instances, employs a drawer, which is usually either a young boy or girl. This drawer has to perform the most laborious part of the work, and is kept for many hours employed—too many for a growing person, and not only is he obliged regularly to work, but when either idleness, dissipation, or any other cause, prevents the weaver attending to his work at the beginning of the week, the drawer, whether boy or girl, is obliged to wait his time, and frequently to work 15 or 18 hours incessantly, to get the piece finished . . .

Nor is this all; for, from the constant opportunity in the workshops, great immorality takes place, even at a very early age, between the drawers, and frequent instances of seduction on the part of married men and fathers of families takes place, from the facilities afforded by the solitary night-working, with their draw girls.

This early slavery . . . must have and does have a baneful effect upon them in after-life. Consumption, diseases of the joints, and ruptures, are of frequent occurrence; and . . . the mortality among children at an early age is alarmingly great.

S. SCRIVEN; P.P. 1843, vol. XIV, p. C 27.

16

Behind the Scenes in a Staffordshire Pottery

The manufacturers are a highly influential, wealthy, and intelligent class of men; they evince a warm-hearted sympathy for those about them in difficulty or distress, contribute as much as possible to their happiness, and are never known to inflict punishment on the children, or to allow others to do so . . .

Many of the manufactories of most recent structure are built upon scales of great magnitude, in some instances of beauty; they contain large, well ventilated, light, airy, commodious rooms, in all respects adapted to the nature of the processes carried on in them. [But] most of them have been erected many years, and as the trade has increased, so the rooms appear to have increased . . . upon, around, and about the first premises; so that there is neither order, regularity, nor proportion; the consequence of this is, that men, women, and children are to be seen passing in and out, to and fro, to their respective departments all hours of the day, no matter what the weather, warm, cold, wet, or dry; the rooms, with very few exceptions, are either low, damp, close, small, dark, hot, dirty, ill ventilated, or unwholesome, or have all these disadvantages.

The third class, which include the Egyptian-ware and figure manufactures, are even still worse; but the children to be found in them are very few, and in many of them there are none. In eight cases out of ten of the whole, the places of convenience for the sexes are indecently and disgustingly exposed and filthy . . . In some places the women and girls are compelled to pass through the hovels where men and boys of the lowest character work, to relieve the calls of nature; others sit under the same shed slightly partitioned off, exposed to the vulgar gaze of half the men on the premises, to avoid which the better disposed either wait their return home, perhaps, at some considerable distance, or run to some opposite, or next door neighbour for relief . . .

The operatives are in their general character a quiet, orderly people, possessing not only the necessaries but in most instances the comforts and luxuries of life; their habitations are respectable, cleanly, and well furnished . . . Their wages are considered the best of any staple trade in the kingdom, averaging, when in full work—that is, 12 hours per day, or 72 hours per week (deducting 1½ hours for meals):—Slip makers £1 19s, throwers £2, turners £1 12s, plate, dish, and saucer makers £1 18s, painters (landscape and flowers) £2, . . . sorters 9s, jiggers, mould-runners, oven boys . . . boys and girls between the ages of 8 and 13 average weekly 2s 0½d.

The processes being such as to admit of the employment of whole families—father, mother, and some two, three, or more children—their united earnings are sometimes £3 or £4 per week; but, proverbially improvident, and adopting the adage, 'sufficient unto the day is the evil thereof', they squander the proceeds of their labour in gaudy dress, or at the skittle-ground and ale-house; so that, when overtaken by illness or other casualty, and thrown for a few days out of work, they resort to their masters for a *loan*, or to the parish workhouse for relief.

The employments of children are various and dissimilar; in some of the rooms great numbers are congregated together, while in others there are only one or two; the painting, burnishing, gilding, flower-making, moulding, figure-making, and engraving, constitute literally schools of art, under the superintendence of masters and mistresses ... They are seen sitting at their clean tables, at a comfortable distance from each other, and in an airy, commodious, and warm room, well ventilated, and heated by a stove or hot plate, on which they dress their meals. They commence their duties at six in the morning in summer, and at seven in winter, and leave at six. In the midst of their occupations (which have in reality more the character of accomplishments), they arc allowed the indulgence of singing hymns. I have often visited the rooms unexpectedly, and been charmed with the melody of their voices. In personal appearance they are healthy, clean, and well conducted ...

The class of children whose physical condition has the strongest claims to consideration is that of the 'jiggers' and 'mould runners', who, by the very nature of their work, are rendered pale, weak, diminutive, and unhealthy; they are employed by the dish, saucer, and plate makers; their hours are from half-past five in the morning to six at night, but in numberless instances they are required to labour on to eight, nine, or ten, and this in an atmosphere varying from 100 to 120 degrees; all these extra hours being occasioned, nine times out of ten, by the selfishness or irregularities of their unworthy taskmasters. The men work by the piece; however much there may be on hand to accomplish they seldom or ever work after Saturday noon, and often not before the following Tuesday or Wednesday morning, but spend the hard earnings of the previous days idly and unprofitably; once gone, they again 'buckle to,' and work like horses.

Each man employs two boys, one to turn the jigger, or horizontal wheel, from morning to night; the other to carry the ware just formed from the 'whirler' to the hot-house and moulds back. These hot-houses are rooms within rooms, closely confined except at the doors, and without windows. In the centre stands a large cast-iron stove, heated to redness, increasing the temperature often to 130 degrees. I have burst two thermometers at that point. During this inclement season I have seen these boys running to and fro on errands, or to their dinners, without stockings, shoes, or jackets, and with perspiration standing on their foreheads, after labouring like little slaves, with the mercury 20 degrees below freezing. The results of such transitions are soon realized, and many die of consumption, asthma, and acute inflammations . . .

MR SAMUEL SCRIVEN's report on the Staffordshire potteries; P.P. 1843, vol. XIV, C 2 to 5.

17

Tea and Cakes for Good Little Girls

In the Potteries [in the West of England] in general the children are seldom harshly and often very kindly treated. Even in those establishments in which corporal punishment is occasionally inflicted, the tenor of the evidence shows that it is rarely severe, while in many establishments it is altogether prohibited; and in some of the departments, as in that of painting, in which the children are under the charge of some respectable women, they are sometimes 'watched over with the eye of a mother'.

The children are not encouraged by rewards, neither is their labour enforced by punishment . . . 'I never hear of any case of cruelty or oppression; if I did I should immediately correct it.'

'If one should be short of food, I'm sure the rest would help her; I endeavour to inculcate a spirit of good feeling and kindness towards each other; I do not know of any cases of punishment exercised by the master or myself; we can manage them without; if I see or hear anything wrong I talk to them; if they are good girls, master gives us a sovereign to be expended in tea, milk, sugar, and cakes, which they take in the room, and enjoy themselves after with a game or so, or singing hymns; master and mistress and their friends look in on these occasions; no children can be happier!'

'If they conduct themselves well (and I have never found that we had occasion to make an exception), they get a treat once a year. The women who overlook them receive from the masters a sum of money, which they expend on tea and cakes, with a bowl of punch or something of that sort, when they are as merry as crickets; they have games, or some kind of amusement. At other times, when a wedding has occurred in the family of the master or the coming-of-age of one of his children, there is a general treat of roast beef and plum-pudding for all the men, women, and children in the works, the family joining.'

'They behave very well to the children generally; if they did not, the children would leave, as they are not bound for any specific time, and the parties exercising any cruelties would doubtless be brought before the stipendiary magistrates; the people think this is a great protection to them.' 'Tis a common saying here, if an offence or assault is committed, "I'll Bailey Rose him!" ' (referring to the name of the stipendiary magistrate).

MR SCRIVEN's report; P.P. 1843, vol. XIII, pp. 85–86.

18

Spurring Them On

Jacob Ball, 12-year-old runner of dish-moulds at Mr Rowley's earthenware factory, Tunstall: I come in the morning to work at 6 o'clock, gets fires in, sweep my place, get coals up, and ash out. I go home to breakfast, and sometimes takes my ha'f hour. I go home to dinner at ha'f-past one, sometimes quarter-past. My hour allowed me is from one to two, but John Wareham won't allow me to go before. I always come back at 2, and go home sometimes at 8 and 9. I get 3s 6d a week if I work from 6 to 6; I do not get more than 3s 6d if I work till 9.

John is paid by the dozen. I am paid by the day. He sometimes gives a 1d at week's end, but not always. He lays on me sometimes; the other men lay on their lads; they are always laying on them for nothing; some of them put red-hot corks under the feet of the jiggers and runners to burn the feet; some on 'em put cock-spurs up the floor to hurt our feet when running. We work without shoes or stockings.

I am very tired when I get home a-nights. Get my supper, and go to bed, and up again at ha'f past foive. I get bread and cheese, sometimes bread and treacle, for breakfast, tatees and beef for dinner. If I had my choice I would sooner work from 6 to 6 at 7d a day, than to nine. If I wor to cut away from work at six, I should play me a bit. I should loike to go to school, evenings; I should do that too.

P.P. 1843, vol. XIV, p. C 78.

19

In a London Match Factory

Report by Dr Mitchell on a visit to a lucifer-match factory in Finsbury, London: There was considerable unwillingness to show the work, which was overcome. One part is for men, to cut from wood the stalks, which fall on the ground, and children gather them and tie them together in large bundles, as large as can be handled by the hands of boys. In another room is the dipping of these bundles of stalks in melted sulphur. There is an iron stove, and there is near it a pan full of the liquid sulphur. A boy places a bundle of the stalks on their end on the stove, which heats them much. Another takes the same bundle, and dips it into the melted sulphur, and hands it to another boy, who rolls it about on a block, to keep the stalks from adhering. This completes the sulphuring part of the process. The fumes of the sulphur are exceedingly disagreeable, and make a stranger cough very much.

In another room is the process of putting on the chlorate of potass. It is combined with some adhesive matter, and forms a half-liquid mass. A portion of this mass is poured upon a board, and the bundles already sulphured are set on their ends on this mass upon the board, and removed, and set to dry. There were a great many children, obviously under 12 and 13, and not looking well nor cheerful. The room was most disagreeable to be in.

There are other rooms where the boxes are made, and where the matches are put up in those boxes. These rooms are remote from the offensive parts of the operations.

It was stated that there were upwards of 180 employed, men, women, boys, and children. The children were more numerous than the grown people, and some of them, in appearance, were about 10, and the larger part under 13. It was stated that the work was done by the piece, also the children made from 5s to 7s a week. This is double the usual wages of children in London, and is a proof of the difficulty of getting persons to encounter the disagreeable nature of this business.

It was stated that the children, in many instances, took their meals in the working-rooms. It was impossible to hear this without the most painful feelings. If ever a breathing of the pure air of heaven was needful, it must be so to children employed in rooms which, if we may judge from the sensations experienced, are not only disagreeable but most noxious to health.

P.P. 1843, vol. XIV, pp. 251–252.

20

Down by the Glasgow Tobacco-Works

The tobacco-spinning appears to employ, in all the large towns in which it is carried on, the children of the most wretched class of the population, the factories being sometimes contiguous to their abodes. Thus, of the children so employed in Glasgow, the Sub-Commissioner (Mr Tancred) reports that . . . 'Nakedness, hunger, shortness of stature, filth, scrofulous tumours, all combine to render their youth the prelude to a vicious and wretched manhood. Without affecting particular sensibility, I must say that no man of ordinary feeling could pass down the Trongate last winter, with the snow frozen fast to the pavement, and meeting the cutting, piercing east wind, without his heart aching at the sights he saw.

'Scores of children of both sexes were to be seen, in groups of two or three, scuffling along the snowy streets, with feet either quite naked or only protected by the remnant of a slipper, and mere rags over the rest of the body, the boys often without hats, and the girls with a sort of *mantilla*, consisting of a coarse bit of sackcloth hung over their heads and held together beneath the chin, sometimes clothed in a large woman's gown cut short, with the original sleeves like bags on either side. The wind showed the lightness of the garments worn by others, and the ease with which it could pierce to their very bones. The abode of such specimens of the population could be guessed. They belong to the neighbourhood of the tobacco-works . . . It is evident that to children so circumstanced the employment in a tobacco manufactory must be an object of ambition. They are there at least sheltered from the elements and kept warm for several hours a day.'

P.P. 1843, vol. XIII, pp. 113–114.

21

Hot Work for the Stove-girls

Children are employed to assist adults in most of the processes in bleaching, dyeing, and printing [of calico and other textile fabrics] . . . In the Turkey-red works there is a class of girls employed, amounting in some to about fifty, whose office is to hang the goods in the Turkey-red stoves, and hence called stove-girls. These stoves are usually constructed with barred floors two or three stories high, and over the bars the pieces are suspended by the middle with their ends hanging down on either side. The temperature at which I usually found these stoves when the girls were filling them was 110°, or fever heat; and the steam rising from the wet goods as they are hung up is still more suffocating and oppressive than dry heat would be.

The stove-girls go in and out of this heat with bare feet, and hardly any clothes, carrying the goods on their backs to the dyeing department, or to the field or park where the goods have been exposed on the grass, and where the park-girls collect them in heaps. The stove-girls are then loaded by each other, and carry their burdens into the stove, going and coming till they have taken in the whole . . . The hours of the stove and park girls are very irregular, and often excessive, not that they are kept late at night, but from being obliged to come generally about five, but often as early as three o'clock in the morning.

T. TANCRED, report on Print Works in the West of Scotland: P.P. 1843, vol. XV, I, 14–15.

22

Little Sarah of the Brick-fields

Sarah Griffiths, age 12:

'Please, sir, all the family are very small.' Works in the brick-yards; works under one of the men, who pays her 4s a week; gives the money to her mother; the man never beats her; was never beated by anybody; nobody sees any of the girls beaten except they don't behave themselves, and won't do their work, and run away to play, when they don't like work, and then the men smack 'em with their hands—only on their faces and backs—not badly; thinks it's only when the girls deserve it.

Works from 6 in the morning till 8 or 9 at night, according to the weather, because the rain would spoil the fire-bricks while they are soft; when the weather's fine they are all obliged to work for their lives. Is sometimes very tired at night; has to carry very heavy weights, bricks or clay; 4 or 5 or 6 bricks at a time, as many as each one can; the girls sometimes fall down with them, or drop 'em and spoil 'em, and have to bring them back; then they get smacked, or turned off from the work.

Finds her legs swell sometimes with running about and has pains and aches between the shoulders, and her hands swell; all this goes off when they get used to it. Can read, not write. (N.B. Growth appearing somewhat stunted, health good; clean, and well clothed.)

From R. H. HORNE's report; P.P. 1843, vol. XV, p. q 76.

23

Home Work Worse than in the Factory

There are a large number of young persons employed in weaving in this district [Lancashire], but from the work being carried on in separate cottages by one or two persons together, they would scarcely come within the terms of this Commission, which only embraces those children employed in numbers together. The children and young persons, however, who are employed in this branch of manufacture at their own houses are more to be commiserated than most of the operatives in large manufactories. I have frequently seen them at work in their cold, dark, damp cellars, without any fire or means of ventilation, and the atmosphere, on entering the room, was literally foetid with the breath of the inmates. They are at liberty to work what hours they please; but many of them work from very early in the morning till late at night to make the smallest pittance. I have frequently been told by young boys in this trade that they have worked from 5 in the morning till 12 at night for many days without intermission.

J. L. KENNEDY; P.P. 1843, vol. XIV, B 40, para. 278.

24

Moral Condition of the Child Workers

From the whole of the evidence collected under the present Commission relative to the *Moral Condition* of the Children and Young Persons included within its terms, whether employed in *Collieries* and *Mines*, or in *Trades* and *Manufactures*, we find—

1. That there are few classes of these Children and Young Persons 'working together in numbers', of whom a large proportion are not in a lamentably low moral condition.

2. That this low moral condition is evinced by a general ignorance of moral duties and sanctions, and by an absence of moral and religious restraint, shown among some classes chiefly by coarseness of manners, and the use of profane and indecent language; but in other classes by the practice of gross immorality, which is prevalent to a great extent, in both sexes, at very early ages.

3. That this absence of restraint is the result of a general want of moral and religious training, comparatively few of these classes having the advantage of moral and religious parents to instruct and guide them; their low moral condition, on the contrary, often having its very origin in the degradation of the parents, who, themselves brought up without

virtuous habits, can set no good example to their Children, nor have a beneficial control over their conduct.

4. That the parents, urged on by poverty and improvidence, generally seek employment for the Children as soon as they can earn the lowest amount of wages; paying but little regard to the probable injury of their Children's health by early labour, and still less regard to the certain injury to their minds by early removal from school, or even by the total neglect of their education; seldom, when questioned, expressing any desire for the regulation of the hours of work, with a view to the protection and welfare of their Children, but constantly expressing the greatest apprehension lest any legislative restriction should deprive them of the profits of their Children's labour; the natural parental instinct to provide, during childhood, for the Children's subsistence, being, in great numbers of instances, wholly extinguished, and the order of nature even reversed—the Children supporting, instead of being supported by, their parents.

5. That the girls are prevented, by their early removal from home and from the day-schools, to be employed in labour, from learning needlework, and from acquiring those habits of cleanliness, neatness, and order, without which they cannot, when they grow up to woman-hood, and have the charge of families of their own, economize their husbands' earnings, or give to their homes any degree of comfort . . .

6. That among the great body of employers it is very uncommon, even for those who are considered the best masters, to do anything more, in the moral care of their young workpeople, than merely to suspend in the place of work printed regulations, defining the duties and behaviour of the Children, and prohibiting the adult workmen from beating and otherwise ill-using them, without, either by themselves or their agents, taking any personal care that these regulations are observed: while, in the great majority of instances, even this is not done, but the young people come to their work at a fixed hour; during the hours of labour they work constantly; when the task is done, they leave their place of work; and then all connexion ends between the employers and the employed . . .

12. That the means of secular and religious instruction . . . are so grievously defective, that, in all the districts, great numbers of Children and Young Persons are growing up without any religious, moral, or intellectual training; nothing being done to form them to habits of order, sobriety, honesty, and forethought, or even to restrain them from vice and crime.

13. That neither in the new Colliery and Mining towns which have suddenly collected together large bodies of the people in new localities, nor in the towns which have suddenly sprung up under the successful pursuit of some new branch of Trade and Manufacture, is any provision made for Education by the establishment of Schools with properly qualified teachers, nor for supplying the spiritual wants of the people . . .

15. That, were schools ever so abundant and excellent, they would be wholly beyond the reach of a large portion of the Children employed in labour, on account of the early ages at which they are put to work.

16. That great numbers of Children and Young Persons attend no day-school before they commence work; that even those who do go for a brief period to a day-school are very commonly removed to be put to labour at five, six, seven, and eight years old; and that the instances are extremely rare in which they attend an evening-school after regular employment has once begun.

18. That in all the districts, many Children and Young Persons, whether employed in the mines of coal and iron, or in trades and manufactures, never go to any school, and some have never been at any school.

20. That in regard, particularly, to the Children and Young Persons employed in the Mines of coal and iron, the fatigue produced by their labour is in general so great, that they cannot, with any advantage, attend School after the work of the day is over . . .

21. That even in the day-schools which do exist, and which are provided with funds adequate to their support, the teachers, with some striking exceptions, are wholly unqualified for their office . . .

22. That in almost all instances the sole dependence for the education and moral and religious training of the Children and Young Persons, after they have begun to work, is on the Sunday-schools; the teachers volunteering their meritorious efforts, which, however, are altogether unsystematic and feeble.

23. That in all districts, great numbers of those Children who had been in regular attendance on Sunday-schools for a period of from five to nine years, were found, on examination, to be incapable of reading an easy book, or of spelling the commonest word; and they were not only altogether ignorant of Christian principles, doctrines, and precepts, but they knew nothing whatever of any of the events of Scripture history, nor anything even of the names most commonly occurring in the Scriptures.

24. That in all the districts many Children who had been returned as

able to read, when examined were found to know only the letters of the alphabet; a very small proportion indeed being able to read well an easy book . . .

25. That of those who could read fluently, very few, when questioned, were found to have any conception of the meaning of the words they uttered, or were able to give any intelligible account of what seemed to the examiners to be simple and easy terms and things; so that, as far as regards the acquisition of any useful knowledge, or the accomplishment of any higher purpose to be answered by education, these Children, in great numbers of instances, were as little benefited, after years of so-called tuition, as if they had never been at school.

29. That, whatever may be the state of ignorance and demoralization of the classes included in this inquiry, the instances in which efforts have been perseveringly made to improve their condition have generally been attended with success; as is shown, among others, in some of the mining districts, more especially in the West of England and North Wales, where, under the zealous and devoted care of the Wesleyan and other ministers, men, who were formerly almost lawless, who spent their leisure hours in noise and riot, who delighted in all sorts of cruel sports, who were the terror of the surrounding neighbourhoods, and who, for gross ignorance, rudeness, and irreligion, were almost without a parallel in any Christian country, are now so far reformed, that there is as much decorum in their manners as is witnessed in the generality of the rural districts . . .

32. That there are parents who not only anxiously endeavour to afford their Children, even at the expense of some personal sacrifice and self-denial, good and sufficient clothing, but also the best education within their reach, and who themselves superintend, as well as they are able, their Children's education and conduct; but this attention to their moral condition is rare.

33. That there are some masters of large works, and proprietors of mining and manufacturing establishments, who take great pains to afford the Children and Young Persons employed in their service, not only the opportunity of innocent and healthful amusement and recreation in the intervals of their labour, but also the means of intellectual, moral, and religious instruction and improvement, and who, by their own personal superintendence and exertion, do much to induce and direct their work-people so to avail themselves of those means as really to profit by them.

35. That from the whole body of evidence it appears, however, that

there are at present in existence no means adequate to effect any material and general improvement in the Physical and Moral Condition of the Children and Young Persons employed in labour . . .

All which we humbly certify to Your Majesty,

THOMAS TOOKE, T. SOUTHWOOD SMITH,
LEONARD HORNER, ROBERT J. SAUNDERS.

Westminster, January 30th, 1843

2nd Report of the Commission on the Employment of Children (Trades and Manufactures), 1843; P.P. vol. XIII, pp. 195–204.

(g) CHILD LABOUR: FOR AND AGAINST

There is a story told of William Pitt, Prime Minister during the great war with Revolutionary France, that when the British manufacturers warned him that owing to the high wages they had to pay their workmen they would be unable to pay their taxes, he returned the terrible answer, 'Then take the children'. The story has been denied, but that he was generally supposed to have said something of the kind is clear from the first document in this section. It comes from one of the numerous books written by William Cooke Taylor (1800–1849), an Irishman who became a 'miscellaneous writer' in London and achieved prominence as an opponent of factory legislation. Another of his books is drawn upon for No. 2, in which we are reminded that, whatever the hard fate of the factory child, the condition of the child working at home under the Domestic system was sometimes harder. Edward Baines (1800–1890) was likewise inclined to be critical of factory legislation, although in other fields he was a prominent reformer; he followed his father as proprietor of the *Leeds Mercury* and as Liberal M.P. for Leeds, and wrote a history of the Cotton Manufacture that became a standard work (No. 3). Dr Andrew Ure (1778–1857) was another antagonist of factory legislation, and his almost lyrical descriptions of factory life aroused the ire of the reformers; he was professor of chemistry at Glasgow, and lectured on scientific subjects. Powerfully eloquent on the other side was John Fielden, who spoke, unlike the literary men, out of his 'own bodily experience' (Nos. 5 and 6). Particularly interesting is the document (No. 7), in which Carleton Tufnell, a highly experienced investigator of social conditions, told the Factory Commission of 1833 that the parents of the children employed in factories were more often to blame than the employers for any ill-treatment (such as it was, and he thought it exaggerated); what was really necessary, he argued, was not special factory legislation so much as the education of working-class parents in proper child care. Finally, in No. 8 we have another defence of factory life, but it is significant that it is stated that conditions had much improved since the passing of the Factory Act in 1833. The author, John James (1811–1867), was a Yorkshireman, born of humble parents, who worked in lime-kilns as a boy and became a solicitor's clerk and engaged in journalism in Bradford. He was a keen antiquarian, and his history of the Worsted Manufacture is as authoritative as it is informative.

I

Why Children Must Work

Every man acquainted with the political history of the last half-century must know, that the labour of children was actually pointed out to the manufacturers by Mr William Pitt, as a new resource by which they might be enabled to bear the additional load of taxation which the necessities of the state compelled him to impose.

The necessity for labour created by this taxation has not yet abated; because the immense capital taken away by the enormous expenditure of the great wars arising out of the French Revolution—an expenditure which was mainly supported out of the industrial resources of the country—has not been replaced. But even independent of these considerations . . . we mean to assert that the infant labour—or the juvenile labour, as it should be called—in factories, is in fact a national blessing, and absolutely necessary for the support of the manifold fiscal burthens which have been placed upon the industry of this country. It is quite sufficient to say that the children of the operatives have mouths, and must be fed; they have limbs, and must be clothed; they have minds, which ought to be instructed; and they have passions, which must be controlled.

Now, if the parents are unable to provide these requisites—and their inability to do so is just as notorious as their existence—it becomes absolutely necessary that the children should aid in obtaining them for themselves. To abolish juvenile labour is plainly nothing less than to abolish juvenile means of support; and to confine it within very narrow limits is just to subtract a dinner or a supper from the unhappy objects of mistaken benevolence . . .

It comes within our knowledge that children who were deprived of the easy work of the factories have been sent to toil in the coal-mines, and to other avocations equally injurious to health, and far more ruinous to morals. The parents are compelled by sheer necessity to send their children to work; they could not otherwise support them in comfort, and in many cases they could not keep them from contact with perilous pollution . . . The house-accommodations of the operatives in large towns are necessarily very limited; if the children were excluded from the factories and workshops it is not very clear what would become of them. At home they could not remain even if they were disposed to do so; there is no legal provision for compelling them to attend schools —their only resource would be the street, with all its perils and temptations . . .

Persons enter a mill . . . they see the figures of the little piecers and cleaners employed in their monotonous routine, . . . and they think how much more delightful would have been the gambol of free limbs on the hill-side, the inhaling of the fresh breeze, the sight of the green mead with its spangles of buttercups and daisies, the song of the bird, and the humming of the bee! But they should compare the aspect of the youthful operatives with other sights which they must have met in the course of their experience, as we too often have in ours: we have seen children perishing from sheer hunger in the mud-hovel, or in the ditch by the way-side . . . the juvenile mendicant, and the juvenile vagrant, with famine in their cheeks and despair in their hearts. We have seen the juvenile delinquent, his conscience seared by misery, his moral nature destroyed by suffering, his intellectual powers trained to perversity by the irresistible force of the circumstances that surrounded him. It is a sad confession to make, but owing, perhaps, to some peculiar obliquity of intellect or hardness of heart—we would rather see boys and girls earning the means of support in the mill than starving by the road-side, shivering on the pavement, or even conveyed in an omnibus to Bridewell . . .

W. COOKE TAYLOR, *Factories and the Factory System* (1844), pp. 23–24.

2

Now When We *Were Children*

My excellent host has induced me to visit some of those who may be called the philosophers of the operatives. Our first visit was to a village patriarch, over 80 years of age . . . He had been a weaver, and remembered the condition of the trade before the introduction of machinery . . . These were, according to his account, really the days of infant slavery. 'The creatures were set to work', he said, 'as soon as they could crawl; and their parents were the hardest taskmasters.'

I may remark that on a previous occasion I received a similar account from an old man in the vale of Todmorden, who declared that he would not accept an offer to live his whole life over again, if it were to be accompanied with the condition of passing through the same servitude and misery which he had endured in infancy.

Both these old men expressed great indignation at the clamour which had been raised for infant protection: my Todmorden friend quite lost his temper whenever any reference was made to the subject, contrasting in very strong terms the severities he had endured, and the heavy labours he had to perform, both in his father's house and afterwards as an apprentice, with the light toil and positive comfort of the factory children.

W. COOKE TAYLOR, *Notes of a Tour in the Manufacturing Districts of Lancashire,*
1842; pp. 145–146.

3

Long Hours, Light Labour

That there have been instances of abuse and cruelty in some of the manufacturing establishments, is doubtless true; that the labour is not so healthful as labour in husbandry, must be at once admitted; and that some children have unquestionably suffered from working beyond their strength. But abuse is the exception, not the rule. Factory labour is far less injurious than many of the most common and necessary employments of civilized life. It is much less irksome than that of the weaver, less arduous than that of the smith, less prejudicial to the lungs, the spine, and the limbs, than those of the shoemaker and the tailor. Colliers, miners, forgemen, cutlers, machine-makers, masons, bakers, corn-millers, painters, plumbers, letter-press printers, potters, and many other classes of artisans and labourers, have employments which in one way or another are more inimical to health and longevity than the labour of cotton mills. Some classes of professional men, students, clerks in counting-houses, shopkeepers, milliners, etc., are subject to as great, and in many cases to much greater, confinement and exhaustion than the mill operatives . . .

I am far from contending, that the labour of mills is of the most agreeable and healthful kind; or that there have not been abuses in them, which required exposure and correction; or that legislative interference was not justifiable, to protect children of tender years from being overworked. It must be admitted that the hours of labour in cotton mills are long, being twelve hours a day on five days of the week, and nine hours on Saturday: but . . . none of the species of work in which children and young persons are engaged requires constant attention; most of them admit even of the attention being remitted every few minutes; and where the eye must be kept on the watch, habit makes the task of observation perfectly easy. It is scarcely possible for any employment to be lighter. The position of the body is not injurious: the general attitude is erect, but the children walk about, and have opportunity of frequently sitting if they are so disposed.

On visiting mills, I have generally remarked the coolness and equanimity of the work-people, even of the children, whose manner seldom, as far as my observation goes, indicates anxious care, and is more frequently sportive than gloomy. The noise and whirl of the machinery, which are unpleasant and confusing to a spectator unaccustomed to the scene, produce not the slightest effect on the operatives habituated to it.

The only thing which makes factory labour trying even to delicate children is, that they are confined for long hours, and deprived of fresh air: this makes them pale, and reduces their vigour, but it rarely brings on disease. The minute fibres of cotton which float in the rooms, and

are called *fly*, are admitted, even by medical men, not to be injurious
to young persons . . .

SIR EDWARD BAINES, *History of the Cotton Manufacture in Great Britain*
(1835), pp. 453–457.

4

'Lively Elves'

I have visited many factories, both in Manchester and in the surrounding districts, during a period of several months, entering the spinning
rooms, unexpectedly, and often alone, at different times of the day,
and I never saw a single instance of corporal chastisement inflicted on
a child, nor indeed did I ever see children in ill-humour. They seemed
to be always cheerful and alert, taking pleasure in the light play of their
muscles,—enjoying the mobility natural to their age. The scene of
industry, so far from exciting sad emotions in my mind, was always
exhilarating . . . The work of these lively elves seemed to resemble a
sport, in which habit gave them a pleasing dexterity. Conscious of
their skill, they were delighted to show it off to any stranger.

As to exhaustion by the day's work, they evinced no trace of it on
emerging from the mill in the evening; for they immediately began to
skip about any neighbouring play-ground, and to commence their little
amusements with the same alacrity as boys issuing from a school.

ANDREW URE, M.D., F.R.S., *The Philosophy of Manufactures* (1835), p. 301.

5

'My own bodily experience'

As I have been personally and from an early age engaged in the operations connected with factory labour; that is to say, for about forty years,
a short account of my own experience may not be useless in this place,

as it is this experience which teaches me to scoff at the representations of those who speak of the labour of factories as 'very light', and 'so easy, as to require no muscular exertion'.

I well remember being set to work in my father's mill when I was little more than ten years old; my associates, too, in the labour and in recreation are fresh in my memory. Only a few of them are now alive; some dying very young, others living to become men and women; but many of those who lived, have died off before they attained the age of fifty years, having the appearance of being much older, a premature appearance of age which I verily believe was caused by the nature of the employment in which they had been brought up.

For several years after I began to work in the mill, the hours of labour at our works did not exceed *ten* in the day, winter and summer; and even with the labour of those hours, I shall never forget the fatigue I often felt before the day ended, and the anxiety of us all to be relieved from the unvarying and irksome toil we had gone through before we could obtain relief by such play and amusement as we resorted to when liberated from our work. I allude to this fact, because it is not un-common for persons to infer, that, because the children who work in factories are seen to play like other children when they have time to do so, the labour is, therefore, light, and does not fatigue them. The reverse of this conclusion I know to be the truth. I know the effect which ten hours' labour had on myself; I who had the attention of parents better able than those of my companions to allow me extraordinary occasional indulgence. And he knows very little of human nature who does not know, that, to a child, diversion is so essential, that it will undergo even exhaustion in its amusements. I protest, therefore, against the reasoning, that, because a child is not brought so low in spirit as to be incapable of enjoying the diversions of a child, it is not worked to the utmost that its feeble frame and constitution will bear . . .

Another remarkable fact within my own knowledge I must also state: when my father introduced the machinery that is now used, into his own mill, the hours of labour were increased to *twelve*, for five days in the week, and *eleven* for Saturdays, making seventy-one hours in the week This he was obliged to do in his own defence, because others who used the same sort of machinery, worked their hands *seventy-seven* hours; and some even so much as *eighty-four* hours a week, a practice which continued until 1819, when the 59th of Geo. 3 was passed, and which limited the time-labour for children under sixteen years of age to seventy-two hours in the week, that is, one hour more than the time of work for both children and adults at the establishment in which I had worked myself, but in which I had now become interested as a partner. These hours I always thought and said were excessive; I thought so from my own bodily experience; and, therefore, I have always been an advocate for a reduction by legislative enactment . . .

JOHN FIELDEN, M.P.: *The Curse of the Factory System* (1836), pp. 31-34.

6

All in a Day's Walk

This question [of the distance walked by a factory child in a day's work] was mooted at Manchester on the 1st of December last year, by certain delegates from the factory people, who were appointed from Bolton, Bury, Ashton, Oldham, Chorley, Preston, and Manchester, to meet a few Members of Parliament . . .

One of these delegates gave a statement, with particulars, of a minute calculation of the number of miles which a child had to walk in a day in following the spinning machine: it amounted to *twenty-five*!

The statement excited great surprise; but this delegate was followed by another, who had also made calculations . . . that a child has to walk twenty-four miles in the day; and, if the distance that it frequently has to walk to and from home be thrown in, it makes, not unfrequently, a distance of nearly *thirty miles*.

Observing the impression that these statements made on the minds of my brother Members of Parliament, and being myself desirous of testing their accuracy, I resolved, on my return home, to make a calculation myself, by watching a child at work in the factory in which I am myself concerned. To my own surprise, I found that the distance was not less than *twenty miles* in twelve hours; and, therefore, I can easily believe the statements of the delegates, seeing that the machinery in my own works is not driven at anything like the speed of that on which their calculations are founded.

JOHN FIELDEN, M.P.: *The Curse of the Factory System* (1836), pp. 39-40.

7

Who Is Really to Blame?

The most prominent charge that has been brought against the factories is, that either the masters, or persons by their sanction and authority, are in the habit of inflicting corporal punishment, sometimes of the most cruel description, on children employed in their mills.

To this accusation I can give the most decided and unqualified denial. It is not only not true, but cannot generally be true . . .The charge almost wholly relates to the piecers (children employed in joining the threads that break in the spinning), and the scavengers (children employed to sweep up the waste cotton), as it is only in these departments that children in any numbers are employed; and in no other are they engaged at so tender an age.

Now, with some rare exceptions, all the piecers and scavengers are employed by the working spinners themselves; the master or his immediate agents have little or rather no control whatever over them: if they do their work badly, the spinner, who is always paid piece-work, suffers, and if there is any ill-usage, he, and he only, is to blame . . .

I must, however, defend the workmen against themselves, for truth compels me to record my conviction that the general accusation of cruelty is groundless as respects any body of persons. They dare not be cruel, for fear of the just resentment of those masters whom they charge with cruelty. That individual instances of ill-usage do occur is doubtless true; and they will occur so long as man is actuated by human passions; but they are exceedingly rare. It would be the grossest injustice to assert that they equal in amount one quarter of the cruelties which children have to endure in the glass-house, pin-heading, and colliery trades . . .

MR TUFNELL's report on Lancashire trades; Factory Commission, Supplementary Report; P.P. 1834, vol. XIX, D 2, 193–194.

8

Pleasant, and Well Paid

The worsted spinners are chiefly children and young persons. Since the passing of the Factory Act of 1833, their state has been wonderfully ameliorated, and especially so subsequent to the limitation of factory labour to ten hours a day ... The calling is a clean and active one, and secures sufficient wages to enable the spinners (mostly girls) to be well fed and clothed. According to the age and excellence of the spinner, the earnings average from four to seven shillings a week.

One of the main objections urged against the factory system is the employment of persons of tender age. This is, however, an objection which will apply to the manufactures of our forefathers. In all ages, children have been employed in labour often unsuitable to their strength. For example, in the agricultural districts gangs of them may be seen weeding in the fields during the bitter days of Winter, for nine hours a day, at two shillings a week.

Even superior to that of the spinner is the sanitary state of the power-loom weaver, whose employment ranks among the very best paid, the pleasantest, and the most healthy pursued by females. These weavers will, if of fair ability, earn ten shillings a week, whilst a first-rate hand employed upon fine stuffs will obtain a much higher remuneration. With the exception of the noise from the machinery, there can scarcely be mentioned a disagreeable item which appertains to the labour of a power-loom weaver, in a well conducted mill. The temperature of the rooms is, like that for spinning, moderate, there is little dust, the duties are active, not fatiguing, and the hours of labour, like those of the spinners, not excessive. Most of these weavers are girls, and are as a class well conducted.

JOHN JAMES, *History of the Worsted Manufacture in England*, (1857), pp. 548–550.

WOMAN'S PLACE

(a) THE FACTORY GIRL

Woman, so it has been said, was man's first beast of burden. Women have always worked, in household duties and in husbandry, and also, under the Domestic System, at the spinning-wheel and the cottage loom. But with the coming of the Industrial Revolution, for the first time large numbers of women and girls were employed away from their homes, under the direction of men with whom their relationship was that of paid worker. It is true that for centuries women had had a place in the coal workings, but even there as a rule they worked beside and for their menfolk. Now it was a stranger who gave them their orders, regulated their working lives, paid them their wages. The manufacturers could never get a sufficient number of 'hands', not even when the legions of children had been impressed into service, and they were quick to appreciate the potentialities of female labour. Young women and girls, they found, might be easily induced to undertake the routine jobs of the factory employment; they were cheap, they were (usually) submissive, and they could be easily trained and soon became quite expert.

This was in the second half of the eighteenth century, when the Agricultural Revolution was reducing the value of women's work on the farms, and the Domestic System that was so praised by Gaskell and others was breaking up. There must have been numbers of females engaged in factory employment when Mary Wollstonecraft in 1792 published her *Vindication of the Rights of Woman*—the book which may be taken as the start of the movement for the emancipation of women—and it seems strange that she should have been unaware of the fact. She complained bitterly that there were so few occupations open to a woman; and yet at that very moment there were numbers of her sex—unmarried girls, middle-aged spinsters, widows, deserted wives—who were earning their own livings in industry.

Among the human types engendered by the Industrial Revolution the Factory Girl stands out in bold individuality and apparent unconcern for the conventions. In her clogs and rough working clothes, the shawl pinned across her waist or thrown over her head, we see her emerging from her lodging into the street at dawn, or before it, and going to her work, alone; and at nightfall, or later, making her return, again alone or in the company of workmates. She was so much a newcomer to the industrial scene that she was suspect from the beginning. As we have seen from Peter Gaskell's account her reputation was none of the best, and predatory males were inclined to look upon her as easy game.

But there was another Gaskell—no relation, it would appear, of the doctor—who painted a very different picture. Mrs Gaskell was the wife of a Unitarian minister in Manchester, and out of her own personal knowledge of the cotton towns in the cruel thirties and hungry forties of the last century she wrote novels that are of abiding worth. There is little in common between the precocious females of Peter Gaskell's pages and the often noble women that Mrs Gaskell introduces us to in *Mary Barton* and *North and South*.

In what follows, Gaskell and Cooke Taylor and Ure . . . are reinforced by the collected testimonies of those employed under the various Commissions, etc. Worthy of particular attention is the statement by Mr Hickson (No. 11), that 'one of the greatest advantages resulting from the progress of manufacturing industry . . . is its tendency to raise the condition of women'. If Mary Wollstonecraft could have read *that* she would indeed have been gratified to learn that, what her arguments had failed to accomplish, the hard facts of the economic situation were bringing about.

I

Lancashire Witches

Lancashire has long been celebrated for the beauty of its women; 'the Lancashire witches' being a standing toast in all private and public convivialities. In the higher and middle classes of society, there are certainly to be found many exquisite specimens of female loveliness—many exceedingly graceful and feminine beings. They may be seen in abundance in all the social circles, in places of amusement and parade, in which, like the sex all the world over, they naturally assemble—a passion for admiration and attention forming an essential and important part of woman's character, and one too of the utmost value, and worthy every cultivation.

But these must not be sought for amongst the precociously developed girls herding in factories. Here, on the contrary, will be found an utter absence of grace and feminine manners—a peculiar raucous or rough timbre of voice—no such thing as speaking soft and low, 'that most excellent thing in woman', a peculiarity owing to various causes, a principal one of which is, too early sexual excitement, producing a state of vocal organs closely resembling that of the male.

Here is no delicacy of figure, no 'grace in all her steps', no 'heaven within her eye', no elegance of tournure, no retiring bashfulness, no coy reserve, no indication that a woman's soul dwells there in all its young loveliness, with its host of hidden delights, waiting but the touch of some congenial spirit to awaken all its sensibilities and passions; but in their place an awkward and ungainly figure;—limbs badly moulded from imperfect nutrition—a bony frame-work, in many points widely divergent from the line of womanly beauty—a beauty founded upon utility—and a general aspect of coarseness and a vulgarity of expression quite opposed to all ideas of excellencies in the moral and physical attributes of the sex.

There is something in the female figure strongly indicative of its aptitude for the performance of certain functions peculiar to her sex. Child bearing is one of these, and the nourishment she is subsequently destined to afford her offspring another. The gait of women who labour under any material alteration in the axis of the thigh-bone is singular—a sort of waddle, an alternate sidelong progression . . . This gait may be detected in great numbers of factory girls and women, and is exceedingly ungraceful—ungraceful in itself, and still more so in its impression upon the mind, by the evidence it gives of certain alterations in form peculiarly unsexual.

Neither is the condition of those organs from which the child is to derive its first aliment less strikingly illustrative of their habits. Very early in life, from ten to fourteen years, the breasts are often found large and firm, and highly sensitive, whilst at a later period and a period indeed when they should shew the greatest activity and vital energy—when in fact they have children to support from them, they are soft, flaccid, pendulous, and very unirritable—both states giving the most decisive proofs of perversion in the usual functional adaptation of parts . . .

P. GASKELL, *The Manufacturing Population of England* (1833), pp. 162–164.

2

Not so ugly !

A writer on the factory question heads one of his sections, 'On the general ugliness of the manufacturing population'.—This is a mere question of taste; prejudice would not discern a particle of beauty in Venus herself . . . and it might therefore equally blind a spectator of the brides that present themselves at the collegiate church of Manchester. Factory labour does not indeed improve the form or the complexion, but it is less injurious to either than many of the ordinary employments of females,—far less so than the trade of the milliner, the embroiderer, and the straw-plaiter. Lancashire has its fair proportion of beautiful women, and the factories have not yet abated its ancient fame for the witchery of female charms.

W. COOKE TAYLOR, *Notes of a Tour in the Manufacturing Districts of Lancashire*, 1842; p. 261.

3

Belles of the Loom

So much nonsense has been uttered about the deformities and diseases of factory children, that I may hardly be credited by some of my readers, when I assert that I have never seen, among a like number of young women of the lower ranks in any country, so many pleasing countenances and handsome figures as I saw in Mr Ashton's nine power-weaving galleries [at Hyde]. Their light labour and erect posture in tending the looms, and the habit which many of them have of exercising their arms and shoulders, as if with dumb-bells, by resting their hands on the lay or shuttle-bearer, as it oscillates alternately backwards and forwards with the machinery, opens their chest, and gives them generally a graceful carriage.

Many of them have adopted tasteful modes of wearing neat handkerchiefs on their heads, and have altogether not a little of the Grecian style of beauty. One of them, whose cheeks had a fine rosy hue, being asked how long she had been at factory work, said nine years, and blushed from bashfulness at being so slightly spoken to.

DR ANDREW URE, *The Philosophy of Manufactures* (1835), pp. 350–351.

4

You Should See Her on Sunday!

Though the general appearance of the operative is squalid, and the majority of the middle-aged badly dressed, the young women and girls expend considerable sums upon their persons. They exhibit in the style of dress a very striking contrast with the inhabitants of the rural districts, a distinction always observable between town and country girls. A taste for showy clothing has been no doubt given by the extreme cheapness of printed calicoes and muslins, and indeed by the lowness of price in all manufactured articles of middling quality; and the factory girl, with her pale face and languid expression, offers, when decked out in her Sunday and holiday apparel, a strange anomaly with the dirty, unfurnished, and miserable home from which she issues.

The females employed in silk mills go a step still further as to dress than the cotton spinner or weaver. Many of these are really well and handsomely clad, and present an appearance of outward respectability, equal if not superior to that of hundreds in the middle walks of life.

P. GASKELL, op. cit., ch. 5.

In many cases the young women employed in factories do not make their own clothes at all; their working clothes they obtain at the slop-shops which abound in the manufacturing districts, where ready-made clothes are to be had; and their Sunday dress is, of course, of a very smart description, wherever they can afford it, and is manufactured by some notable milliner who knows how to set those matters off to the best advantage.

P.P. 1831–32, vol. XV, p. 423.

5

Miss Eighteen's Dress Bill

Jane L., aged 18, born in Manchester of Irish parents; began to be a silk-winder at nine years of age, and earned 4s a week at it. After twelve months learned weaving, and has been a power-loom weaver ever since. Has four looms, earns 13s a week, and pays her 'little helper' 3s a week besides, so her gross earnings are 16s. Gives her mother 7s a week and keeps the rest of her wages herself. She can cook a little; knows she could cut out and make a shirt, though she never tried. Could cut out and make up such a gown as she wears now. (It was of beautiful silk and well made.)

The gown she has on cost her £1 16s 6d, her bonnet cost £1 9s. She wears silk gloves; they cost her about 1s 6d per pair. Shoes cost her about 15s a year. Makes her own caps, such as she has got on; learnt to make them from one of the teachers at the school. She sells caps which she makes; they are of different prices; she sells one like that she has on at 6s, without the riband; the cheapest she makes are 4s 6d, the dearest 8s, both without the riband; can't make more than four or five in a year for sale; it would take two months' working very late at night to make an 8s one. She is a girl of high spirit for work.

Examinations by Mr Cowell; P.P. 1833, vol. XX, D 1, 34–35.

Windlass Girls and Coal Wheelers of Pembrokeshire.

Sectional View of Diagram No. 1, with Girls winding Coal from the Workings in the Dip.

11. Windlass Girls in the Pembrokeshire coal-field (P.P. 1842, vol. XVII)
(*photo:* British Museum)

12. Girl Coal-bearers in Scotland
(P.P. 1842, vol. XV)
(*photo:* British Museum)

6

Factory Dress—and Undress

How are the women and girls drest in the Factory when at work?
—They take off their Bedgown and Apron, and some their upper
Petticoats, and hang them up, and put on others.

Do they put them on again when they go out?—Yes. They are more
warmly clad when they go out than when at work.

JAMES KNOTT, manager in Holywell Cotton Twist Companies mills; P.P.
Lords, 1819, vol. XVI, p. 408.

* * *

When you come of a morning, do you all take off your clothes?—Yes,
sir.

Do the piecers see one another take off their clothes?—Yes, sir; as
fast as they come in they slip off their clothes, and the girls put on their
bishops [smocks].

What do you take off?—Hat and shawl, shoes and stockings.

What do the lads take off?—They take off their shoes and stockings,
hat, coat, and waistcoat; all works barefoot, boys and lasses.

Do the big lads see the big girls take off their stockings?—Yes, sir;
some big piecers is married women; they have to do the same.

Do the boys ever say anything naughty and pert?—Yes, sir; some
big boys is always doing it . . .

Do the girls care about it?—Some doesn't like it; some doesn't
mind it.

From the evidence taken by MR COWELL, Manchester; P.P. 1833, vol. XX,
pp. 76–77.

* * *

I have only one circumstance to mention connected with my visit to
Messrs J. & G. Mills' spinning-mill [near Nottingham], which happened to be on Saturday afternoon, just before the mill stopped . . .

I had learned from one of the girls that time was always given to them
to wash themselves before they left the mill; and soon afterwards, when
the engine had already stopped, as I chanced to return suddenly from

one room to another in search of a lad [Parker] whom I wished to examine, I found a group of girls and young women together, some of them naked to the waist, occupied in cleansing themselves. There was considerable confusion among them at the sight of me, and a huddling on of clothes; but although there appeared this sense of shame in the exposure to a stranger, none seemed to be felt with regard to the workpeople; for Parker, a lad of sixteen, came to me from among them, and obviously had not discomposed them any more than the presence of two other men who were with me at the other end of the room.

This incident may appear trifling to the Central Board, but I have thought it worth mentioning, as illustrative of a demoralizing habit, even arising, in this instance, out of a practice in other respects laudable.

MR DRINKWATER's report; Factory Commission, 1833; P.P., vol. XX, C I, 41.

7

Bradford's Mill Girls

The factory girl of Bradford . . . is cleanly, prone to smart dressing, and astonishes the stranger on Sundays or holidays by the respectability of her appearance. That licentiousness does not exist to any alarming extent among the female worsted operatives seems obvious from the small number of illegitimate children born in Bradford, compared with other districts . . . It must also be remarked that married female operatives in worsted factories have not been found to be less prolific than those engaged in agricultural labours.

To the often repeated allegations, that females employed in factories neglect their homes and families, that they are deficient in the practice of cookery, domestic economy, and needlework, it may be counterstated that such is also the condition of females engaged in agricultural labours, whose homes are, in like manner, left uncared for whilst working in the fields. Wherever the married woman has to pursue any avocation to earn her bread, so far will her domestic duties be neglected. The factory operative, however, is in cleanliness and domestic management vastly superior to the female labourers of Wilts, Devon, and Dorset.

JOHN JAMES, *History of the Worsted Manufacture in England* (1857), p. 556.

8

The London Milliner

Miss H. Baker, in business as a milliner in the West End; learnt the business in the country, and came to London as an 'improver' at the age of 16:

The young women who come as improvers are generally 16 or 17 years of age; they have in most cases served an apprenticeship previously either in London or the country. The apprenticeship is usually for two years; for this, if board and lodging are included, £30 or £40 are paid.

There are many young women employed after their apprenticeship as journeywomen, receiving from £15 to £50 a year and board and lodging. The journeywomen and the improvers are worked the longest; the apprentices, being beginners and not knowing the business so well, are sent to bed earlier.

In some of the establishments the hours of work are regulated; in others, not. The common hours are from 8 a.m. till 11 p.m. The breakfast is eaten as quick as possible at about half past 8, about 20 minutes are allowed for dinner, which is also taken as quickly as possible, the hour being half-past one. For tea, at 5, no time is allowed; it is taken as quick as the other meals. Supper is at 9 or 10.

In the houses which are regulated, by which is meant those which do not make a practice of working all night, it happens that if any particular order is to be executed they go on later than 11, often till 2 or 3 in the morning, and, if required, all night. In those houses which are not so well-regulated they often work all night; in the season they usually go on till one or two in the morning. In the summer it is common to commence at 5 in the morning.

In one establishment where the witness formerly worked, during three months successively, she had never more than 4 hours' rest, regularly going to bed between 12 and one, and getting up at 4 in the morning. On the occasion of the general mourning for His Majesty William IV witness worked without going to bed from 4 o'clock on Thursday morning till half-past 10 on Sunday morning; during this time witness did not sleep at all; of this she is certain. In order to keep awake she stood nearly the whole of Friday night, Saturday, and Saturday night, only sitting down for half an hour for rest. Two other young persons worked at the same house for the same time; these two dozed occasionally in a chair. Witness, who was then nineteen, was made very ill by this exertion, and when on Sunday she went to bed she could not sleep. Her feet and legs were much swelled, and her feet seemed to overhang the shoes . . .

The young persons are often so much fatigued that they lay in bed so late on Sunday so as not to be able to go to church . . .

If any become sick, they must either go on with their work, or leave the house. 'They often sit at work when they are so ill as to be scarcely able to stick to their needle.' Employers in general pay little or no attention to the health of the young people who work for them.

P.P. 1843, vol. XIV, pp. 204–205.

9

The Milliner's Apprentice

John Dalrymple, assistant surgeon, Royal London Ophthalmic Hospital, Moorfields:

A few years ago, a delicate and beautiful young woman, an orphan, applied at the hospital for very defective vision. Upon inquiry it was ascertained that she had been apprenticed to a milliner, and was in the last year of indentureship. Her working hours were 18 in the day, occasionally even more; her meals snatched with scarcely an interval of a few minutes from work, and her general health was evidently assuming a tendency to consumption.

An application was made, by my directions, to the mistress for relaxation; but the reply was, that in this last year of her apprenticeship her labours had become valuable, and that her mistress was entitled to them, as recompense for teaching.

Subsequently, a threat of appeal to the Lord Mayor, and a belief that a continuance of the occupation would soon render the apprentice incapable of labour, induced the mistress to cancel the indentures, and the victim was saved. It was not until many months afterwards that her health was re-established.

P.P. 1843, vol. XIV, p. 235.

10

The Girl at the Hanging

―――――――――

Girl. It [lace-running] is a very bad trade for the eyes. Where I sit I can't see the hands and figures on the clock-face a bit.
Second girl. Me! I can see the clock very well, but I can't tell what time it is. I can't see which is hands and which is figures. I went a long way to see a man hanged t'other day, and couldn't see him a bit after all. I heard folks talking; that was something. I got very near at last, A man asked me couldn't I see him now. I said I could, I was so ashamed, but I could not. None of us [five girls] can see much except the youngest; she has not been at it so long. We earn at this work 3s 6d a week the most of us; some only 3s. We take our lace to Mr Carter's, Rutland Street [Old Radford]. It's a trade that makes you subject to headache.
First girl. I like it better than the factory, though we can't get so much. We have our liberty at home, and get our meals comfortable, such as they are.

P.P. 1833, vol. XX, p. C 2, 18.

11

Independent Young Women

―――――――――

One of the greatest advantages resulting from the progress of manufacturing industry, and from severe manual labour being superseded by machinery, is its tendency to raise the condition of women. Education only is wanting to place the women of Lancashire higher in the social scale than in any other part of the world.

The great drawback to female happiness, among the middle and working classes is, their complete dependence and almost helplessness in securing the means of subsistence. The want of other employment than the needle cheapens their labour, in ordinary cases, until it is almost valueless. In Lancashire profitable employment for females is abundant. Domestic servants are in consequence so scarce, that they can only be obtained from the neighbouring counties.

A young woman, prudent and careful, and living with her parents, from the age of 16 to 25, may, in that time, by factory employment, save £100 as a wedding portion. I believe it to be the interest of the community that every young woman should have this in her power. She is not then driven into an early marriage by the necessity of seeking a home; and the consciousness of independence, in being able to earn her own living, is favourable to the development of her best moral energies.

HICKSON's report; Hand-loom Weavers' Report; P.P. 1840, vol. XXIV, p. 44.

(b) FACTORY WIVES

What sort of a wife did the 'Factory Girl' make? From all accounts, a very indifferent one. Even Parson Bull and Rowland Detrosier admit as much, although they have their apologies ready for the unfortunate girls who were expected to manage a home without having had the least instruction. Considerably less understanding is No. 3, in which a Birmingham button-burnisher tells the story of his own mother's married life; 'poor thing' he calls her, but it is his father who really arouses his sympathy. Equally masculine and even more selfish is the tribute of Mr A. B. to his first wife and to his second, who turned out to be much easier to live with (No. 4). The note of genuine human concern is struck again in Dr Hawkins's criticism of the young mother who has to go out to work (No. 5), and this is followed by an informative little piece on how they kept the baby quiet. Then in No. 7 we have a moving little real-life story of a Bolton husband and wife who had shared good times and bad, and although things seemed black at the moment were determined to see it through together. From this it is an easy transition to No. 7, in which we have one of the earliest accounts of that remarkably honest and courageous woman, Mrs Kitty Wilkinson (1786–1860) who is among the 'noble women' commemorated in stained glass in the Lady Chapel in Liverpool Cathedral. The 'rules' of the municipal wash-house that was established as a result of her enterprise, and of which she and her husband were appointed caretakers, are given in No. 9. No. 10 contains tributes to the housewives who so gallantly strove to keep their homes and children clean and decent in the midst of abominable surroundings, and No. 11 illustrates another of the hardships of working-class wives: the payment of part of their husbands' wages in the form of 'tommy', i.e. in goods obtainable at their employers' own stores. To the literary-minded this document has a special interest, as it suggested to Benjamin Disraeli (Lord Beaconsfield) the very similar incident described in his novel *Sybil* (1845). Then in No. 12 we have a sidelight on domestic arrangements in Birmingham, where the wife was not strictly a 'factory wife' but went out to work in one of the engineering workshops with which the city abounded. Once more it is the poor man who gets all the sympathy!

I

Parson Bull's Opinion

I would do an injustice to many young persons who are brought up in the factory system, if I did not say that their industry, neatness, and disposition to improve themselves, are beyond the power of my commendation ... But I would say that these are exceptions; I would say that the generality of them are as unfit as they possibly can be to fill the important station of a cottager's wife.

How should they, considering the length of labour to which they are subject, from their youth up, until the time of their marriage, be able to learn the duties of the cottage? I am acquainted with many that can scarcely mend a hole in their garments; I have heard it from their mothers and their relations, that they scarcely know how to darn a stocking; and I know a case in which the father of a child was so anxious that his little girl should acquire the use of the needle, that during a considerable period, when he was confined at home himself by a lameness, he sat with her, after her return from work, with a little light rod in his hand, and insisted upon her mending her stockings, although she was falling asleep continually, and when she nodded over it, he gave her a very gentle tap upon the head with the rod.

REV. G. S. BULL, in evidence; P.P. 1831–32, vol. XV, p. 423.

2

Apology for Factory Wives

One of the greatest evils to the working man is the ignorance of the women of his own class, who are generally incapable of becoming either good wives or good mothers . . . Brought up in the factory until they are married, and sometimes working there long after that event has taken place, even when they have become mothers, they are almost entirely ignorant of household duties, and are incapable of laying out the money their husbands have earned to the best advantage. They are equally incapable of preparing his victuals, in an economical and comfortable manner; and not unfrequently as much money is spent on a Sunday's dinner as in other and better hands would have procured a dinner for two or three days. A working man is fortunate, indeed, who happens to marry a young woman who has been brought up in service, and whose habits of cleanliness and knowledge of household duties secures him a comfortable home and economical management.

The practice of the working men in general is to entrust the laying out of their money to their wives, and hence a knowledge of household duties, combined with habits of industry, cleanliness and economy, is of first-rate importance amongst the females of this class of society to the working men. In thousands of instances the very contrary of these desirable virtues prevails, and the industrious working man lives in misery and debt from the conduct of an ignorant gin-drinking woman called his wife. Every apology, however, may be offered for some of these unfortunate creatures, for they have never had the opportunity of learning better . . .

ROWLAND DETROSIER, in evidence; Factories Commission, 1st Report, 1833; P.P. vol. XX, p. E 13.

3

My Mother, Poor Thing!

———

Mr Joseph Corbett, employed for more than 40 years past as a button burnisher at Messrs Turner's, Birmingham; often consulted by mechanics generally when they need advice; statement made and signed, December, 7, 1840:—

My mother worked in a manufactory from a very early age. She was clever and industrious; and, moreover, she had the reputation of being virtuous. She was regarded as an excellent match for a working man.

She was married early. She became the mother of eleven children. I am the eldest. To the best of her ability she performed the important duties of a wife and mother. She was lamentably deficient in domestic knowledge; in that most important of all human instruction, how to make the home and the fire-side to possess a charm for her husband and children, she had never received one single lesson.

She had children apace. As she recovered from her lying-in, so she went to work, the babe being brought to her at stated times to receive nourishment. As the family increased, so anything like comfort disappeared altogether.

Poor thing, the power to make home cheerful and comfortable was never given to her. She knew not the value of cherishing in my father's mind a love of domestic objects. My heart aches when I reflect upon her anxious and laborious situation.

Not one moment's happiness did I ever see under my father's roof. All this dismal state of things I can distinctly trace to the entire and perfect absence of all training and instruction to my mother. He became intemperate; *and his intemperance made her necessitous*. She made many efforts to abstain from shop-work; but her pecuniary necessities forced her back into the shop. The family was large, and every moment was required at home.

I have known her, after the close of a hard day's work, sit up nearly all night for several nights together washing and mending of clothes. My father could have no comfort here. These domestic obligations, which in a well-regulated house, (even in that of a working man, where there are prudence and good management), would be done so as not to annoy the husband; to my father, they were a source of annoyance, and he from an ignorant and mistaken notion sought comfort in an alehouse.

My mother's ignorance of household duties; my father's consequent irritability and intemperance; the frightful poverty; the constant quarrelling; the pernicious example to my brothers and sisters; the bad effect upon the future conduct of my brothers; one and all of us forced out to work, so young, that our feeble earnings would produce only 1s a week; cold and hunger, and the innumerable sufferings of my childhood, crowd upon my mind and overpower me . . .

P.P. 1842, vol. XIV, p. f 131.

4

My Two Wives

'Do those women who have been brought up at mills make useful wives ?'—Not many of them; not useful wives with regard to household work; they very generally go out to work after marriage to pay for washing and making of clothes, which many of them are unable to perform, which necessitates them to carry their infants out in the morning, winter and summer, to a nurse.

Fortunately for myself, my first wife was a pretty good one, considering I had her out of the mill, with regard to her abilities in household work; but unfortunately for me, she was often sick, and lame in one ankle from overstrain during her factory work; so that with her lameness and sickness together, we had very little pleasure the five years we were tied together. But with regard to my second wife, I have advantages which I had not with the first, her enjoying and her child much better health, and being more handy in household work, having been a servant in gentlemen's families.

Is she worth as much to you in a money point of view ?—Yes, I consider she has the advantage by being able to get me what she does get at home, and at the same time being able to make me comfortable. By being not in such an emaciated and sickly state she retains her temper better, which enables us to live a more peaceable life.

A. B., factory worker at Manchester, in evidence; P.P. 1833, vol. XX, pp. D 2, 8–9.

5

The Woman with Two Jobs

But let us suppose one of these young females about to assume the character of wife, mother, nurse, housekeeper,—which she too often undertakes prematurely and improvidently. She has had no time, no means, no opportunities of learning the common duties of domestic life; and even if she had acquired the knowledge, she has still no time to practise them. In addition to the twelve hours' labour is an additional absence from home in the going and returning. Here is the young mother absent from her child above twelve hours daily. And who has the charge of the infant in her absence? Usually some little girl or aged woman, who is hired for a trifle, and whose services are equivalent to the reward. Too often the dwelling of the factory family is no home; it sometimes is a cellar, which includes no cooking, no washing, no making, no mending, no decencies of life, no invitations to the fireside. I cannot help on these and on other grounds, especially for the better preservation of infant life, expressing my hope that a period may arrive when married women shall be rarely employed in a factory.

From DR HAWKINS's medical reports; P.P. 1833, vol. XXI, pp. D3, 3–5.

6

Keeping Baby Quiet

Mary Colton, 20-years-old lace-runner [embroiderer]. Has worked at lace-piece since she was six years old, for 14 or 15 hours a day on the average . . . could earn from 4s to 5s a week. Was confined of an illegitimate child in November, 1839. When the child was a week old she gave it half a teaspoonful of Godfrey's [a proprietary mixture of laudanum and treacle] twice a day. She could not afford to pay for the nursing of the child, and so gave it Godfrey's to keep it quiet, that she might not be interrupted at the lace piece; she gradually increased the quantity by a drop or two at a time until it reached a teaspoonful; when the infant was four months old it was so 'wankle' and thin that folks persuaded her to give it laudanum to bring it on, as it did other children . . . She now buys a halfpenny worth of laudanum and a halfpenny worth of Godfrey's mixed, which lasts her three days . . . If it had not been for having to sit so close to work she would never have given the child the Godfrey's. She has tried to break it off many times but cannot, for if she did, she would not have anything to eat . . .

P.P. 1843, vol. XIV, p. f 62.

* * *

Priscilla Hatton, aged 'ten years old'. Works at home at nursing; the child is one month old. Is considered a good nurse by her mother; the child is a good child, but it squeaks a little sometimes when her wants tittee; mother gives it a teaspoonful of Godfrey's cordial, about three times a day; sometimes she (witness) gives the child a teaspoonful of Godfrey's cordial when mother's out, and the child is noisy and restless . . .

P.P. 1843, vol. XV, p. q 77 (No. 385).

7

Married Love in Bolton

I visited several families of the distressed operatives in Bolton, accompanied by a gentleman well acquainted with the locality. The invariable account given in every place was 'no work', and, as a consequence, 'no food, no furniture, and no clothing'. We entered one house tenanted by a young couple whom I at first mistook for brother and sister; they were a husband and wife, about six years married, but fortunately without children. On a table of the coarsest wood, but perfectly clean, stood what we were assured was the only meal they had tasted for twenty-four hours, and the only one they had any reasonable prospect of tasting for twenty-four hours to come. It consisted of two small plates of meal porridge, a thin oaten cake, some tea so diluted that it had scarcely a tinge of colour, and a small portion of the coarsest sugar in the fragment of a broken bowl.

The husband had been a cotton-spinner, but the factory to which he belonged had been closed for several weeks; the wife had also been employed in the same establishment. When in good work the united earnings of both average about 30s weekly; but for several (I think they said thirteen) weeks they had not been able to earn so many pence. Their furniture had been sold piecemeal to supply pressing necessities, their clothes had been pawned, they had hoped for better times; but they felt their condition was 'worsening'. The man would have gone to a foreign land, but he could not leave his wife alone to die, and her constitution would not bear the rough travelling which falls to the lot of light pockets.

My friend asked whether, under the circumstances, he did not lament his early imprudent marriage. He paused, looked fondly at his wife, who reciprocated his gaze with a melancholy smile of enduring affection; tears gathered in his manly eye, and his lip quivered with strong emotion; he dashed the tear aside, mastered his emotions with one convulsive effort, which, however, shook his entire frame, and with calm firmness replied, 'Never! We have been happy and we have suffered together; she has been the same to me all through'.

W. COOKE TAYLOR, *Notes of a Tour in the Manufacturing Districts of Lancashire*, (1842), pp. 41–42.

8

The Woman with a Mangle

Among the many females in humble life who have been exemplary for their extraordinary perseverance under difficulties, their ingenious industry, and their self-sacrificing benevolence, a poor woman now living in an obscure situation in Liverpool is deserving of being placed in the foremost rank. This heroine in humble life—whom we shall describe under the name of Catherine or Kitty, by which she is usually known to her friends—was born in a populous village in Lancashire about the year 1786. Her parents . . . were in poor circumstances, and Catherine was sent with her brother to work at a cotton mill in a village at some distance. This was in 1798, when she was only twelve years of age. [The now accepted account says that she was Catherine Seaward, born in Londonderry, in Ireland, and was taken to Liverpool as a child. The cotton mill has been identified as Messrs Greg's, at Caton, near Lancaster] . . .

The mill was one of the better regulated class. The hours were not long, and were precisely fixed. All had their appointed duty, which, if they attended to, no complaint was made. There was an open airing-ground for recreation in good weather, and a library from which books were given freely out to those who chose to read. Great care was likewise taken to prevent any impropriety of behaviour. In short, nothing was wanting to render the attendance agreeable, or to encourage the diligent and orderly.

In this mill Catherine passed a few years, improving in health and intelligence . . . and her good feelings prompted her to be grateful for the care taken of her, as well as others, at the mill. She has often been hard to say, 'If ever there was a heaven on earth, it was that apprentice-house, where we were brought up in such ignorance of evil, and where Mr Norton, the manager of the mill, was a father to us all'.

Catherine left the cotton-mill to go to service in a family, (and then) was married to a person deserving her affection . . . A small house was taken, and furnished, and the marriage promised every prospect of happiness. But when she had become the mother of two children, her [first] husband died . . . The difficulty of obtaining work at this time was very great. The only employment of which Catherine could obtain an offer was work at a nail factory, for which she was not well fitted . . . The employment was hard, and poorly paid. She generally wrought at large nails, of which she was able to make about 800 daily; but of the same kind some men can make double that number. Her earnings were, on an average, fifteen pence per day . . . She has been known to work in this factory until her fingers were blistered, and she could do no more; she would then remain at home, and poultice them till they were sufficiently recovered to enable her to resume her work. She and her mother at that time often suffered from hunger . . .

After Catherine left the nail factory, she supported her family by mangling, a benevolent gentleman in the neighbourhood, who was struck with her character, having assisted her to purchase a mangle at a sale of effects. By means of it and a little charring work she lived for several years, till her mother died . . . and she removed with her only surviving son to Liverpool. She took her mangle with her . . .

At the first appearance of cholera in England [in 1832], great anxiety was manifested to guard against it, and cleanliness was especially enjoined. The habits of the very poor, and their few conveniences, made the washing and drying of clothing and bedding very difficult. Catherine's house at this time consisted of a small kitchen, a little parlour, two or three chambers, and a small yard at the back of the house. In the kitchen she had a copper. She fastened ropes across the yard, and offered her poor neighbours the free use of them and her kitchen for washing and drying their clothes. She also took charge of clothes and bedding which were lent for the use of the poor. So apparent was the benefit derived by the families who availed themselves of Catherine's kindness, that a benevolent society was led to provide a common cellar where families might wash every week. The establishment thus begun has been found so useful that it is still maintained . . .

Catherine still lives, and is a credit to her station. Her economy in regard to both food and clothing is admirable. Nothing is wasted. She has been known to stew fish-bones into broth for the sick poor, and from the refuse of fruit to make a pleasant drink for fever patients . . . The owner of the house in which Catherine lives is a single lady, and a cripple, with a very small income. Catherine expresses her unwillingness to apply to her poor landlady for necessary repairs, and as far as possible has made those repairs herself. She buys paint, and paints her rooms with her own hand. She receives payment from her lodgers on Friday, and the sum, although only a few shillings altogether, she lends to some poor women, who purchase certain goods which they sell in the market on Saturday, and make their returns to her on Saturday night. She has mixed but little with her neighbours, except for such offices of kindness as she could render to them; and most unwillingly asks for any aid for her own personal friends . . .

Chambers's Miscellany of Useful and Entertaining Tracts, Edinburgh, 1844; vol. 3, No. 26, pp. 1–10.

9

Liverpool's Public Wash-house: Rules

Each woman to pay 1d for a length of time not exceeding 6 hours, for the use of tubs, water, and having her clothes dried.

Each woman to have the choice of any tub vacant at the time of her coming; if there is not then room, to be served in the order of application. The matron to decide whose clothes shall go into the boiler together, and to see that each washer puts in a proper proportion of soap and soda, to direct who shall clean out the boiler on clothes being taken out, and to see that it is immediately filled again.

Each person to put her small things into the boiler enclosed in a bag.

Great care must be taken that the boiler be not left without water or it will burn.

The matron to superintend the placing of each person's clothes on the drying horses, and see that they be kept separate . . .

Many of the clothes are full of vermin, which boiling does not destroy; the clothes of the clean should therefore be boiled together, and those of the dirty together, in a second boiler when it is not wanted for infectious clothes. The woman must be very cautious, however, how she gives such reason, or she will give great offence.

From the Rules for the management of Liverpool's corporation baths: State of Large Towns, Appendix to 1st Report; P.P. 1844, vol. XVII, pp. 197–198.

10

The Housewives' Endless Battle

Amidst these scenes of wretchedness, the lot of the female sex is much the hardest. The man, if, as is usually the case, in employment, is taken away from the annoyances around his dwelling during the day, and is generally disposed to sleep soundly after his labours during the night; but the woman is obliged to remain constantly in the close court or neglected narrow alley where she lives, surrounded by all the evils adverted to; dirty children, domestic brawls, and drunken disputes meet her on every side and every hour. Under such circumstances, the appropriate employments of a tidy housewife in brushing, washing, or cleansing, seem vain and useless efforts, and she soon abandons them.

R. A. SLANEY, MP, reporting on the state of Birmingham, etc. State of Large Towns, 2nd Report; P.P. 1845, vol. XVIII, Appendix, p. 18.

*   *   *

In the perambulation of the lower districts inhabited by the poorer classes, it was often very affecting to see how resolutely they strove for decency and cleanliness amidst the adverse circumstances; to see the floors of their houses and the steps washed clean, made white with the hearth-stone, when the first persons coming into the house must spoil their labours, with the mud from the street, kept filthy by neglect of proper scavenging; to see their clothes washed and hung out to dry, but befouled by soot from the neighbouring furnaces; and to see their children attempted to be kept clean, but made dirty from like causes; and sometimes to see those children, notwithstanding all their care, pale, sickly, and drooping, evidently from the pestilential miasma of a natural stream converted into a sewer, and dammed up for the sake of mill power, in the hands of persons of great influence in the return of members to the town council, who are deaf to all statements of evidence of the evil, or of the possibility of amendment.

JAMES SMITH of Deanston, on Yorkshire manufacturing towns; P.P. 1845, vol. XVIII, p. 317.

II

'Cruel work' at the Tommy Shop

I never went to the shop but there were twelve or thirteen standing round the door in rain, snow, or whatever weather it may be; they do not allow you to come in. I have seen [it] when it was supposed near two hundred were there. When there has not been any flour for some days, the women will be fighting and tearing to get in.

About a month or six weeks ago, one Thursday, I went from home at 11 o'clock in the day; I was there certainly before 12, having only gone to my mother-in-law's on the way, and I was 8 o'clock at night before I got home, having only called to leave some tommy [goods obtained by this truck system] on the road and was not delayed five minutes. There was a great crowd to get flour, and when I got it I was forced to stay or else I should not have got anything for my children or my husband. He was hurt in the knee, and his field-pay, or most of it, was to be paid in goods; 15s was paid out of 20s. When at last I got into the shop my bonnet was off, and my apron was all torn, with the women all trying who should get in first.

There were two women carried off who had fainted, and I helped them to come to themselves, and that got me out of my turn and made me longer. And there was a little boy who wanted a loaf of bread for his mother; and having no dinner, he was quite smothered and I thought he was dead and the sweat poured off him. They carried him up to bed, but he went home afterwards.

Ah it's cruel work is the tommy shop. Banks's shop has got much worse of late, since young Mr Charles Banks came to the shop; he swears at the women when the women are trying to crush in, with children crying in their arms. He is a shocking little dog . . .

A pit-man's wife, at Bilston, South Staffs coalfield; P.P. 1843, vol. XIII, p. 93.

12

Dyspepsia in Brummagem

To the extreme ignorance of domestic management on the part of the wives of the mechanics is much of their misery and want of comfort to be traced. Numerous instances have occurred to us of the confirmed drunkard who attributes his habits of dissipation to a wretched home, and a respectable working-man is rarely met with whose house is not managed by a prudent and industrious wife. We believe, however, that much improvement in this respect is not to be looked for so long as the early years of the females are so generally spent in the workshops. ... It very frequently happens that when the working-man returns home to his dinner he finds it unprepared: his wife has been at her shop, and she leaves the cooking of her husband's dinner to a neighbour who forgets it, and the poor man is obliged to swallow hastily his half-cooked meal, and to return to his labour with his stomach loaded with indigestible materials. To this cause, we believe, is not unfrequently to be attributed much of the dyspepsia from which this class of persons suffer ...

From evidence collected in Birmingham by R. D. GRAINGER: P.P. 1843, vol. XIV, f 180.

(c) WOMEN IN COAL MINES

When the 18-year-old Victoria became Queen in 1837 there were several thousands of her sex (many of them even younger than she was) working in coal mines in Britain. There was nothing new in this; it had been going on for centuries, since the Middle Ages in fact, when coal mining was first undertaken in this country. But the mines in those days were only shallow pits or cuttings made in the hillside where there were outcrops of easily accessible coal, and the women worked in conjunction with their menfolk, usually in helping to transport the mineral to the carts or barges. With the development of mining technique, shafts were sunk to ever deeper levels, and in most pits horses and later the steam engine were employed to raise the coals to the surface. Not in all pits, however. In some places women were still preferred, either because they were cheaper or because the output of the mines was insufficient to make the introduction of machinery worth while. This was particularly the case in Scotland.

The deplorable condition of the Scottish women miners was first brought to public attention in 1793 by Lord Dundonald, and in 1808 Robert Bald, a civil engineer and mineral surveyor in practice at Alloa, published the results of his inquiry 'into the condition of those Women who carry coals under ground in Scotland, known by the name of Bearers'. As will be seen from the passages reprinted here (No. 1) from Bald's book, he had no hesitation in denouncing this form of female labour as slavery. The historical background to the practice is shortly reviewed in the letter to the Duchess of Hamilton from her agent (No. 2).

But the condition of the females employed in English and Welsh mines was almost as bad. The employment of women and girls underground in pits in the Tyne and Wear district of England had ceased about 1780, but there were parts of the country where it continued to be general long after that date. One of these was Cumberland, where Richard Ayton was so shocked to encounter 'beastly girls' in the 'dismal shades' when he summoned up sufficient nerve to descend some 600 feet into one of Lord Lonsdale's pits (No. 3). Mr Tufnell made an examination of the Lancashire collieries for the Factory Commission of 1833 (see *Child Labour* (*d*) No. 9), and his report came in useful to Lord Ashley when in 1840 he moved for the setting up of a commission of inquiry into the condition of children and young persons employed in mines. The inclusion of women in the survey was an afterthought, dating from the next year. According to the Census taken in 1841 there were then employed in British coal mines, in underground labour, 1,185 females over the age of twenty and 1,165 girls under that age, while another 3,650 women and girls were employed in pit workings above ground. Of this total of 6,000, there were 2,240 employed in collieries in Scotland, where most of the pits had a hundred, or a hundred and fifty, women and girls on their strength.

The report of the Children's Employment Commission that was published in 1842 presented a horrifying picture. 'Female children of tender age and young and adult women' were stated to be employed regularly underground just as men and boys were in some of the coal pits in Lancashire and Yorkshire, and also in South Wales, while in Scotland this was the common practice. The Commissioners did not mince their words. Thus Mr Symons declared that the state of female employment in the West Riding collieries was such that 'no brothel could beat it' (No. 4), and Mr Scriven described women and girls presenting an appearance that was 'indescribably disgusting' (No. 5).

The Report made a tremendous impact on public opinion, and a good deal of this was attributable to the pictures. Sex and sadism, debauchery, violence and cruelty, and the foulest obscenities—all were there in full measure, in those hundreds of closely printed pages, sufficient to make the Victorian middle-class male burst his waistcoat buttons in righteous indignation. No one who reads the passages given here will wonder why the revelations should have caused such a stir.

Lord Ashley seized the opportunity when public interest and indignation were at their height. On June 7, 1842, when the Report was only a month old, he introduced into the House of

Commons a Bill that not only gave some protection to boys employed in coal mines but prohibited the employment of women and girls. His speeches convinced the House, but in the Lords it was a very different matter. Here Lord Londonderry put up a strong defence of female labour; there were some pits, he averred, where the coal could be got only by female workers. Many of the coal-owning peers, however, were not greatly concerned, since in most pits in England no women were employed, and even in the remainder, the women and girls were employed not by the masters but by their menfolk. Londonderry was unable to secure the Bill's rejection, but he did manage to get retained the employment of females in coal mines above ground. The Bill became law as the Coal Mines Regulation Act 1842.

Although so well intentioned and necessary, the Act was not altogether happy in its results. When the Negro slaves were emancipated in 1833, the Government had compensated their owners to the extent of twenty millions sterling, but there was no such consideration for the women who were so suddenly thrown out of the employment in which they had been engaged, many of them, all their working lives, and which was the only one they knew or were fitted for. In Scotland their fate was particularly harsh, since there they were refused parish assistance (No. 21). Lord Ashley forwarded a cheque for £100 which a benevolent lady had given him, and made a contribution from his own slender means, but some at least of the women most affected were not at all grateful (No. 23). In Scotland and in Wales some of the displaced women workers even managed to slip back into the mines, and it was several years before the Inspectors could claim that there were no more females working underground.

I

Scotland's Women Slaves

We consider it proper to bring into view the condition of a class in the community, intimately connected with the coal-trade, who endure a slavery scarcely tolerated in the ages of darkness and barbarism. The class alluded to is that of the women who carry coals underground, in Scotland—known by the name of Bearers.

At present, there are four modes practised in Scotland, for transporting of coals from the wall-face to the hill. The first, most approved of, is to draw the basket of coals from the wall-face to the pit bottom by means of horses, from whence it is drawn to the hill by machinery. The next method resorted to is to draw the coals in small wheel-carriages, by men, women, or boys hired for the purpose, or by the collier himself, as practised in the west country. In the third mode, the coals are carried by women, known by the name of Bearers, who transport them from the wall-face to the pit-bottom, from whence they are drawn by machinery to the hill. The fourth and last mode is the most severe and slavish; for the women are not only employed to carry the coals from the wall-face to the pit bottom, but also to ascend with them to the hill. This latter mode is unknown in England, and is abolished in the neighbourhood of Glasgow.

Severe and laborious as this employment is, still there are young women to be found who, from early habits, have no particular aversion to the work, and who are as cheerful and light in heart as the gayest of the fair sex; and as they have it in their power to betake themselves to other work if they choose, the carrying of coals is a matter of free choice; and therefore no blame can be particularly attached to the coalmaster. Yet, still it must, even in the most favourable point of view, be looked upon as a very bad, old, and disgraceful custom. But, as married women are also as much engaged in this servitude as the young, it is in this instance that the practice is absolutely injurious and bad, even although they submit to it without repining . . .

In those collieries where this mode is in practice, the collier leaves his house for the pit about eleven o'clock at night, (attended by his sons, if he has any sufficiently old), when the rest of mankind are retiring to rest. Their first work is to prepare coals, by hewing them down from the wall. In about three hours after, his wife (attended by her daughters, if she has any sufficiently grown) sets out for the pit, having previously wrapped her infant child in a blanket, and left it to the care of an old woman, who, for a small gratuity, keeps three or four children at a time, and who, in their mothers' absence, feeds them with ale or whisky mixed with water. The children who are a little more advanced, are left to the care of a neighbour; and under such treatment, it is surprising that they ever grow up or thrive.

The mother, having thus disposed of her younger children, descends the pit with her older daughters, when each, having a basket of a suitable form, lays it down, and into it the large coals are rolled; and such is the weight carried, that it frequently takes two men to lift the burden upon their backs: the girls are loaded according to their strength. The mother sets out first, carrying a lighted candle in her teeth; the girls follow, and in this manner they proceed to the pit bottom, and with weary steps and slow, ascend the stairs, halting occasionally to draw breath, till they arrive at the hill or pit-top, where the coals are laid down for sale; and in this manner they go for eight or ten hours almost without resting. It is no uncommon thing to see them, when ascending the pit, weeping most bitterly, from the excessive severity of the labour; but the instant they have laid down their burden on the hill, they resume their cheerfulness, and return down the pit singing.

The execution of work performed by a stout woman in that way is beyond conception. For instance, we have seen a woman, during the space of time above mentioned, take on a load of at least 170 pounds avoirdupois, travel with this 150 yards up the slope of the coal below ground, ascend a pit by stairs 117 feet, and travel upon the hill 20 yards more to where the coals are laid down. All this she will perform no less than twenty-four times as a day's work . . . The weight of coals thus brought to the pit top by a woman in a day amounts to 4,080 pounds, or above 36 hundredweight English, and there have been frequent instances of two tons being carried. The wages paid for this work, are eightpence per day!—a circumstance as surprising almost as the work performed . . .

From this view of the work performed by bearers in Scotland, some faint idea may be formed of the slavery and severity of the toil, particularly when it is considered that they are entered to this work when seven years of age, and frequently continue till they are upwards of fifty, or even sixty years old.

The collier, with his wife and children, having performed their daily task, return home, where no comfort awaits them; their clothes are frequently soaked with water and covered with mud; their shoes so very bad as scarcely to deserve the name. In this situation they are exposed to all the rigours of winter, the cold frequently freezing their clothes.

On getting home, all is cheerless and devoid of comfort; the fire is generally out, the culinary utensils dirty and unprepared, and the mother naturally seeks first after her infant child, which she nurses even before her pit clothes are thrown off . . .

How different is the state of matters, where horses are substituted for women, and when the wife of the collier remains at home. The husband, when he returns home from his hard labour with his sons, finds a comfortable house, a blazing fire, and his breakfast ready in an instant, which cheer his heart, and make him forget all the severities of toil; while his wife, by her industry, enables him to procure good clothes and furniture, which constitute the chief riches of this class of the community. A chest of mahogany drawers, and an eight-day clock, with a mahogany case, are the great objects of their ambition; and when the latter is brought home, all their relations and neighbours are invited upon the occasion, when a feast is given, and the whole night spent in jovial mirth . . .

In surveying the workings of an extensive colliery below ground, a married woman came forward, groaning under an excessive weight of coals, trembling in every nerve, and almost unable to keep her knees from sinking under her. On coming up, she said in a most plaintive and melancholy voice, 'O Sir, this is sore, sore work. I wish to God the first woman who tried to bear coals had broken her back, and none would have tried it again'.

ROBERT BALD, civil engineer and mineral surveyor of Alloa, in *Inquiry into the Condition of Women who carry Coals under Ground in Scotland, known by the name of Bearers* (Edinburgh, 1812).

2

'Better than she is bonny'

Coal was wrought on the Duke of Hamilton's estate of Corrinden, Bo'ness, by the then proprietor, William de Vereponte, before the end of the twelfth century . . . From the end of that century, down to the year 1799, during a period of 700 years, colliers merely by entering upon work in a colliery were bound to perpetual service thereof; and if the owner sold or alienated the ground upon which the work stood, the right of the service of the colliers passed over to the purchaser. By an Act of Parliament passed on the 13th June 1799, the collier population were freed from this servitude.

During the whole of this long time the female sex of the collier population were serfs or slaves like their husbands, fathers, or brothers, and wrought with them in the mines, and were liable to be seized and brought back to servitude if they attempted to escape, and subjected to a fine of £100 Scots each.

While the males were employed digging in the pits with pickaxes and shovels, the women were engaged in carrying the coal on their backs from the extremity of the mines, to the pit bottoms or mouths of the mines, or in dragging that mineral there by means of hutches or hurleys along the underground roads. Muscular strength in a female, not beauty, was the grand qualification by which she was estimated, and a strong young woman was sure of finding a husband readily. There is an old Scotch saying, 'She is like the collier's daughter, better than she is bonny', proving the value put upon this description of female excellence.

From a letter dated January 2, 1851, addressed to the Duchess of Hamilton by the principal agent of the Hamilton Estates on the subject of the education of females in the mining districts of Lanarkshire; quoted in P.P. 1851, vol. XXIII, p. 3.

3

'Beastly girls' in the 'Dismal shades'

Having seen all the operations connected with the coals above-ground, I was determined before I left Whitehaven to descend down one of the pits and see the wonders below. A gentleman of the place, who had himself frequently made the experiment, kindly consented to bear me company. The William Pitt mine was the scene of my adventure, the last opened and said to be the best planned work of the kind, and the most complete in all its conveniences of any in the kingdom.

Preparatory to our descent, our guide, one of the stewards, cried out 'Coming down', to the people below . . . The voice was answered from the depths below by a strange, hollow, distant, but loud cry, which thrilled through my marrow . . . We fixed ourselves in the basket, standing, with our hands grasping the chain; the word was given, and down we glided with a smooth and scarcely perceptible motion through a duct about 6 feet in diameter and wooded all round . . . At length the basket stopped, and we found ourselves on our feet at the bottom, 630 feet from the light.

I could here distinguish nothing but a single candle, with the obscure form of a man by it—all around was pitch dark . . . While we were conversing here on the possible accidents that might occur, we were told of a poor woman who lately had an extraordinary escape. It was her business to attach the chain to the basket, and while she was in the act of doing this, her hand somehow became entangled, and the man at the engine setting it in motion before the proper time, she was pulled from the ground before she could extricate herself, and dragged up, as she hung by one arm, to the top of the pit, with no injury but a slight laceration of her hand.

From the foot of the shaft we proceeded through a very long passage cut through the rock, with the roof arched, and like the sides faced with bricks and whitewashed . . . As far as I could ascertain as I groped my way through the darkness, the mine appeared, in the meeting and crossing of its numerous passages, to resemble the streets of a city—and of a city of no mean extent . . . A dreariness pervaded the place which struck upon my heart—one felt as of beyond the bounds allotted to man or any living being, and transported to some hideous region unblest by every charm that cheers and adorns the habitable world. We traced our way through passage after passage in the blackest darkness, sometimes rendered more awful by a death-like silence, which was now and then broken by the banging of some distant door, or the explosion of gunpowder . . .

Occasionally a light appeared in the distance before us, which advanced like a meteor through the gloom, accompanied by a loud rumbling noise, the cause of which was not explained to the eye till we were called upon to make way for a horse, which passed by with its long line of baskets, and driven by a young girl, covered with filth, debased and profligate, and uttering some low obscenity as she hurried by. We were frequently interrupted in our march by the horses proceeding in this manner with their cargoes to the shaft, and always driven by girls, all of the same description, ragged and beastly in their appearance, and with a shameless indecency in their behaviour, which, awe-struck as one was by the gloom and loneliness around one, had something quite frightful in it, and gave the place the character of a hell.

All the people whom we met with were distinguished by an extraordinary wretchedness; immoderate labour and a noxious atmosphere had marked their countenance with the signs of disease and decay; they were mostly half naked, blackened all over with dirt, and altogether so miserably disfigured and abused, that they looked like a race fallen from the common rank of men, and doomed, as in a kind of purgatory, to wear away their lives in these dismal shades . . .

After rambling about for nearly an hour through the mazes of the mine, occasionally meeting a passenger, or visiting a labourer in his solitary cell, we were conducted to a spacious apartment, where our ears were saluted with the sound of many voices mingling together in noisy merriment. This was a place of rendezvous whither the baskets of coals were brought from the workings and fixed on the trams, and a party of men and girls had met together here, who were joining in a general expression of mirth, that was strangely contrasted with the apparent misery of their condition, and the dreariness of the spot where they were assembled.

There was an unusual quantity of light in this chamber which showed its black roof and walls, and shone upon the haggard faces and ruffian-like figures of the people, who were roaring with laughter at a conversation which outraged all decency, and resembled, as it appeared to my imagination, a band of devils. Some coarse jokes levelled at myself and my companion, which we did not think it prudent either to parry or return, drove us from this boisterous assembly, and we were soon again in the silent and lonely depths of the mine . . .

RICHARD AYTON, *A Voyage round Great Britain undertaken in the Summer of 1813* (1814), vol. 2, pp. 155–160.

4

'No brothel can beat it'

In England, exclusive of Wales, it is only in some of the colliery districts of Yorkshire and Lancashire that female Children of tender age and young and adult women are allowed to descend into the coal mines and regularly to perform the same kinds of underground work, and to work for the same number of hours, as boys and men; but in the East of Scotland their employment in the pits is general; and in South Wales it is not uncommon.

West Riding of Yorkshire: Southern Part.—In many of the collieries in this district, as far as relates to the underground employment, there is no distinction of sex, but the labour is distributed indifferently among both sexes, except that it is comparatively rare for the women to hew or get the coals, although there are numerous instances in which they regularly perform even this work. In great numbers of the coal-pits in this district the men work in a state of perfect nakedness, and are in this state assisted in their labour by females of all ages, from girls of six years old to women of twenty-one, these females being themselves quite naked down to the waist.

'Girls', says the Sub-Commissioner [J. C. Symons], 'regularly perform all the various offices of trapping, hurrying [Yorkshire term for drawing the loaded corves], filling, riddling, tipping, and occasionally getting, just as they are performed by boys. One of the most disgusting sights I have ever seen was that of young females, dressed like boys in trousers, crawling on all fours, with belts round their waists and chains passing between their legs, at day pits at Hunshelf Bank, and in many small pits near Holmfirth and New Mills: it exists also in several other places. I visited the Hunshelf Colliery on the 18th of January: it is a day pit; that is, there is no shaft or descent; the gate or entrance is at the side of a bank, and nearly horizontal. The gate was not more than a yard high, and in some places not above 2 feet.

'When I arrived at the board or workings of the pit I found at one of the side-boards down a narrow passage a girl of fourteen years of age in boy's clothes, picking down the coal with the regular pick used by the men. She was half sitting half lying at her work, and said she found it tired her very much, and 'of course she didn't like it'. The place where she was at work was not 2 feet high. Further on were men lying on their sides and getting. No less than six girls out of eighteen men and children are employed in this pit.

'Whilst I was in the pit the Rev Mr Bruce, of Wadsley, and the Rev Mr Nelson, of Rotherham, who accompanied me, and remained outside, saw another girl of ten years of age, also dressed in boy's clothes, who was employed in hurrying, and these gentlemen saw her at work. She was a nice-looking little child, but of course as black as a tinker, and with a little necklace round her throat.

'In two other pits in the Huddersfield Union I have seen the same sight. In one near New Mills, the chain, passing high up between the legs of two of these girls, had worn large holes in their trousers; and any sight more disgustingly indecent or revolting can scarcely be imagined than these girls at work—no brothel can beat it.

'On descending Messrs Hopwood's pit at Barnsley, I found assembled round a fire a group of men, boys, and girls, some of whom were of the age of puberty; the girls as well as the boys stark naked down to the waist, their hair bound up with a tight cap, and trousers supported by their hips. (At Silkstone and at Flockton they work in their shifts and trousers.) Their sex was recognizable only by their breasts, and some little difficulty occasionally arose in pointing out to me which were girls and which were boys, and which caused a good deal of laughing and joking. In the Flockton and Thornhill pits the system is even more indecent; for though the girls are clothed, at least three-fourths of the men for whom they "hurry" work *stark naked*, or with a flannel waistcoat only, and in this state they assist one another to fill the corves 18 or 20 times a day: I have seen this done myself frequently.

'When it is remembered that these girls hurry chiefly for men who are *not* their parents; that they go from 15 to 20 times a day into a dark chamber (the bank face), which is often 50 yards apart from any one, to a man working naked, or next to naked, it is not to be supposed but that where opportunity thus prevails sexual vices are of common occurrence. Add to this the free intercourse, and the rendez-vous at the shaft or bullstake, where the corves are brought, and consider the language to which the young ear is habituated, the absence of religious instruction, and the early age at which contamination begins, and you will have before you, in the coal-pits where females are employed, the picture of a nursery for juvenile vice which you will go far and wide above ground to equal.'

P.P. 1842, vol. XVI, pp. 24, 196.

5

Indescribably Disgusting

The estimation of the sex has ever been held a test of the civilization of a people. Shall it then be said, that in the very heart of our own country—from which missions are daily sent to teach God's law, and millions upon millions have been generously poured forth for the manumission of hosts in a distant land—that there shall exist a state of society in which hundreds of young girls are sacrificed to such shameless indecencies, filthy abominations, and cruel slavery as is found to exist in our coal pits? Chained, belted, harnessed, like dogs in a gocart—black, saturated with wet, and more than half naked—crawling upon their hands and feet, and dragging their heavy loads behind them—they present an appearance indescribably disgusting and unnatural.

S. S. SCRIVEN's report; P.P. 1842, vol. XVII, p. 75.

6

Betty Harris's Belt and Chain

Betty Harris, age 37: I was married at 23, and went into a colliery when I was married. I used to weave when about 12 years old; can neither read nor write. I work for Andrew Knowles, of Little Bolton (Lancs), and make sometimes 7s a week, sometimes not so much. I am a drawer, and work from 6 in the morning to 6 at night. Stop about an hour at noon to eat my dinner; have bread and butter for dinner; I get no drink. I have two children, but they are too young to work. I worked at drawing when I was in the family way. I know a woman who has gone home and washed herself, taken to her bed, been delivered of a child, and gone to work again under the week.

I have a belt round my waist, and a chain passing between my legs, and I go on my hands and feet. The road is very steep, and we have to hold by a rope; and when there is no rope, by anything we can catch hold of. There are six women and about six boys and girls in the pit I work in; it is very hard work for a woman. The pit is very wet where I work, and the water comes over our clog-tops always, and I have seen it up to my thighs; it rains in at the roof terribly. My clothes are wet through almost all day long. I never was ill in my life, but when I was lying in.

My cousin looks after my children in the day time. I am very tired when I get home at night; I fall asleep sometimes before I get washed.

13. The Girl Miner (P.P. 1842, vol. XVII)
(*photo:* British Museum)

14. Snow's Rents, Westminster, from the Report on the State of the Large
Towns (P.P. 1844, vol. XVII)
(*photo:* British Museum)

I am not so strong as I was, and cannot stand my work so well as I used to. I have drawn till I have had the skin off me; the belt and chain is worse when we are in the family way. My feller (husband) has beaten me many a time for not being ready. I were not used to it at first, and he had little patience.

I have known many a man beat his drawer. I have known men take liberties with the drawers, and some of the women have bastards.

P.P. 1842, vol. XV, p. 84.

7

'Tell the Queen Victoria'

Isabel Hogg, 53 years old, coal-bearer. Been married 37 years; it was the practice to marry early, when the coals were all carried on women's back, men needed us; from the great sore labour false births are frequent and very dangerous. I have four daughters married, and all work below till they bear their bairns—one is very badly now from working while pregnant, which brought on a miscarriage from which she is not expected to recover.

Collier-people suffer much more than others—my guid man died nine years since with bad breath; he lingered some years, and was entirely off work eleven years before he died.

You must just tell the Queen Victoria that we are guid loyal subjects; women people here don't mind work, but they object to horse-work; and that she would have the blessings of all the Scotch coal-women if she would get them out of the pits, and send them to other labour.

(*Note* by the Sub-Commissioner: Mrs Hogg is one of the most respectable coal-wives in Penston; her rooms are well furnished, and the house the cleanest I have seen in East Lothian.)

R. H. FRANKS' report; P.P. 1842, vol. XVI, p. 460.

8

'Brought it up in my skirt'

Betty Wardle, housewife, Outwood, near Lever, was asked: Have you ever worked in a coal-pit?—Ay, I have worked in a pit since I was six years old.

Have you any children?—Yes. I have had four children; two of them were born while I worked in the pits.

Did you work in the pits while you were in the family way?—Ay, to be sure. I had a child born in the pits, and I brought it up the pit-shaft in my skirt.

Are you sure that you are telling the truth?—Ay, that I am; it was born the day after I were married, that makes me to know.

Did you wear belt and chain?—Yes, sure I did.

P.P. 1842, vol. XVII, p. 163.

* * *

Isabel Wilson, 38-years-old coal-putter, Elphingstone colliery, East Lothian: When women have children thick (fast) they are compelled to take them down early. I have been married 19 years and have had ten bairns; seven are in life. When on Sir John's work [I] was a carrier of coals, which caused me to miscarry five times from the strains, and was gai ill after each. Pushing is so oppressive; last child was born on Saturday morning, and I was at work on the Friday night.

Note by Mr Franks: Nine sleep in two bedsteads; there did not appear to be any beds, and the whole of the other furniture consisted of 2 chairs, 3 stools, a table, a kail-pot and a few broken basins and cups. Upon asking if the furniture was all they had, the guid wife said, furniture was of no use, as it was so troublesome to flit with.

P.P. 1842, vol. XVI, p. 461.

9

Why Women Were Preferred

When asked, Do you prefer women to boys as drawers, Peter Gaskell, a collier at Mr Lancaster's, near Worsley, Lancs, replied: Yes, they are better to manage, and keep the time better; they will fight and shriek and do every thing but let anybody pass them, and they never get to be coal-getters, that is another good thing.

P.P. 1842, vol. XVII, p. 217.

*   *   *

One reason why women are used so frequently as drawers in the coal-pits is, that a girl of twenty will work for 2s a day or less, and a man of that age would want 3s 6d; it makes little difference to the coal-master, he pays the same whoever does the work. The only difference is that the collier can spend 1s or 1s 6d more at the ale-house, and very often the woman helps him to spend it. Not one woman in a hundred ever becomes a coal-getter, and that is one of the reasons why the men prefer them.

MR MILLER, undertaker at Mr Woodley's collieries, near Stalybridge; P.P. 1842, vol. XV, p. 27.

*   *   *

The employment of women induces early marriages. Where women carry coal on their backs they are more frequently chosen for their strength than for any aptitude for domestic duties; they in fact are chosen as good bearers, and are often bad wives. The very nature of the employment is degrading, as females are wrought only where no man can be induced to draw or work—in one word, they are mere beasts of burden.

MR JAMES WRIGHT, manager of the Duke of Buccleugh's collieries at Dalkeith; P.P. 1842, vol. XVI, p. 442.

*   *   *

'Men only marry us early because we are of advantage to them', said Janet Selkirk; and the truth of her statement was borne out by an old collier who said he had been 'obliged to get a woman early', to avoid paying away all his profits.

P.P. 1842, vol. XVI, p. 475.

259

10

The Trials of Patience

Patience Kershaw, age 17, Halifax: I go to pit at 5 o'clock in the morning and come out at 5 in the evening; I get my breakfast, porridge and milk, first; I take my dinner with me, a cake, and eat it as I go; I do not stop or rest at any time for the purpose, I get nothing else until I get home, and then have potatoes and meat, not every day meat.

I hurry in the clothes I have now got on—trousers and a ragged jacket; the bald place upon my head is made by thrusting the corves; I hurry the corves a mile and more under ground and back; they weigh 3 cwt. I hurry eleven a day. I wear a belt and chain at the workings to get the corves out. The getters that I work for are naked except their caps; they pull off all their clothes; I see them at work when I go up.

Sometimes they beat me if I am not quick enough, with their hands; they strike me upon my back. The boys take liberties with me sometimes; they pull me about. I am the only girl in the pit; there are about 20 boys and 15 men; all the men are naked. I would rather work in mill than in coal-pit.

Note by Sub-Commissioner Scriven: This girl is an ignorant, filthy, ragged, and deplorable looking object, and such a one as the uncivilized natives of the prairies would be shocked to look upon.

P.P. 1842, vol. XVII, p. 108

11

A Good Pair of Trousers

Mary Glover, age 38, employed in the collieries of Messrs Foster, Ringleybridge, Lancs.:

I went into a coal-pit when I was seven years old, and began by being a drawer. I have five children alive now, and I have buried two.

I never worked much in the pit when I was in the family way, but since I gave up having children I have begun again a bit. My husband is a collier. I go at half-past five in the morning, and I come out between 4 and 5 in the afternoon, and sometimes later. I wear a shift and a pair of trousers when at work, and I will always have a good pair of trousers. I have had many a twopence given me by the boatmen on the canal to show my breeches, I never saw women work naked, but I have seen men work without breeches in the neighbourhood of Bolton. I remember seeing a man who worked stark naked, and we could not go near him; we used to throw coals at him. He was killed afterwards; some coals fell on him.

Have you ever seen the men take liberties with the women?—Ay, mony a time.

Are any of your children in the pits?—No, they are too young at present; but I don't think I shall let my children into the pits—that is the girls; the boys may go there if they have a mind, but I don't think it is proper for a woman . . .

Who takes care of your children whilst you are in the pits?—A wench of mine takes care of the children; she has been struck with a palsy, and cannot do any great deal of work. I have a father and mother that live with us, but they are old people.

Note by Mr J. L. Kennedy, the Sub-Commissioner: I saw the house of this family myself. The old people, her father and mother, was 84 and 80 years of age respectively. The husband of this woman, when in work, will earn 25s to 30s per week, and his wife about 14s or 15s, yet the house was wretched in the extreme, and the children were covered with lice . . .

P.P. 1842, vol. XVII, p. 214.

12

Women's Underground Dress

Whilst at work, the women wear a pair of drawers which come down nearly to the knees, and some women a small handkerchief about their necks; but I have seen many a one with her breasts hanging out.

The girls are not a bit ashamed amongst their own pit set; it is the same as if they were one family.

JOHN MILLINGTON, superintendent of colliers at Mr Ashton's pits, Hyde; P.P. 1842, vol. XV, p. 203.

*   *   *

I do not like working in pit, but I am obliged to get a living. I work always without stockings, or shoes, or trousers; I wear nothing but my chemise. I have to go up to the headings with the men; they are all naked there. I am got well used to that, and don't care much about it; I was afraid at first, and did not like it; they never behave rudely to me.

MARY BARRETT, aged 14; Halifax; P.P. 1642, vol. XVII, p. 122.

*   *   *

In the West Riding of Yorkshire district, girls are almost universally employed as trappers and hurriers with boys. The girls employed as hurriers are of all ages, from 7 to 21; they commonly work quite naked down to the waist; the boys who work with them are also naked to the waist; and both (for the garment is pretty much the same in both) are dressed, as far as they are dressed at all, in a loose pair of trousers, seldom whole in either sex. In many of the collieries, the adult colliers, whom these girls serve, work perfectly naked.

P.P. 1842, vol. XV, p. 72.

13

Mary Holme's Breeches

———————

I have been eight years working in pits. I have always hurried. I have never thrust much. I always hurry as you saw me, with a belt round my waist and the chain through my legs. I always wear boys' clothes. The trousers don't get torn at all. It tires me middling; my back doesn't ache at all, nor my legs. I like being in pit, and don't want to do naught else . . . I have a shilling for hurrying two dozen—that is 16 corves. This is my regular stint. I don't know how long I shall stop in the pit. I have two sisters married, and one is at service; they all hurried before.

I am sure I would rather be in the pit, where I am thrashed sometimes, and work in the wet, than do anything else.

MARY HOLMES, age 14½.

*   *   *

I went into a pit to help before I was five years old. I used to thrust; I didn't do it long. I hurry now with a belt and chain in the board-gates. There are no rails there. We have to hurry full corves this way, up hill as well as down. I do this myself, and I have 26 runs a day, for which I have 1s. There are girls that hurry in the same way, with belt and chain. Our breeches are often torn between the legs with the chain. The girls' breeches are torn as often as ours; they are torn many a time, and when they are going along we can see them all between the legs naked; I have often; and that girl, Mary Holmes, was so today; she denies it, but it is true for all that.

EBENEZER HEALEY, age 13; P.P. 1842, vol. XVI, p. 295.

14

Elizabeth's Day

Elizabeth Day, aged 17, working in Messrs Hopwood's pit at Barnsley: I have been nearly nine years in the pit. I trapped for two years when I first went, and have hurried ever since. I have to riddle and fill, and sometimes I have to fill by myself. I have hurried by myself going fast on three years. I have to hurry up hill with the loaded corves, quite as much up as down, but not many have to hurry up hill with the loaded corve. When I riddle I hold the riddle, and have to shake the slack out of it, and then I throw the rest into the corf.

We always hurry in trousers as you saw us today when you were in the pit. Generally I work naked down to the waist like the rest. I had my shift on today when I saw you, because I had had to wait and was cold; but generally the girls hurry naked down to the waist. It is very hard work for us all. It is harder work than we ought to do a deal. I have been lamed in my ancle, and strained my back; it caused a great lump to rise on my ancle-bone once.

The men behave well to us, and never insult or ill-use us, I am sure of that. We have to work between 5 and 6, but we begin to hurry when we get down. We stop an hour to dinner at 12; we generally have bread and a bit of fat for dinner, and some of them a sup of beer; that's all; we have a whole hour for dinner, and we get out from 4 to 5 in the evening; so that it will be eleven hours before we get out. We drink the water that runs through the pit. I am not paid wages myself; the man who employs me pays my father, but I don't know how much it is. I have never been at school. I had to begin working when I ought to have been at school. I don't go to Sunday-school. The truth is, we are confined enough on week-days, and want to walk about on Sundays; but I go to chapel on Sunday night. I can't read at all. Jesus Christ was Adam's son, and they nailed him to a tree; but I don't rightly understand these things.

P.P. 1842, vol. XVI, p. 244.

15

'I never learnt nought'

Ann Eggley, 18-years-old hurrier in Messrs. Thorpe's colliery: I'm sure I don't know how to spell my name. We go at four in the morning and sometimes at half-past four. We begin to work as soon as we get down. We get out after four, sometimes at five, in the evening. I hurry by myself, and have done so for long.

I know the corves are very heavy, they are the biggest corves anywhere about. The work is far too hard for me; the sweat runs off me all over sometimes. I am very tired at night. Sometimes when we get home at night we have not power to wash us, and then we go to bed. Sometimes we fall asleep in the chair.

Father said last night it was both a shame and a disgrace for girls to work as we do, but there is naught else for us to do . . . I don't know my letters. I never learnt nought . . .

P.P. 1842, vol. XVI, p. 252.

16

Feminine Ablutions

At Silkstone there are a great many girls who work in the pits, and I have seen them washing themselves naked much below the waist as I passed their doors, and whilst they are doing this, they will be talking and chatting with any man who happen to be there with the utmost unconcern, and men young and old would be washing in the same place, at the same time.

The moral effects of the system must be exceedingly bad. They dress, however, so well after their work and on Sundays that it is impossible to recognize them. They wear earrings even whilst they work, and I have seen them with them nearly two inches long ... Their dress when they come out of the pit is a kind of skull-cap which hides all the hair; trousers without stockings, and thick wooden clogs ...

Evidence of Edward Newman, Solicitor of Barnsley; P.P. 1842, vol. XV, p. 250.

* * *

Peter Gaskell, a collier in the Worsley pits, Lancashire, when asked, 'How often do the drawers wash their bodies?' replied, 'None of the drawers does wash their bodies; I never wash my body; I let my shirt rub the dirt off, my shirt will show that; I wash my neck and ears and face, of course.'

To the further question, 'Do you think it is usual for the young women to do the same as you do?' he replied, 'I don't think it is usual for the lasses to wash their bodies; my sisters never wash themselves, and seeing is believing; they wash their faces and necks and ears.'

[N.B. It was a common belief among colliers that washing the back had a weakening effect.]

P.P. 1842, vol. XVII, p. 217.

17

'Best out of pits, the lasses'

I would not have a lass seen in the pit if I had my will, and nobody will allow them who has any spirit or sense. They can see nought but blackguardism and debauchery. They are best out of pits, the lasses.

JOHN HARGREAVE, collier, Thorpe's colliery, Barnsley; P.P. 1842, vol. XV, p. 32.

* * *

I wish the Government would expel all girls and females from mines. I can give proof that they are very immoral, and I am certain that the girls are worse than the men in point of morals, and use far more indecent language. It unbecomes them in every way; there is not one in ten of them that know how to cut a shirt out or make one, and they learn neither to knit nor sew. I have known myself of a case where a married man and a girl who hurried for him had sexual intercourse often in the bank where he worked.

MATTHEW LINDLEY, collier, Day & Twibell's, Barnsley; P.P. 1842, vol. XVI, p. 251.

* * *

I consider it [women in pits] to be a most awfully demoralizing practice. The youth of both sexes work often in a half-naked state, and the passions are excited before they arrive at puberty. Sexual intercourse decidedly frequently occurs in consequence. Cases of bastardy frequently also occur; and I am decidedly of the opinion that women brought up in this way lay aside all modesty, and scarcely know what it is by name. I sincerely trust that before I die I shall have the satisfaction of seeing it prevented and entirely done away with.

JOHN THORNLEY, JP; P.P. 1842, vol. XVI, p. 246.

* * *

I have worked a great deal where girls were employed in pits. I have had children by them myself, and have frequently had connexion with them in the pits. I am sure that this is the case, especially in pits about Lancashire.

JOHN SIMPKIN, collier, Drighlington; P.P. 1842, vol. XVI, p. 204.

There are no girls in pits here. I make no more than the colliers at Silkstone, nor so much, but I would be hard put to it before I would bring a lass of mine to the pits—no, not if I was ever so ill put to it. I would live upon one meal a day sooner. I don't consider it right, no way; it is never done here . . . I am sure the colliers could do without putting their lasses in the pits . . . It's a shameful practice.

GEORGE CARR, aged about 50, employed in Messrs Graham's ironstone pits at Tankersley, Yorks; P.P. 1842, vol. XVI, p. 266.

* * *

I have wrought below ground since 10 years of age. Have been married now 18 years. Have had eight children; six are alive. I have not allowed my wife to work below since she was first in the family way. That is not the usual practice with men, who too frequently marry women for their labour than any liking they may have.

Where women are encouraged to work below they get husbands very early, and have large families, and the children are as much neglected as they have been themselves. There are a vast of women work in the pits, and the employment very much unfits them for the performance of mother's duties; and they frequently cause men to leave their homes, if homes they may be called, and drink hard; the poor bairns are neglected; for in time the women follow the men and drink hard also.

Women work till the ninth month of pregnancy, and frequently go home and bear the child. Respectable workmen would be glad to keep females and young boys out of the pits.

JOSEPH FRASER, age 37, coal hewer; P.P. 1842, vol. XVI, p. 442.

18

Work Hard, Marry Later

It is now four years since the practice of employing females and very young children ceased in these mines, and I have evidenced the advantage of the change religiously, morally, and socially.

In these works, since the discharge of women, marriages have been formed with greater care, and more appropriately: few now marry till 23 or 24, and we have not had a bastard child since the disemployment of females. On the old system men married more from the advantage their physical strength might procure them, than any degree of affection. Men labour here regularly and average eleven or twelve days in the fortnight, whereas, when they depended on their wives and children, they rarely wrought nine days in the same period. Colliers are now stationary, with very few exceptions; the women themselves are opposed to moving since they have felt the benefit of homes . . .

JOHN WRIGHT, manager of coal-mines in Lasswade, east of Scotland; P.P. 1842, vol. XVI, p. 451.

19

'I wouldna gang down again'

While working in the pit I was worth to my husband 7s a week, out of which we had to pay 2s 6d to a woman for looking after the younger bairns. I used to take them to her house at 4 o'clock in the morning, out of their own beds, to put them into hers. Then there was 1s a week for washing; besides, there was mending to pay for, and other things. The house was not guided. The other children broke things; they did not go to school when they were sent; they would be playing about, and get ill-used by other children, and their clothes torn. Then when I came home in the evening, everything was to do after the day's labour, and I was so tired I had no heart for it; no fire lit, nothing cooked, no water fetched, the house dirty, and nothing comfortable for my husband. It is all far better now, and I wouldna gang down again.

A mother of four children, formerly working in Pencaitland colliery. Mining Commissioner's Report, P.P. 1844, vol. XVI, p. 4.

20

What Happened to the Women Miners

We had about 100 females in our pits when the Act came into operation. Many of these have got work in brick fields and out-door labour from the farmers; some have gone to service; one or two are married. Some are maintained by their relations; others earn a little by sewing. At first, after the Act was passed, we took five or six widows on our private poor-list, and provided them with a meal, etc. till their daughters found employment. We have still two or three on the list, and not likely to get off; these are widows whose daughters have left the place, and are only just able to support themselves. There are one or two able-bodied girls who partake of this support with their widowed mothers; these will get out-door employment as the spring advances . . .

The men who had wives or daughters working with them in the pit are not much worse off than they were before. If their daughters are at work they are off their parents' hands. The women earned in the pits from 10d to 1s 1d a day. Now the men draw the coal for themselves. We give them the same as before for hewing, and pay them over and above for the putting. Being no longer dependent on the women, who often worked irregularly, and our horses, which we have since introduced assisting them, the men can now earn as much as before.

MR F. GRIER, manager of Fordel Colliery, Fifeshire; P.P. 1844, vol. XVI, p. 52.

21

No Parish Relief

Some few women may possibly go down by stealth where the mines are accessible by means of stairs . . . The few who may still, for a time, persevere in their endeavour to obtain work in this way, are those of mature or advanced age, who have been so long accustomed to labour in the pits that they are little suited to anything else . . . If they are able-bodied, they have, by the usages of Scotland in regard to the treatment of the poor, no claim on the parish for relief; and the small assistance they may receive from their late employers, or from their neighbours, falls far short of what they had been in the habit of earning at labour, which however objectionable in other respects, had at least afforded them for many years the means of decent subsistence and comfort.

The usage of Scotland in refusing all relief from the parochial funds to the able-bodied rests on the assumption that every such person can find employment—a presumption which, in the case of this class of females, is far from being sustained by the fact. In a country where female labour is in excess, and where large numbers of women were suddenly displaced from their usual occupations and thrown upon the general market in search of new spheres of industry, the last to meet with success in the more crowded race of competition will naturally be those who had grown up to maturity in the dull routine of dragging or carrying heavy burdens in the coal pits.

Accordingly, in all parts of the coal districts where women had been employed, complaints were numerous of the hardships that the Act had occasioned to elder females, widows, orphan daughters of mature age, families where there were no sons to aid a father who was old and ailing; and other similar cases. All these were assisted by the proprietors, and others their neighbours, to a certain extent, but they were still exposed to privations. Their case merits particular sympathy.

I had opportunities of seeing many of these women. They were anxious to relate their simple tales of distress consequent on their enforced idleness, and to testify their anxiety to get work. Their scanty dress, and general aspect of depression, sufficiently showed that, nothwithstanding the helping hand of charity which had been held out to them by their late employers, they felt severely the change that had struck them so suddenly with the deprivation of the means of living to which they had been accustomed from their childhood . . .

Mining Commissioner's Report, P.P. 1844, vol. XVI, p. 4

22

Three-pence a Day

The daughters, of the ages of 49 and 50 respectively, of a father aged 75, have been left to shift for themselves, and have had recourse to making and mending camstone (a kind of white clay used for washing the earthen and stone floors of houses), since they cannot hope to be received as domestic servants, after having been for so long a period nothing better than beasts of burden. In this occupation, when the weather admits of their going abroad, they make on an average about *three-pence a day*, and to do this they have sometimes to travel as far as Haddington, a distance of 14 miles.

REV. J. ADAMSON, minister of parish of Newton, Mid-Lothian; Mining Commissioner's report; P.P. 1844, vol. XVI, p. 4.

23

Ungrateful Females!

Instead of allowing any hope to be indulged in that the Act [prohibiting the employment of women in coal mines underground] would not be put strictly in force, the course at once most humane and most consistent with duty has been to forward as much as possible the transference of the most suffering class of females to other occupations; or, failing that, the alleviation of their distress by benevolent assistance. The latter process has been encouraged and stimulated by the act of a charitable lady in England, who, in the course of last autumn, placed anonymously in Lord Ashley's hands the sum of £100 for the benefit of those labouring women who, in Scotland, were still suffering most from the operation of the law which excluded them from their accustomed work in the collieries. To this donation Lord Ashley added a sum of his own.

Having been consulted as to the distribution, I recommended the division of the sum among four parishes . . . Lord Ashley accompanied the transmission of these sums with a letter to the minister of each of those parishes . . . In the parish of Newton (Mid-Lothian), near Dalkeith the letter and accompanying donations were received in an excellent spirit. The recipients, to the number of forty, were chiefly widows, who had no sons to work for them; daughters, who could receive no help from their parents; and unmarried women, upwards of 30 years of age, who had no chance of getting into domestic service. The clergyman states, that 'clothing and shoes were distributed to the whole of these according to their ascertained wants, the expenditure being at an average of 5s 6d for each person . . .'

A very proper feeling towards their unknown benefactress was exhibited by those selected, [but] I regret to have to state that a very different spirit manifested itself on the occasion in the mining village of Tranent. The assistant minister (the incumbent being advanced in age) informs me, that every care was taken by the kirk session, in conjunction with himself, in examining individually the applicants, and selecting the proper objects for relief. A sum was allotted to each, from 5s to 10s, in proportion to their need. The minister acquaints me, with expressions of pain, that 'in the great majority of cases, the intended kindness has not been productive of the good that was designed. Those who were not admitted to a participation of it, stirred up those who were; and the abuse that was heaped on us, both by those who were and those who were not recipients, was beyond your conception'. The interposition of the village police became necessary, and the evening closed amidst intoxication.

Report of the Commissioners . . . Mining Districts; P.P. 1845, vol. XXVII, p. 5.

24

The Women Who Went Back

The convictions obtained in this district in the course of 1847, for employing females under ground . . . had the effect at the time of so far checking the practice, that the services of those so engaged were shortly after dispensed with.

I regret to say, that some of the larger companies, the proprietors of iron works and mines, have failed to exercise their authority in support of the law with the vigilance and determination that might have been expected, and the result has been that I was lately informed that at the large and important works of Blaenavon, Clydach, Nantyglo, Beaufort, Blaina, Coalbrook, and probably at one or two more, females were again at work below ground.

It is but justice to the gentlemen who are the resident managers of these works, and to their mineral agents, to state, that on my acquainting them with what has been reported to me, they did not attempt to deny it, but offered as excuses, that these mines were accessible by 'levels' on the sides of the hills, that the women went in before it was light and came out after dark, and that they hid themselves from the mineral agent whenever a search was made for them . . .

Mr Robert Smith stated, that he became mineral agent to the Blaenavon Colliery (employing between 800 and 900 colliers and miners) in March 1849. Hearing that women were employed under ground . . . he searched the pits. Notice was, however, always conveyed to them when he was coming, so that it was not until a month after he had been there that he was able to discover them. In April he turned out 70 women and girls, as many as 20 of the latter being not more than eleven or twelve years of age. He has no doubt that since then many have gone back from time to time. He gave notice that he would fine any man whom he found employing them again, and he has fined seven or eight from 5s to 10s each. He gave employment to as many [women] as he could at the pit banks; three or four orphans were obliged at first to apply for relief from the parish, and many of the men went away to go to works where they could take their daughters or other females under ground. These men were earning in the worst times at least 12s 6d a week clear, after deducting powder and candles, and consequently had no excuse of poverty for thus employing their children.

Report of the Commissioner (H. Seymour Tremenheere) on the state of the Mining Districts (Monmouthshire, Brecon, and Glamorganshire): P.P. 1850, XXIII, pp. 59–60.

(d) GIRLS OF THE PIT BANK

There was one class of female workers in the colliery districts which particularly attracted the interest of the investigators of the early eighteen-forties. These were the girls who were employed in banking the coal brought up from the pit and in transporting it and loading it into the canal boats. They were so badly treated, their condition was so miserable, they themselves were so depraved—and yet, in spite of everything, they were, most of them and a good part of the time, so jolly and happy-go-lucky!

I

Singing at Their Work

On the banks of the canals in Staffordshire are seen many girls engaged in loading the boats with coals. These girls are substantially, though coarsely, clothed, and the head and neck more particularly protected from the cold. The work is laborious, but not beyond their strength. The clothing is obviously such that a girl cannot continue to wear it after going home. She therefore lays it aside, and washes herself, and puts on more agreeable clothing for the rest of the day . . .

Many girls are employed under the designation of bankswomen. They stand on the bank near the mouth of the shaft, and when a skip comes up, and the slide is thrust forward, and the skip is let down upon it, they unhook it and push it forward, and then empty out the coals. They also hang an empty skip to the chain, and when the slide is withdrawn it is let down the shaft.

The returns from Staffordshire show the wages of the girls to be as follows:—age 12 to 13, 4s to 4s 6d; 13 to 14, 4s 6d to 5s; 14 to 15, 5s to 6s 6d; 15 to 16, 6s to 7s 6d; 16 to 17, 7s to 8s 6d; 17 to 18, 7s 6d to 9s.

Many girls are employed on the banks of the ironstone pits, in picking out the ironstone boulders from the measures in which they are contained.

There are some persons who object to girls being employed in out-door, and what is supposed to be laborious, employment; but when we consider how many employments men have engrossed to themselves, and how few ways there are for women to gain their living, we must be cautious not to attempt to narrow what is already so limited. As to the laboriousness of their occupations, the young women are best able to judge for themselves, and they are able to show that they possess a physical vigour far surpassing that of the young women brought up in the close air of great towns. The girls are generally singing at their work, and always appear smiling and cheerful.

Children's Employment Commission (Mines), P.P. 1842, vol. XVI, p. 11.

2

So Very Unfeminine!

———————

The girls who work on the pit-banks are well grown, healthy, and strong; but thin, sinewy, bony, and very unfeminine . . . They are in most instances as gross and immoral in their language and conduct as the men who first made them so.

From their constant association with men, and from the nature of their work, one of these girls, in her coarse great coat, with her hands in her side-pockets, presents a picture of rude jovial independence of life, and recklessness of all refinements and delicacies of sex, which often makes an observer forget the objectionable characteristics of the individual in his sense of the uncivilized circumstances by which she has become so unlike the rest of her countrywomen.

They drive coal-carts, ride astride upon horses—sometimes two or three together upon a large long-backed horse—drink, swear, fight, smoke, whistle, and sing, and care for nobody. Being very happy, they are certainly no objects for pity, but surely their circumstances are of a kind in which girls should never be placed.

Report on the town of Bilston, Staffs; P.P. 1843, vol. XV, Q 65.

3

The Hovel at the Pit Mouth

———

The banks-women are the lowest and most degraded class; they stand at the pit-mouth all day, and receive the skips as they come up; there are generally two at each pit-mouth; they are there from six in the morning till six at night; their dinners are sent up to them; and if they are mothers they do not see their children all day . . .

The girls on the pit-bank do that kind of work which men ought to do; exposed to the weather all day; there is a little house near the pit-mouth for them to run into occasionally. When the men come up at night half stripped, they change their clothes in this hovel, and these girls are there mixing with them; these girls are generally in their teens, seldom above twenty, and become very immoral and obscene.

Evidence of Robert Bew, chemist and druggist, Bilston; P.P. 1843, vol. XV, p. q 49.

4

They Call for Their Pints

———

There are a great number of illegitimate children born here (Darlaston); many of the girls have from three to four children each; and they work for and support their children and themselves without a murmur.

The effects of early work, particularly in forges and on the pit-bank, render these girls perfectly independent. They often enter the beer-shops, call for their pints, and smoke their pipes, like men; indeed, there seems little difference in their circumstances from those of the men, except that they are the chief sufferers.

P.P. 1843, vol. XV, Q 62.

5

Good-looking Welsh Girls

It is only in the collieries of Ruabon that girls under 18 are employed; *in* the mines no females have any employment. I have great satisfaction in reporting that, though girls find work at the pit mouth, they never go under ground, such a practice has not yet found its way into the northern parts of the principality. The number who work on the surface is comparatively few, and the custom of employing females at all is confined to the district around Wrexham.

At each pit two females are placed to assist in *banking* the coal, and, where there is no steam-engine or horse-whimsey, also in turning the winding-barrel, by which the coal and ironstone are brought to the surface. In most cases the females employed exceed the age of 18; as strength is required there are but few under that age and rarely any to be found under 13.

There is nothing in the employment of banking coal which is repugnant to the feelings; and the manner, conduct, and dress of the females so engaged appear respectable and decorous. They work generally from six in the mornings till six in the evening, and have their meals brought to them. They are hired by the charter-masters, and paid by them; their wages being from 6d to 1s a day.

From the evidence I have taken it will be seen that the girls 'on the bank' usually marry early, that they are not deficient in the knowledge and discharge of the domestic duties, and that they make good wives and mothers. In respect to their health and physical condition, the evidence of the medical men proves that the work they are engaged in rather tends to improve than to detract from either; they are represented by them as enjoying excellent health. By the constant exertion of their strength the muscles acquire a development, and their carriage a manner, which may be somewhat out of character with feminine appearance; in other respects they suffer nothing when put in comparison with any class among the lower orders; on the contrary, in figure and complexion they have the advantage of most.

In some of the useful domestic duties they may be somewhat deficient, such as sewing, washing, and baking, but as their time is not completely occupied at the pits, and as they are always at home on Saturday and most evenings, they are not wholly without the knowledge of those necessary acquirements, which require no great talent or industry in being learnt.

Few females on the bank have been at school, and very few can read, though they all, or nearly all, attend Sunday-school, and seldom absent themselves from Divine worship. Their morals are considered not inferior to those of other females of the working classes. They are frequently pregnant, it is true, previous to marriage, but this is not unusual amongst the lower orders in Wales, and appears to throw no great slur on the character, whether afterwards married or forsaken by the putative father; marriage, however, in 99 cases in 100 takes place, and though the immorality is greatly to be lamented, it is to the honour of the parties concerned that marriage so frequently follows pregnancy, and that bastardy is not more common . . .

Report on North Wales mining districts by MR H. H. JONES; P.P. 1482, vol. XVII, pp. 365–366.

SEXUAL RELATIONS

In those heady days of change beyond any that had been experienced before, what kind of sex life did the workers lead? In the nature of the case an answer is hard to come by, but from the sources that have been drawn upon for our account of conditions in factory and mine and workshop we may discover, now and again, a piece of 'sexual relation' that is all the more valuable for being so rare.

Peter Gaskell has quite a lot to say on the subject, and, as might be expected, his picture of Sex in the Factory (No. 1) is most highly coloured. The facts disclosed by the two midwives who gave evidence before the Factory Commission of 1833 are much more reliable (No. 2). The temptations that assailed the young women and girls employed in the factories are well illustrated in Nos. 3, 4, and 5; and No. 7—taken from Mr Riddall Wood's account of his investigation on behalf of the Manchester Statistical Society as to the effects of overcrowding on moral habits—show all too clearly that 'home' was often as bad as, or even worse than, the mill. The extent to which the juvenile workers were morally depraved was a matter in dispute: 'Parson Bull' considered that promiscuity was pretty general (No. 7), but others (Nos. 8 and 9) thought that there was a good deal of misunderstanding and exaggeration in the stories of juvenile vice. The 'shocking incident' in No. 10 was reported as a piece of corroboration of the most unfavourable view of juvenile character, and Mr Symons's account of a visit to Leeds places of amusement on a Saturday night is a particularly vivid piece of social reporting.

Prostitution was practised in the manufacturing districts both by professionals and by factory girls who found it impossible to make both ends meet on their meagre earnings (Nos. 12 and 13). Léon Faucher, describing Manchester life for his French readers, insisted that the factory girls were 'strangers to modesty', but his stay in Manchester was hardly long enough to enable him to speak with authority (No. 14). In his evidence before the Factory Commission in 1833 Dr Hawkins admitted that only a small number of factory girls seem to have taken to prostitution, although he had a rather low opinion of their state of morals (No. 15). Statistics of prostitution, as of moral phenomena in general, are in any case notoriously unreliable.

The 'very curious fact' given in No. 16 may serve as an introduction to the documents illustrating the birth-control techniques of the period. In No. 19 there is mentioned a book dealing with what we should call contraception that had been circulated among the females '. . . when Carlile came round to lecture.' The reference is to that doughty journalist Richard Carlile (1790–1843), who was sentenced in 1819 (a particularly bad year for reformers) to imprisonment and fine for having published Thomas Paine's *Age of Reason*. While in Dorchester gaol he was allowed to continue with his writing activities, and he was still in prison when in 1825 the issue of his journal *The Republican* appeared in which is printed the article 'What is Love?' that is given in our document No. 20. As will be seen, Carlile included in his article the text of a handbill addressed 'To the married of both sexes of the working people', and this was one of the earliest pieces of birth-control instruction to appear in England.

I

Sex in the Factory

The crowding together numbers of the young of both sexes in factories, is a prolific source of moral delinquency. The stimulus of a heated atmosphere (the average temperature of the atmosphere in mills is 70 to 75° Fahrenheit; formerly it was much higher), the contact of opposite sexes, the example of lasciviousness upon the animal passions —all have conspired to produce a very early development of sexual appetencies. Indeed, in this respect, the female population engaged in manufactures, approximates very closely to that found in tropical climates; puberty, or at least sexual propensities, being attained almost coeval with girlhood.

It may be questioned whether puberty in the common acceptation of the term, is necessary for the display and exercise of functions of sex. Observation has taught, that the usual marks accompanying and preceding this epoch in the female, have very frequently been wanting in instances where unequivocal proofs were given that the individuals had not only suffered, but also enjoyed intercourse. Not only this, but in some examples pregnancy has occurred, where the usual physiological data, generally esteemed requisite for its production, have been entirely wanting.

Independently of this, however, the usual accompaniments of puberty shew themselves very early, stimulated into premature activity by the above causes, and unchecked in their effects upon manners by the absence of moral discipline, whether at home or abroad.

So far indeed is this from being the case, that at the mill the factory girl is subjected to a series of excitements, which inevitably lead to the ultimatum of desire. She can hardly be said to have a home—certainly she has none in the proper sense of the word—for the whole of the day is passed from it, and she visits it merely for the purpose of rest. It has no moral ties upon her; and her parents are perhaps positively injurious to her in this respect . . .

Unfortunately no regard, however slight, is paid to these matters by the majority of millowners. A certain number of hands are required to superintend the labours of their untiring engine, with its complement of looms, etc. for a certain number of hours, and for a certain amount of wages; so long as these are attained, he looks no further. He considers the human beings who crowd his mill, from five o'clock in the morning to seven o'clock in the evening, but as so many accessaries to his machinery, destined to produce a certain and well-known quantity of work, at the lowest possible outlay of capital. To him their passions, habits, or crimes are as little interesting, as if they bore no relation to the errors of a system, of which he was a member and supporter.

Added to this, those who hold the higher rank in his mill, from the overlooker downwards, are all tinged with the same carelessness or coarseness—and in place of being checks and stays, rather lead the train of mischief. Springing from the diseased body themselves, they too often show their origin by a course of conduct to those over whom they are placed, calculated for the gratification of their own satyr-like feelings, and the baseness of their own minds . . .

The evil unfortunately does not end with the party first yielding to temptation . . . The mother who has never felt her own moral and social rank injured by her sexual indulgences—who looks around her, and sees that all are like herself—who has experienced no difficulty in settling herself as a wife—who even, if, after her marriage, she has continued her former practices, has derived positive and substantial benefits in consequence, by improving the condition of her husband, and adding to the comforts of her family, forgets—if she ever felt—that she was sinning. Her family inherit the same lax feelings; her sons and daughters are both subjected to the same causes which prematurely evolved her own propensities; are themselves in the same state of precociousness; have the same failings, and become fathers and mothers in their turn . . .

It is not denied that there are many girls who, from a coincidence of favourable causes, or from their possessing a higher and more just sense of what is due to themselves, escape some of the many evils that beset them, and grow up decent and moral women, fitted to make good wives and good mothers. These are, nevertheless, exceptions; not so rare as to be extremely remarkable, but still standing out in strong relief from the mass to which they are attached.

P. GASKELL, *The Manufacturing Population of England*, ch. 2.

2

What the Midwives Revealed

Mary Woodhouse, midwife, age 58; for the last 12 years one of the midwives to the lying-in hospital of Manchester:

At what age are the women belonging to the factory classes generally delivered of their first child?—Sometimes, but seldom, at 16; very often at 18; generally before 20.

Are the factory women often pregnant before marriage?—Too often.

Are the unmarried women often deserted by their seducers?—Often.

Have the unmarried women often the venereal disease at the time when you deliver them?—Sometimes; it does not very often come under my observation.

Have the married women often the venereal disease at the time when you deliver them?—Sometimes; some have it very bad.

What recompence do the factory wives usually make you for your attendance?—Five shillings is the charge I make.

Do the factory women miscarry more frequently than the other classes whom you attend?—Why, I cannot speak positively, but, however, it does happen that the factory women generally do miscarry; but the others sometimes.

Do you find still births more common among the factory classes than among others?—No, I cannot say that I do.

How do the factory women manage about suckling their children? —They give them the breast at breakfast, and at noon, and in the evening.

Does the child ever suffer from the separation from its mother at the intermediate times?—Sometimes. They give it to a nurse while they are away.

What nurses do they employ in their absence?—Often old people; and I must say that it hurts my feelings, it seems so unnatural.

Do the factory girls menstruate earlier or later than the other classes with whom you mix?—On the whole, I think earlier. Some suffer very severely and have it very late; and some never have it at all . . .

How soon after labour do factory women generally go to work?— Some go back in nine or ten days; some stay at home even three weeks or a month.

Have they generally as many children as other women?—Well, I think they have.

Are they subject to the whites [Leucorrhoea] more than other women?—I cannot say positively, but they are very subject to it; I often hear them complain of it.

*   *   *

Elizabeth Taylor, midwife, age 52; midwife attached to Manchester lying-in hospital, been in the habit of delivering women since she was 12:

Do many of the factory women live with men without being married? —That I cannot tell. I attend many for love-children, but I cannot tell what becomes of them afterwards.

Do you find that the children of factory women are as healthy when first born as those of other women?—No, certainly not; they are more delicate.

To what do you ascribe their being more delicate?—To the mother's being more delicate, from heat and want of proper food.

How long do factory women generally work up to the time of their being confined?—Many of them up to the very day; some up to the very hour, as I may say. Some have gone to work before breakfast, and I have had them in bed at two o'clock the same day. A girl has gone to work after her breakfast, and I have delivered her, and all over, by twelve o'clock the same forenoon.

How soon do they go back to the factory after confinement?—Many at the end of a fortnight; three weeks they think a great bit.

Have they generally got baby-linen?—In a general way, the English have, but the Irish not often.

At what age do factory wives generally begin to lose their good looks? —They generally lose them two months or so after they are married. Their colour gets quite pale and wan.

But some of the factory girls have a good colour?—Yes; but some use paint. Are you positive of that?—Yes; I have seen them put it on.

Examined by Dr Hawkins; Employment of Children in Factories, 1833; P.P. XXI. D 3, pp. 11 and 12.

3

A Girl's Road to Ruin

It is not difficult to imagine a young female, of pleasing face and person, exposed, by being placed in a manufactory, to the lewd remarks and familiarities of the coarse and dissipated of the other sex.

Perhaps not one idea of virtue was ever established in the mind of this susceptible and credulous creature. She is now in the certain path to ruin and seduction. She is often treated as an inferior being; until some infamous seducer flatters to obtain her ruin. She is the victim of her own confiding and unsuspecting nature; but she is branded for being extremely vicious.

Suppose the weekly earnings of a female to be 6s, and this is above the average; out of this she has to pay for lodgings, for clothes, and for the making of them, too; for she cannot make them herself, never having been taught; her washing after work-hours, she will do herself; in her outlay she must be frugal to keep clear of the inconveniences of debt.

There can be little or no saving in this instance. Suppose the poor creature to be put to half-time, or to be thrown out of work all together, she has no parents, no friends to fall back upon, resources she can have none, what then is the alternative ? The answer is obvious.

Children's Employment Commission (Mines), P.P. 1843, vol. XIV, p. 132.

4

Seduction in the Mill

[In factories] there are great temptations both for old and young; there are boys of a very young age, and few young women will go to these places who have any character; if they do they must take great care, or it will be blasted. Indecencies and immoralities were talked of, but I saw but one, that was of my own setter-on. I had sent the bobbin-carrier for bobbins, and she not coming, I sent my setter-on, and she not returning as soon as she ought, I went to look for her, and found her and the overlooker in an indecent situation; she told me that she would stand it no longer, and would leave me the next morning; I said that she must tell the master of what the overlooker had been doing to her. She told the manager the next morning, who sent for the over-looker, who, when he came, denied it; then they sent for me, and I told them in what manner I saw him having hold of her, with one hand round her neck and the other in a very indecent situation: then the manager asked him again, and he did not then deny it, but said he was only searching her to see if she had any bobbing waste about her. I had no doubt of his real intent from what I saw if the girl would comply. The girl was about seventeen, and she told me that the over-looker had attacked her before in a similar manner, but not in the mill...

JOHN AINSWORTH, age 26, stretcher in Mr Bolling's mill, Bolton: Factory Commission Report; P.P. 1834, vol. XIX, D 1, 168–169.

5

In the Theatre Gallery

John Upton, police constable, Birmingham: Has been specially employed in obtaining information respecting the juvenile prostitutes and thieves. Knows that the fact of boys and girls working together at the same factory leads to much of the prostitution and stealing. The fact of the mechanics, male and female, leaving the manufactory at the same hour, facilitates the making of assignations. Assignations are made at the time, usually between 4 and 5 p.m., allowed for tea.

Girls who are seduced in this way frequently become prostitutes. They rarely marry the party who is the seducer. If a child is born, the mother in general returns to her former employment in the manufactory, and the child is usually supported by the mother and her friends, occasionally by the father. Many prostitutes in the town come from the country, either already of abandoned character, or as servants, etc.

Having been on duty at the gallery of the theatre, has had opportunities of knowing the class of persons who frequent that place. On Monday evening the majority of the audience in the gallery are boys and girls of the age of 12, 14, 16, or 18. Thinks that the facility of this meeting is a frequent cause of prostitution, and tends very much to an increase of that vice.

It is a very frequent case for an apprentice, a very numerous class of mechanics in this town, to obtain leave to quit his work at half-past five on Monday to go to the theatre, and to keep a place for a female companion, who comes when she leaves her work at 7; or this arrangement, as to the female, may be merely to spare her the crush at the entrance to the theatre. Believes that in general the girls employed in the manufactories of this town are not virtuous.

Employment of Children (Mines), P.P. 1843, vol. XIV, pp. f 172–173.

6

Bad Housing, Bad Morals

The towns in which I found instances of the greatest crowding were Manchester, Liverpool, Ashton-under-Lyne, and Pendleton. In a cellar in Pendleton, I recollect there were three beds in the two apartments of which the habitation consisted, but having no door between them, in one of which a man and his wife slept; in another, a man, his wife, and child; and in a third two unmarried females . . . In a cellar in Liverpool, I found a mother and her grown-up daughters sleeping on a bed of chaff on the ground in one corner of the cellar, and in the other corner three sailors had their bed. I have met with upwards of forty persons sleeping in the same room, married and single, including, of course, children and several young adult persons of either sex. In Manchester I could enumerate a variety of instances in which I found such promiscuous mixture of the sexes in sleeping-rooms. I may mention one: a man, his wife and child sleeping in one bed; in another bed, two grown-up females; and in the same room two young men, unmarried. I have met with instances of a man, his wife, and his wife's sister, sleeping in the same bed together. I have known at least half-a-dozen cases in Manchester in which that has been regularly practised. the unmarried sister being an adult . . .

Early in my visitation of Pendleton, I called at the dwelling of a person whose sons worked with himself in a colliery. It was in the afternoon, when a young man, one of the sons, came down stairs in his shirt and stood before the fire where a very decently-dressed young female was sitting. The son asked his mother for a clean shirt, and on its being given to him, very deliberately threw off the shirt he had on, and after warming the clean one, put it on. In another dwelling in Pendleton, a young girl of 18 years of age, sat by the fire in her chemise during the whole time of my visit. Both these were houses of working people (colliers) and not by any means of ill-fame.

I have frequently met with instances in which the parties themselves have traced their own depravity to these circumstances. As, for example, when I was following my inquiries in Hull, I found in one room a prostitute, with whom I remonstrated on her course of life, and asked her whether she would not be in a better condition if she were an honest servant instead of living in vice and wretchedness. She admitted she should, and on asking the cause of her being brought to her present condition, she stated that she had lodged with her married sister, and slept in the same bed with her and her husband; that hence improper intercourse took place, and from that she gradually became more and more depraved; and at length was thrown upon the town, because, having lost her character, the town was her only resource.

Another female of this description admitted that her first false step was in consequence of her sleeping in the same room with a married couple. In the instance I have mentioned of the two single women sleeping in the same room with the married people, I have good authority for believing that they were common to the men. In the case I have mentioned of the two daughters and the woman where I found the sailors, I learned, from the mother's admission, that they were common to the lodgers. In all these cases the sense of decency was obliterated.

J. RIDDALL WOOD: Sanitary Condition of the Labouring Population; House of Lords Sessional Papers, 1842, vol. 26, pp. 124–126.

7

What Impressed the Vicar

I can conceive it very possible that there may be more illegitimate children in an agricultural district of a given population, than in a manufacturing district of the same population; but I should attribute [this] to the fact that a still more vicious and general promiscuous intercourse takes place in the manufacturing population where the factory system prevails. In proof of this view of the subject, I just now recollected one instance at least of a child, a mere child, in my own Sunday-school, whom I had every reason to believe, from the reports that were made to me, was, at a very tender age, quite a common prostitute, and I fear has continued such since. But I am yet to learn, as far as my observations upon this physiological subject has gone,

15. Bradford, drawn by Henry Warren (from John James's *History of the Worsted Manufacture in England* (1857)) (*photo*: Mansell Collection)

Factory Girls in a Manchester Mill, from a drawing of 1842. (21.102 Mansell Collection.)

that the consequence of very frequent promiscuous intercourse will
be offspring . . . I have never yet observed that prostitutes generally
become mothers . . .

My impression is . . . that a very considerable number of the young
females employed in the factories are accustomed to promiscuous
intercourse; but when I say this, I by no means intend to refer to my
own neighbourhood as the worst, or to deny that there are very many
instances of great propriety and modesty of character in young females
employed in factories . . . and I beg to say that I do not by any means
consider that the immoral character of the manufacturing districts is
to be attributed in the way of blame exclusively to the young persons
themselves; for besides the blame which may attach to the system, I
have been very sorry to observe, or to learn upon authority which I
could by no means doubt, that they have seen very corrupt and infamous examples not unfrequently in their overlookers and superiors,
and in some cases their employers.

REV. G. S. BULL in evidence to Sadler's Committee; P.P. 1831–32, vol. XV,
   pp. 487–488.

8

'Keeping company together'

I do not consider the factory population in this town [Leeds] more
immoral than the same class out of the mills; there may be, and no
doubt is, a great deal of loose slang-talk passes among them in going
and returning from meals; or in the burling-rooms, where women only
are admitted, but they have not the opportunity for actual guilt; and
I have always found them, both male and female, as modest in demean-
our as any other class of working people. Consequently, I do not
believe that bastardy or abortion is unusually prevalent amongst them . . .

I have also the means of knowing that promiscuous sexual intercourse
is much less frequent among them than might be supposed, and for
this reason: a couple become attached early in life, which they express
by the term, 'keeping company together'. The term certainly admits
of an equivocal meaning, and I am sorry to say I have known of some

most unequivocal results from 'keeping company'; but, innocent or guilty, the parties in the great majority of cases are faithful to each other; and when anything does occur to alter the girl's shape the mother and neighbours call it a 'misfortune', and the parties are then married, if they can afford it. This is farther confirmed by the fact that I have met with much fewer cases of the venereal disease, in all its varieties, among the factory population.

DR HUNTER, in practice in Leeds since 1818, examined at Leeds by Dr Loudon, sub-commissioner; Employment of Children in Factories; P.P. 1833, vol. XXI, C 3, p. 18.

9

Sex and the Young Factory Workers

I believe the intercourse between the *great majority* of the boys and girls employed in manufactories, under the age of 14 or 15, to be that of simple indifference as to sex. The exceptions are chiefly those who are of much finer growth and health than the average; and of these there are but very few. I do not consider them to possess any moral restraints; but that poorness of blood, and constant exhaustion, leaves them neither time, nor inclination, nor stamina, for the excitement of the imagination and the senses. There is a balance maintained even where all seems evil. They are protected by their injuries.

The erroneous opinions given me on the foregoing point, I consider to have been induced by my informants drawing false and extreme conclusions from the certainly very obvious fact of a want of delicacy or decency in general conduct and language, especially on the part of the girls.

But how should the language of these boys and girls be other than it is, when that of the adults among whom, and under whose authority they work, is so bad?—and how should the girls (or boys either) be able to retain personal delicacy or decency when there is usually only one place in a manufactory for men and women, boys and girls, to answer the calls of physical nature?—or where the ladders and steps are so high and so nearly perpendicular that girls ascending and descending are exposed to all who are in the room beneath ? If they are carrying any weight which extends the arms, the exposure is quite unavoidable. The circumstance is much too common to excite any particular observation; but, in this process of commonizing, the individuals lose the sense of delicacy.

R. H. HORNE, sub-commissioner; P.P. 1843, vol. XV, p. Q 15.

10

Shocking Incident in Sheffield

———————

Whilst this Report was in the press an occurrence took place in Sheffield which corroborates the debased character of the juvenile classes. An inquest was held on the body of a girl who, after lying in the street in the broad day-light for three-quarters of an hour, had eventually died in fits. The following is an extract from the evidence of the policeman who found her:—'Thomas Wakefield, Policeman No. 22. Between 2 and 3 on Saturday afternoon, I was going home on Division-street, and was called back by a neighbour. I was not on duty, but in plain clothes. I was told there was a woman very drunk in the street, and *the boys were taking very indecent liberties with her.* I went to the place, and found her laid on the causeway, by the house side, *with her petticoats round her middle.* I pulled them down, and asked if any one knew her.' The following is from the summing up of the coroner:— 'It appeared that *after the people in Division-street had permitted her to lie and be tumbled about by a crowd of boys for three quarters of an hour,* she was then brought to the office by Wakefield, who was not then on duty . . .'

Report by J. C. SYMONS, on the trades of Sheffield; P.P. 1843, vol. XIV, p. E 16.

II

Saturday Night in Leeds

On Saturday evening, the 24th of April, I went, accompanied by Inspector Childs and three police officers, to visit the low places resort of the working classes of Leeds. We started soon after nine o'clock, and visited about a score of beer and public houses and as many lodging houses. We found the former crowded with lads and girls—a motley assemblage of thieves and youths of both sexes from the factories.

There were, on an average, about thirty in each house, and in each case ranged on the benches round the walls of the room, with a blazing fire, and well-lighted. I am confident that, of the 600 persons I saw in these places, not above one quarter, if so many, were turned of 25 years of age, and at least two-thirds were under age. In the beer-houses there were several more children. In almost all there was a sprinkling of professed prostitutes. In some, perhaps a third of them, several men and boys were pointed out to me as professed thieves. In some of these houses there was a speedy clearance of the company out of one room as we entered another, so that we saw only a part of the inmates . . .

A boy of 14 was sitting in one of the more decent houses by the side of his father, who told me he was his son, and that he worked all the week at the factory. This was at half-past ten at night, and yet his father seemed to be wholly unaware that there was anything wrong in bringing his child to a beer-house and keeping him up to that hour after a week's work in the factory. Now this man was to all appearance not below the average of the working classes in Leeds in point of character.

In some of these places we found a fiddle or some other instrument being played: these places were thronged as full as they could hold. In another dancing was going on in a good-sized room upstairs, where I found a dozen couples performing a country-dance; the females were all factory-girls and prostitutes; obscene attitudes and language accompany and form the chief zest to this amusement.

Not one of these dancers, boys or girls, was above 20 or 21 years of age, and most of them 16 and 17. The prostitutes were easily distinguished from the factory-girls by their tawdry finery and the bareness of their necks, although the costume and head-dress of the factory-girls is not altogether dissimilar. In many of these places there was convenience upstairs for the cohabitation of the company below.

The lodging-houses we visited were situated chiefly up narrow alleys running out of the Kirkgate, and are intermixed with working-class brothels. These alleys are wholly without sewerage; there is a gutter down the middle, but no underground channel whatever; they are in a filthy state. Some of the lodging-houses were wretched places—mere dens with no sort of comfort save a good fire: they had all, however, beds of some description, though in some I saw bundles of straw for the accommodation of an occasional surplus of 'company'. With the exception of Glasgow I have seen nothing more wretched than these places . . .

The most motley crew are usually assembled downstairs. In one we found a party having tea. A shabby-genteel youth in a frock coat, who looked like a broken-down swindler, was standing at the fire frying his supper with a frying-pan in his hand. In another corner a women was industriously frilling a cap at a German heater, which she had first been washing and ironing. Three very young dirty children were crouching round the fire; three rough-looking fellows were getting their supper in a corner; one old woman half-drunk abused the police, and another [woman] was suckling her child.

In nearly all we found some young children up at half-past ten o'clock; and in one room we found a girl with another in her lap, and two more sitting by themselves, all four fast asleep; the mother was not with them . . . Several of the smaller brothels were visited, but they were mostly empty, the inmates being at the beer-shops or about the streets. They presented a far more cleanly aspect than the lodging-houses . . .

Not one half of the working classes in Leeds occupy, I am told, above two rooms, one for living in, and one for sleeping in, called 'the lodging room'; occasionally if there is a large family the man and his wife will sleep down stairs, but generally one room serves for all. Hence an early initiation in scenes which blunt all pure feeling and open the road to every licence and debauchery.

Report by J. C. SYMONS; Children's Employment Commission (Trades & Manufactures); P.P. 1843, vol. XIV, pp. E 37–39.

12

Driven to Prostitution

It is impossible for young women to procure the necessaries of life, exclusive of dress, by the present wages they can earn as lace-runners. The consequence is that almost all become prostitutes, though not common street-walkers. This is an usual and, witness believes, a true cause assigned by young women for losing their virtue.

WILLIAM WATTS, MD, resident medical officer of the Nottingham Poor Law Union; P.P. 1843, vol. XIV, p. f 58.

* * *

Vast numbers of girls who have wrought in factories are driven to prostitution when they are deprived of employment; girls not belonging to the parish of Leeds, probably to distant parishes, in some cases to no parish at all, have absolutely no other alternative but that of prostitution when trade is low and times are bad, so that they have no employ in mills; this was the universal complaint when I was at the Workhouse Board.

WILLIAM OSBURN, in evidence; P.P. 1831–32, vol. XV, p. 467.

* * *

I think there is less whoring among the factory girls than among the lace-runners and glove-makers. They have not so much time.

JOSEPH CHAMBERLAYNE, churchwarden of St Mary's, Leicester; P.P. 1833, vol. XX, C 1, 26.

13

Wolverhampton's Prostitutes

We know from applications at the Board of Guardians that there are very dreadful resorts of iniquity and female profligacy in Wolverhampton of the very lowest description. The public prostitutes are chiefly supported by the working classes, such as farm labourers at the ironworks, etc. Thus we may see, that what we call improvident marriages, so prevalent amongst the miners, are indeed provident in this respect, as they go to prevent this debauchery, which is uncommon among miners.

MR PAYNE, clerk of the Wolverhampton Board of Guardians.

*   *   *

Some of the public-houses will have bad women to sit with the men, and bring customers to their house. There's a house close against the Seven Stars in Hall-street, Dudley, and the women go into the public-house and begin to talk and soon take off some of the men into their house with them. (From the evidence of a pikeman; his wife added:) We used to have the coal to carry up from the pit, and then when a parcel of women get together they are bound to talk about all that's transacted, and I used to hear women complaining of their husbands going to bad houses, and I do now sometimes.

*   *   *

The low prostitutes are supported by miners and canal boatmen. From Rolleston Yard, behind the old church, I have with a man or two and a good stick driven out near a hundred men on a Saturday night or Sunday morning. There are about eight brothels and some twenty prostitutes in the yard; and wives often go there to seek for their hsubands . . . Sometimes the wives have dreadful fights with the girls on these occasions. My stick has been the cause of great improvement since I have been here . . . The low order of colliers and canal boatmen know these low public-houses, and go to find the women at them and have drink with them. They are married men as well as single who resort to them.

MR CASTLE, Superintendent of Police, Wolverhampton; P.P. 1843, vol. XIII, pp. 107, 47, 82.

14

'Strangers to modesty'

In a nocturnal ramble [in Manchester] which I made for the purpose of observation . . . I remarked that the mode in which the prostitutes accost passers-by, was far less rude than in most other places. And this fact is explained by two circumstances. First, the more decent prostitutes flock to Manchester, because it is, in regard to promiscuous intercourse, the rendezvous of the wealthier classes (*gens comme il faut*). On this subject Mr Logan (a missionary who has made personal inquiry into this subject) naively says, 'There is not a single first-rate house for assignations in Rochdale, because the *gentlemen* always go to Manchester'. Secondly, prostitution for money has little scope amongst the inferior classes, where clandestine connexions are so common; and where chastity, instead of being the rule among the females, tends more and more to become the exception . . .

In congregating so many men, women, and children, together without any other object than Labour, there is full scope for the birth and growth of passions which eventually refuse to submit to constraint, and which end in unbridled licence. The union of the sexes, and the high temperature of the manufactories, act upon the organization like a tropical sun; and puberty is developed before age and education have matured the moral sentiments. The factory girls are strangers to modesty, their language is gross, and often obscene; and when they do not marry early, they form illicit connexions, which degrade them still more than premature marriage. It is a common occurrence to meet in the intervals of labour in the back streets, couples of males and females, which the caprice of the moment has brought together. Sometimes they accompany each other to the beer-shops, and thus accustom themselves to a double debauch . . .

I will here relate an occurrence which has made a deep impression on me . . . Entering into a brothel of the lowest order, I noticed a young female of decent appearance, who appeared to fill the situation of servant . . . The Superintendent of Police having had the politeness to put some questions to her, we learnt that this young female, after having worked thirteen hours in a factory, came to assist the mistress of the house in cleaning away the traces of the orgies of the preceding night, and when wanted, to supply the deficiency of the Messalines of the place. Habits of Labour, joined to those of Debauch; order and even decency, in the most abject vice!

LÉON FAUCHER, *Manchester in 1844; Its Present Condition and Future Prospects* (1844), trans. from the French, pp. 41–47.

15

Manchester Statistics

The number of factory girls who finally recruit the ranks of public prostitution is perhaps small; at least, out of fifty prostitutes who have entered the Manchester Penitentiary during the last four years, only eight proceeded from the factories, while twenty-nine had been in service. Three of these factory girls were admitted at the age of 15, one at 16, and one at even the age of 14.

The average proportion of illegitimate births at Manchester, during the years 1824, 1825, and 1826, was about one in twelve of all the births.

An estimate of sexual morality is scarcely possible to be reduced into figures; but if I may trust my own observations, and the general opinion of those with whom I have conversed and the spirit of our evidence, then a most discouraging view of the influence of factory life upon the morality of the female youth obtrudes itself . . .

DR HAWKINS'S medical reports to the Factory Commission; P.P. 1833, vol. XXI, D 3 p. 5.

16

A Very Curious Fact

Sir Anthony Carlisle, F.R.S., surgeon; for 40 years principal surgeon at Westminster Hospital, professor of anatomy at the Royal Academy, Royal College of Surgeons, etc.:

Question: It is sometimes alleged, in answer to these assertions and facts, which go to prove that this system of excessive labour [in textile factories] is also an immoral system, that the number of illegitimate children of females employed in mills and factories is fewer than among a similar number of females in other pursuits, should you consider that

that was conclusive evidence as to their superior state of morality?
—Quite the contrary; premature sexual intercourse, or promiscuous
sexual intercourse with very young females, almost invariably prevents
their being prolific; this is notorious with regard to those unfortunate
women who pass their lives in prostitution; they generally begin very
young, and they often pass to the middle period of life without even
once being pregnant; but it is a very curious fact with respect to those
women who have been sent to Botany Bay [the convict settlement in
New South Wales, near Sydney], where they have been kept from sexual
intercourse during a voyage extending to six or eight months, that they
often become prolific afterwards, though they may have been for many
years the lowest and most abandoned prostitutes.

P.P. 1831–2, vol. XV, p. 563.

17

Disgraceful Books

Some observations have been made upon the circumstances of females
in factories not having a greater proportion of illegitimate children
than females otherwise employed; do you conceive that the morality of
females in factories is as high as that of females otherwise occupied?
—As to their not having so many illegitimate children, the reason is
plain enough; there are certain books which have gone forth to inform
depraved persons of a way by which they may indulge their corrupt
passions, and still avoid having illegitimate children.

Do you mean that certain books, the disgrace of the age, have been
put forth and circulated among the females in factories, to the effect
you state?—Yes.

And you attribute the circumstance of there being fewer illegitimate
children to that disgusting fact?—Yes.

BENJAMIN BRADSHAW, cloth-dresser, of Holbeck Moor, near Leeds, in
evidence given to Sadler's Committee; P.P. 1831–32, vol. XV, p. 159.

18

'Drugs and Stuff'

There are a good many that have bastards that work in factories. I do not know that they would be turned away for that ... I have frequently heard that they prevent themselves from having children. They do it by taking drugs and stuff. They go to some old woman for advice when they find themselves going with child. I never heard it said there were any books that they read to teach them that, or anything of the sort. I do remember hearing of one book of that kind. It was found at our place. It is two or three years ago. The overlooker in the other room, I think, got it from one of the girls. I do not think he found her reading it: he found it laid somewhere. If I recollect aright, he returned it back to them.

JOHN HANNAM, in Mr Drinkwater's collection of evidence; Factory Commission; P.P. 1833, vol. XX, C 1.

19

'Most indecent practices'

From other witnesses the Committee has heard evidence respecting means of prevention of breeding in young females ... Do you know any thing of that occurring in your district?—I have frequently heard from the parents of young persons and others engaged in factories, hints and remarks from which I certainly gathered that means of that description were resorted to, to prevent the effect of promiscuous intercourse in the way of progeny; and I believe also, from what I have heard, that there are sometimes practices resorted to in the working-rooms of the most indecent description which have been broadly hinted to me, but which common delicacy prevented my making any further inquiry about.

Do you know whether they were means to prevent abortion or to prevent pregnancy?—I am not aware what they were exactly . . .

Do you know whether any printed papers detailing the use of such means, or books, have been circulated among the females?—It was reported to me more than two years ago, I believe when Carlile came round to lecture in our part of the county, that he had either published or exposed for sale a book of the description which is referred to, but I never had an opportunity of ascertaining the fact; I merely heard the report of it.

REV. G. S. BULL, in evidence; P.P. 1831–32, vol. XV, p. 488.

20

'What is Love'

. . . What a dreadful thing it is, that health and beauty cannot be encouraged and extended, that love cannot be enjoyed, without the danger of a conception, when that conception is not desired, when it is a positive danger to self and to society . . .

What is to be done to remedy this evil? There is something to be done: a means has been discovered, a simple means more criminal in the neglect than in the use . . . Here, as in every other case of disease or other evil, *it is better to prevent than to cure*, and here, *prevention is most simply practicable, a means within the reach of all* . . .

I think this plan for the prevention of conceptions good, and after three years of consideration . . . I publicly say it. Still, it is not my plan; it was not sought after by me; it was submitted to my consideration; and, I am informed, that it was introduced into this country by Mr Owen of New Lanark. It was suggested to Mr Owen, that, in his new establishments, the healthy state of the inhabitants would tend to breed an excess of children. The matter was illustrated and explained to him, so that he felt the force of it. He was also told, that, on the continent, the women used some means of preventing conception, which were uniformly successful. Mr Owen set out for Paris to discover the process. He consulted the most eminent physicians and assured himself of what was the common practice among their women, that the female was always prepared to absorb the semen and its influence by a small piece of sponge, at the time of coition, and not to allow it to impregnate the genital vessel . . .

It shocks the mind of a woman, at first thought, that never dreampt of such a thing; but once practised, all prejudice flies and gratification must be the consequence. To weak and sickly females, to those to whom pregnancy and parturition are dangerous; . . . the discovery is a real blessing. And it is a real blessing in all other cases, where children are not desired. It will become the very bulwark of love and wisdom, of beauty, health, and happiness . . .

Since the subject of this article was first hinted in *The Republican*, I have received a multitude of letters, from all parts of the country, asking, begging, praying for, offering to pay for, more information upon this important subject; some from poor men, who feel that they are getting too large a family; some from medical men, who consider the discovery a great acquisition to professional knowledge; and many of the profession in London, I know have recommended it to delicate ladies; some from persons merely curious to learn the process; some few anonymous letters; but the bulk signed with real name and address.

I have seen copies of two handbills that have been extensively circulated upon the subject. The first was rather coarsely drawn up, and was that which Mary Fildes of Manchester or Stockport sent me and others a copy, of a bundle that was entrusted to her to be distributed. She assumed much offence at it, at the time; but I have since been informed, from good authority, that she has thought better of the matter, and has become a convert to its great utility and importance. The following is a copy of that now in circulation.

To the Married of Both Sexes of the Working People.

'This paper is addressed to the most reasonable and considerate among you, the most numerous and most useful class of society. It is not intended to produce vice and debauchery, but to destroy vice and put an end to debauchery.

'It is a great truth, often told and never denied, that where there are too many working people in any trade or manufacture, they are worse paid than they ought to be paid, and are compelled to work more hours than they ought to work. When the number of working people in any trade or manufacture has for some years been too great, wages are reduced very low, and the working people become little better than slaves. When wages have been thus reduced to a very small sum, working people can no longer maintain their children as all good and respectable people wish to maintain their children, but are compelled to neglect them; to send them to different employments; to Mills and Manufactories, at a very early age. The misery of these poor children cannot be described, and need not be described to you, who witness them and deplore them every day of your lives.

'Many indeed among you are compelled for a bare subsistence to labour incessantly from the moment you rise in the morning to the moment you lie down again at night, without even the hope of ever being better off.

'The sickness of yourselves and your children, the privation and pain and premature death of those you love but cannot cherish as you wish, need only be alluded to. You know all these evils too well.

'And what, you will ask, is the remedy? How are we to avoid these miseries? The answer is short and plain: the means are easy. Do as other people do, to avoid having more children than they wish to have, and can easily maintain.

'What is done by other people is this. A piece of soft sponge is tied by a bobbin or penny ribbon, and inserted before the sexual intercourse takes place, and is withdrawn again as soon as it has taken place. Many tie a piece of sponge to each end of the ribbon, and they take care not to use the same sponge again until it has been washed. If the sponge be large enough, that is, as large as a green walnut, or a small apple, it will prevent conception, and thus, without diminishing the pleasures of married life, or doing the least injury to the health of the most delicate woman, both the woman and her husband will be saved from all the miseries which having too many children produces.

'By limiting the number of children, the wages both of children and of grown up persons will rise; the hours of working will be no more than they ought to be; you will have some time for recreation, some means of enjoying yourselves rationally, some means as well as some time for your own and your children's moral and religious instruction...

'But when it has become the custom here as elsewhere, to limit the number of children, so that none need have more than they wish to have, no man will fear to take a wife, all will be married while young—debauchery will diminish—while good moral and religious duties will be promoted.

'You cannot fail to see that this address is intended solely for your good. It is quite impossible that those who address you can receive any benefit from it, beyond the satisfaction which every benevolent person, every true Christian, must feel, at making you comfortable, healthy, and happy.'

Here, it is clear, that there is nothing injurious to health; nothing but what must promote health, by removing all dread from the necessary practice of intercourse between the sexes. Nor is to be called an indecent matter. The men, who have been instrumental in making this matter known in this country, are all elderly men, fathers of families of children grown up to be men and women, and men of first rate moral character, and first rate learning, and some of the first politicians and philosophers that ever lived in this or in any other country . . .

From RICHARD CARLILE's article in *The Republican*, vol. XI, January 7 to July 1, 1825; pp. 562–564.

THE STATE OF THE TOWNS

(*a*) A GAZETTEER OF DISGUSTING PLACES

The towns, large and small, in which the people lived, were, judged by modern standards, dreadful places, filled with repulsive sights and horrid smells, and lacking in almost everything that make for health and happiness.

The facts are beyond dispute, and indeed it is almost impossible to exaggerate their abominable character. But we should not forget that we are living after more than a hundred years of devoted and persistent attention to the problems of public health. The men of those changeful years, when the population was increasing by leaps and bounds and the rapidly growing towns were never big enough to take the numbers clamouring for house room, were very differently placed. They had next to nothing to go on. They simply did not know what to do.

In themselves the problems were not altogether new. There had usually been overcrowding in the towns, where the houses were close packed within the encircling walls and were unprovided with water supply or drains, when they were poorly lit and ventilated and the accommodation they afforded was cramped and insufficient. There had always been dunghills before the door, which was not always wreathed in roses. Fever and other diseases were regular visitants, and crime and vice were equally commonplace. Poverty was the common lot, and stench and squalor were accepted as part of the natural order.

But the Industrial Revolution, though it did not create the problems, made them infinitely worse. Those dunghills, for instance: in the old towns and villages they were nothing like the menace they assumed when, unblown upon by country breezes, they made such horrid accumulations in the heart of the thickly populated cities. Everyone was agreed on their nastiness; something ought to be done about them—but what? There were no sanitary inspectors, no medical officers of health, no sanitary regulations to be complied with by order of the 'council'. And no 'council' either that could be called upon to take action, since the municipal corporations were not reformed until 1835, and even then required some years to get into their stride. Overcrowding was inevitable, since there were hosts of people requiring to be housed as quickly, and as cheaply, as possible; and since there was no mechanical transport, public or private, the dwellings had to be erected within walking distance of the places of work.

As the years passed, and the problems became ever more pressing, a race of 'sanitarians' arose, most but not all of them medical men. Their efforts were magnificent in the circumstances, but they had so little knowledge to go upon. Why, they did not even know that there are such things as germs! This explains the mention of 'noxious exhalations', 'effluvia', and something that was called 'miasma'.

Appended to the documents that follow in this section are the names of men who ought to be held in high honour as being among the first and most dedicated of preachers and practitioners of public health. Heading the list is Dr Kay, who by this time had moved to London. Hardly second in importance was Dr Southwood Smith (1788–1861) whose name has already appeared in our pages. As a young man he was minister of a Unitarian congregation in Edinburgh, but he turned to medicine and in 1820 set up as a medical practitioner in London. There he came under the influence of the Utilitarian philosopher Jeremy Bentham, and it was he who, in accordance with Bentham's will, carried out an anatomical dissection of his remains and pronounced over them the funeral discourse. In 1824 Southwood Smith was appointed physician to the London Fever Hospital and became known as an authority on epidemics. He came to the conclusion that the main cause was dirt, and in 1838 he was given his chance to prove it, when Chadwick (see the next section) secured his appointment as an investigator of London's worst fever spots.

In this work he was ably assisted by Dr Neil Arnott (1788–1874), a Scottish farmer's son who became a shop assistant and then moved to London, where he 'walked the wards' at St George's Hospital. Aberdeen granted him his M.D. in 1814, and until 1855 he practised in London. Among his contributions to public welfare were the inventions of a water-bed, a smokeless grate, and a ventilator.

Jelinger Cookson Symons (1809–1860) was a country parson's son who was commissioned in 1835 by the Home Office to inquire into the condition of the hand-loom weavers who were among the last (and most unfortunate) survivors of the Domestic system of industry; later, as we have seen, he was a commissioner to enquire into the state of the mining population in the north of England, and in 1848 he was made an inspector of schools. James Smith (1789–1850), of Deanston, was a nephew of Archibald Buchanan (see *Child Labour (b)*), and at the age of 18 was put in charge of the cotton-mills at Deanston, Perthshire; later he specialized in the production of machinery for mills and agriculture. Soon after his removal to London in 1842 he was appointed one of the commissioners to inquire into the sanitary condition of large towns.

Of the descriptions themselves, it may be recalled that Mr and Mrs Sidney Webb in their study of Statutory Authorities for Special Purposes in Local Government expressed their opinion that the 'climax of horrors' was reached in some of the slums of the Scottish towns, mentioning in particular the dunghill at Greenock.

The last document in this section (No. 25) is drawn from the Report of the Committee appointed to inquire into the Health of Towns in 1840, that met under the chairmanship of a sanitary-minded M.P., Robert Aglionby Slaney (1792–1862). This was the first of a series of similar reports that were published in the eighteen-forties (see next section), and the extract is included here since it is, at one and the same time, a concise summary of the prevailing evils, something in the nature of an apologia in its emphasis on the population explosion (as we should call it) of the time, and a plea for Government action.

I

Manchester in 1795

The new streets built within these few years have nearly doubled the size of the town. Most of them are wide and spacious, with excellent and large houses, principally of brick made on the spot, but they have a flight of steps projecting nearly the breadth of the pavement, which makes it very inconvenient for foot passengers. When two people meet, one must either go into the horse road, or over the flight of steps, which in the night time is particularly dangerous, as the lamps are not always lighted. Very few of the streets are yet flagged, which makes the walking in them, to strangers, very disagreeable.

As Manchester may bear comparison with the metropolis itself in the rapidity with which whole streets have been raised, and in its extension on every side towards the surrounding country; so it unfortunately vies with, or exceeds, the metropolis in the closeness with which the poor are crowded in offensive, dark, damp, and incommodious habitations, a too fertile source of disease! The mischievous effects proceeding from this cause are so clearly stated, and the remedies so ably suggested in a paper addressed by Dr Ferriar to the Committee for the regulation of the police in Manchester, that we are persuaded we shall do a useful service in making it more extensively known by reprinting the most material parts of it:

In some parts of the town, cellars are so damp as to be unfit for habitations ... The poor often suffer from the shattered state of cellar windows. This is a trifling circumstance in appearance, but the consequences to the inhabitants are of the most serious kind. Fevers are among the most usual effects; and I have often known consumptions which could be traced to this cause. Inveterate rheumatic complaints, which disable the sufferer from every kind of employment, are often produced in the same manner ... I am persuaded that mischief frequently arises, from a practice common in many back streets, of leaving the vaults of the privies open. I have often observed, that fevers prevail most in houses exposed to the effluvia of dunghills in such situations. In a house in Bootle Street, most of the inhabitants are paralytic, in consequence of their situation in a blind alley, which excludes them from light and air. Consumption, distortion, and idiocy, are common in such recesses . . .

The lodging houses, near the extremities of the town, produce many fevers, not only by want of cleanliness and air, but by receiving the most offensive objects into beds, which never seem to undergo any attempt towards cleansing them, from their first purchase till they rot under their tenants . . . The horror of those houses cannot easily be described; a lodger fresh from the country often lies down in a bed, filled with infection by its last tenant, or from which the corpse of a victim to fever has only been removed a few hours before . . .

The prevalence of fever among persons employed in cotton mills might be lessened by an attention on the part of the overseers to the following circumstances, besides a due regard to ventilation. Personal cleanliness should be strongly recommended and encouraged; and the parents of children so employed, should be enjoined to wash them every morning and evening, to keep their shoes and stockings in good condition, and above all, never to send them to work early in the morning without giving them food.

JOHN AIKIN, MD, *A Description of the Country from thirty to forty miles round Manchester* (1795), p. 192.

2

Dr Kay's Manchester

The greatest portion of those districts inhabited by the labouring population, especially of those situated beyond Great Ancoats-street, are of very recent origin; and from the want of proper police [municipal] regulations are untraversed by common sewers. The houses are ill soughed [drained], often ill ventilated, unprovided with privies, and in consequence, the streets which are narrow, unpaved, and worn into deep ruts, become the common receptacle of mud, refuse, and disgusting ordure . . .

The state of the streets powerfully affects the health of the inhabitants. Sporadic cases of typhus chiefly appear in those which are narrow, ill ventilated, unpaved, or which contain heaps of refuse, or stagnant pools. The confined air and noxious exhalations, which abound in such places, depress the health of the people, and on this account contagious diseases are also most rapidly propagated there.

The operation of these causes is exceedingly promoted by their reflex influence on the manners. The houses, in such situations, are uncleanly, ill provided with furniture; an air of discomfort if not of squalid and loathsome wretchedness pervades them, they are often dilapidated, badly drained, damp; and the habits of their tenants are gross—they are ill-fed, ill-clothed, and uneconomical—at once spendthrifts and destitute—denying themselves the comforts of life, in order that they may wallow in the unrestrained licence of animal appetite. . .

In some districts of the town exist evils so remarkable as to require more minute description. A portion of low, swampy ground, liable to be frequently inundated, and to constant exhalation, is included between a high bank over which the Oxford Road passes, and a bend of the river Medlock, where its course is impeded by weirs. This unhealthy spot lies so low that the chimneys of its houses, some of them three storeys high, are little above the level of the road. About two hundred of these habitations are crowded together in an extremely narrow space, and are inhabited by the lowest Irish. Most of these houses have also cellars, whose floor is scarcely elevated above the level of the water flowing in the Medlock. The soughs are destroyed, or out of repair; and these narrow abodes are in consequence always damp, and on the slightest rise of the river, which is a frequent occurrence, are flooded to the depth of several inches.

This district has been frequently the haunt of thieves and desperadoes who defied the law, and is always inhabited by a class resembling savages in their appetites and habits. It is surrounded on every side by some of the largest factories of the town, whose chimneys vomit forth dense clouds of smoke, which hang heavily over this insalubrious region.

Near the centre of the town, a mass of buildings inhabited by prostitutes and thieves, is intersected by narrow and loathsome streets, and close courts defiled with refuse . . . In Parliament-street there is only one privy for 380 inhabitants, which is placed in a narrow passage, whence its effluvia infest the adjacent houses, and must prove a most fertile source of disease. In this street also, cess pools with open grids have been made, close to the doors of the houses, in which disgusting refuse accumulates, and whence its noxious effluvia constantly exhale.

The state of the streets and houses between Store-street and Travis-street, and London Road, is exceedingly wretched—especially those built on some irregular and broken mounds of clay, on a steep declivity descending into Store-street. These narrow avenues are rough, irregular gullies, down which filthy streams percolate; and the inhabitants are crowded in dilapidated abodes, or obscure and damp cellars, in which it is impossible for the health to be preserved . . .

The Irk, black with the refuse of dye-works erected on its banks, receives excrementitious matters from some sewers in this portion of the town—the drainage from the gas-works, and filth of the most pernicious character from bone-works, tanneries, size manufactories, etc. Immediately beneath Ducie-Bridge, in a deep hollow between two high banks, it sweeps round a large cluster of the most wretched and dilapidated buildings of the town. The course of the river is here impeded by a weir, and a large tannery eight stories high (three of which stories are filled with skins exposed to the atmosphere, in some stage of the processes to which they are subjected), towers close to this crazy labyrinth of buildings. This group of buildings is called 'Gibraltar', and no site can well be more insalubrious than that in which it is built.

Pursuing the course of the river on the other side of Ducie-bridge, other tanneries, size manufactories, and tripe-houses occur. The parish burial ground occupies one side of the stream, and a series of courts of the most singular and unhealthy character the other . . .

One nuisance frequently occurs in these districts of so noxious a character, that it ought, at the earliest period, to be suppressed by legal interference. The houses of the poor sometimes surround a common area, into which the doors and windows open at the back of the dwelling. Porkers, who feed pigs in the town, often contract with the inhabitants to pay some small sum for the rent of their area, which is immediately covered with pig-styes and converted into a dung-heap and receptacle of the putrescent garbage which is now heedlessly flung into it from the surrounding dwellings. The offensive odour which sometimes arises from these areas cannot be conceived.

There is no common slaughter-house in Manchester, and those which exist are chiefly situated in the narrowest and most filthy streets in the town. The drainage from these houses, deeply tinged with blood, and impregnated with other animal matters, frequently flows down the common surface drain of the street, and stagnates in the ruts and pools . . .

These districts are inhabited by a turbulent population, which, rendered reckless by dissipation and want,—misled by the secret intrigues, and excited by the inflammatory harangues of demagogues, has frequently committed daring assaults on the liberty of the more peaceful portions of the working classes, and the most frightful devastations on the property of their masters. . . . The police form, in fact, so weak a screen against the power of the mob, that popular violence is now, in almost every instance, controlled by the presence of military force . . .

DR J. P. KAY, *The Moral and Physical Condition of the Working Classes . . . in Manchester* (1832), pp. 12–34.

3

Manchester's Deficiencies

The conjoined towns of Manchester and Salford, commonly known by the inclusive name of Manchester (consisting of eight townships . . . with a population of probably 260,000 souls) is a huge overgrown village, built according to no definite plan.

The factories have necessarily sprung up along the watercourses, which are the rivers Irk, Irwell, and Medlock, and the Rochdale Canal, and the dwellings of the work-people have kept increasing on the confines of the factory districts. The interest and convenience of individual manufacturers and owners of property has determined the growth of the town and the manner of that growth, while the comfort, health, and happiness of the inhabitants have not been considered till subsequently, if indeed (which is doubtful) they are much regarded even now.

Until twelve years ago there was no paving and sewering Act in any of the townships; and even in the township of Manchester, containing in the year 1831 upwards of 142,000 inhabitants, this was the case; and the disgraceful condition of the streets and sewers on the invasion of the cholera you have no doubt learned from Dr Kay's able and valuable pamphlet. At this present time the paving of the streets proceeds rapidly in every direction, and great attention is given to the drains . . .

Manchester has no building Act, and hence, with the exception of certain central streets, over which the Police Act gives the Commissioners power, each proprietor builds as he pleases.

New cottages, with or without cellars, huddled together row behind row, may be seen springing up in many parts, but especially in the township of Manchester, where the land is higher in price than land for cottage sites in other townships is. With such proceedings as these the authorities cannot interfere. A cottage row may be badly drained, the streets may be full of pits, brimful of stagnant water, the receptacle of dead cats and dogs, yet no one may find fault.

The number of cellar residences is very great in all quarters of the town . . . That it is an evil must be obvious on the slightest consideration, for how can a hole underground of from 12 to 15 feet square admit of ventilation so as to fit it for a human habitation?

We have no authorized inspector of dwellings and streets . . . Manchester has no public park or other ground where the population can walk and breathe the fresh air. New streets are rapidly extending in every direction, and so great already is the expanse of the town, that those who live in the more populous quarters can seldom hope to see the green face of nature . . . In this respect Manchester is disgracefully defective, more so, perhaps, than any other town in the empire. Every advantage of this nature has been sacrificed to the getting of money in the shape of ground rents . . .

From the letter of DR ROBERTON, Manchester surgeon, to the chairman (R. A. Slaney, M.P.) of the Select Committee on the Health of Towns; P.P. 1840, vol. XI, Appendix No. 2, pp. 221–222.

4

Black Spots of Bethnal Green

The district of Bethnal Green contains upwards of 70,000 inhabitants; in the greater part of it the streets are not close, nor are the houses crowded. On the contrary, large open spaces of ground intervene between them; but in one part the population is as densely crowded as in the closest and most thickly populated parts of the city. I notice the places about to be described in the order in which I visited them . . .

Punderson's Gardens. A long narrow street; the houses have no sunk area, and the ground floor is extremely damp. Along the centre of the street is an open, sunk gutter, in which filth of every kind is allowed to accumulate and putrefy. A mud bank on each side commonly keeps the contents of this gutter in their situation; but sometimes, and especially in wet weather, the gutter overflows; its contents are poured into the neighbouring houses, and the street is rendered nearly impassable. The privies are close upon the footpath of the street, being separated from it only by a parting of wood. The street is wholly without drainage of any kind. Fever constantly breaks out in it, and extends from house to house . . .

Lamb's Fields. An open area, of about 700 feet in length, and 300 feet in width; of this space about 300 feet are constantly covered by stagnant water, winter and summer. In the part thus submerged there is always a quantity of putrefying animal and vegetable matter, the odour of which at the present moment is most offensive. An open filthy ditch encircles this place, which at the western extremity is from 8 to 10 feet wide. Into this part of the ditch the privies of all the houses of a street called North-street open; these privies are completely uncovered, and the soil from them is allowed to accumulate in the open ditch. Nothing can be conceived more disgusting than the appearance of this ditch for an extent of from 300 to 400 feet, and the odour of the effluvia from it is at this moment most offensive!

Lamb's Fields is the fruitful source of fever to the houses which immediately surround it, and to the small streets which branch off from it. Particular houses were pointed out to me from which entire families have been swept away, and from several of the streets fever is never absent.

Alfred and Beckwith Rows consist of a number of buildings, each of which is divided into two houses, one back and the other front; each house is divided into two tenements, and each tenement is occupied by a different family. These habitations are surrounded by a broad open drain, in a filthy condition. Heaps of filth are accumulated in the spaces meant for gardens in front of the houses. The houses have common privies open, and in the most offensive condition. I entered several of the tenements. In one of them, on the ground floor, I found six persons occupying a very small room, two in bed, ill with fever. In the room above this were two more persons in one bed, ill with fever. In this same room a woman was carrying on the process of silk-weaving. The window of the room is small, capable, if wide open, of ventilating the room but very imperfectly; yet this window is not only kept permanently closed, but is carefully pasted all round, so that not the slightest breath of air can enter. On remonstrating against this constant and total exclusion of air, I was told by the woman at work that they are obliged to stop up the window, to prevent the drying of the silk, which is always weighed out to them when they receive it, and they are expected to return the same weight.

North-street. The situation is close; the houses are in a most miserable condition, surrounded by vast collections of filth. Most of the houses are occupied by pig-dealers, and the filth produced by the pigs is seldom or never cleaned away. The stench here is dreadful.

Virginia Row. In the centre of this street is a gutter, into which potato parings, the refuse of animal and vegetable matters of all kinds, the dirty water from the washing of clothes and of the houses, are all poured, and there they stagnate and putrefy. In a direct line from Virginia Row to Shoreditch, a mile in extent, all the lanes, courts, and alleys in the neighbourhood pour their contents into the centre of the main street, where they stagnate and putrefy . . .

After this full account of Bethnal Green, I have thought it unnecessary to enter into a minute description of the state of Whitechapel, because for the most part it would be but a repetition of the same circumstances. The greater part of Whitechapel is very badly drained; in many places the population is densely crowded; the streets, courts, and alleys, as at present constructed, admit of no current of air; large collections of putrefying matter are allowed constantly to remain in the neighbourhood of the houses, and the houses themselves are extremely filthy.

DR SOUTHWOOD SMITH, supplement on Bethnal Green and Whitechapel; appended to 4th Report of the Commissioners appointed under the Poor Law Amendment Act, 1838; P.P. vol. XXVIII, pp. 88–91.

5

My Visit to the Wynds of Glasgow

Though in point of wages the cotton hand-loom weavers are decidedly inferior to every other class of operatives, yet in point of physical and social debasement there exists a portion of the population in the district

I have investigated, very many degrees worse—I allude to the dense and motley community who inhabit the low districts of Glasgow, consisting chiefly of the alleys leading out of the High-street, the lanes in the Calton, but particularly the closes and wynds which lie between the Trongate and the Bridgegate, the salt-market and Maxwell-street. These districts contain a motley population, consisting in almost all the lower branches of occupation; but chiefly of a community whose sole means of subsistence consists in plunder and prostitution.

Under the escort of that vigilant officer, Captain Miller, the superintendent of the Glasgow Police, I have four times visited these districts, once in the morning and three times at night; I have seen human degradation in some of its worst phases, both in England and abroad, but I can advisedly say, that I did not believe until I visited the wynds of Glasgow, that so large an amount of filth, crime, misery and disease existed on one spot in any civilized country.

The wynds consist of long lanes, so narrow that a cart could with difficulty pass along them; out of these open the 'closes', which are courts about 15 to 20 feet square, round which the houses, mostly of three stories high, are built; the centre of the court is the dung-hill, which is probably the most lucrative part of the estate to the laird in most instances, and which it would consequently be esteemed an invasion of the rights of property to remove. The houses are for the most part let in flats, either to the lowest class of labourers or prostitutes, or to lodging-keepers; these latter places are the grand resort and favourite abodes of all those to whom a local habitation and a name are professionally inconvenient. They are likewise the resting place of outcasts of every grade of wretchedness and destitution. In the more costly of these abodes, where separate beds are furnished at the price of 3d per night, the thieves and prostitutes chiefly congregate.

I shall not easily forget the cool sangfroid with which a housebreaker whom the superintendent of police detected in bed in a snug corner of these dens, obeyed his invitation to accompany him to the office, or the composure with which his comrades (of whom there were at least a dozen), male and female in the apartment, contemplated the scene from their respective beds. Considering that our party consisted of five unarmed men, in the dead of the night, and in the centre of a savage and desperate population of at least 7,000 or 8,000 persons—the calmness of the whole proceeding, the perfect recognition of the moral power of discipline, and its ascendancy in the very stronghold of outrage, was, to say the least, singularly impressive . . . As soon as the housebreaker had completed his toilet, an operation which he diversified with various pleasantries, divided between the officers and his fair bedfellow, who was making sundry vain efforts to conceal herself from their scrutiny, we proceeded to other lairs in the neighbourhood without molestation or hindrance. Such is the discipline preserved by the police, who are the only persons who ever visit these habitations, at least *at night*, when its population are alone assembled.

In the lower lodging-houses ten, twelve, and sometimes twenty persons of both sexes and all ages sleep promiscuously on the floor in different degrees of nakedness. These places are, generally as regards dirt, damp and decay, such as no person of common humanity to animals would stable his horse in . . . It is my firm belief that penury, dirt, misery, drunkenness, disease and crime culminate in Glasgow to a pitch unparalleled in Great Britain.

Reports from Assistant Hand-loom Weavers' Commissioners: J. C. SYMONS on the South of Scotland; P.P. 1839, vol. XLII, p. 51.

6

'Worse off than wild animals'

There were no privies or drains there, and the dungheaps received all the filth which the swarm of wretched inhabitants could give; and we learnt that a considerable part of the rent of the houses was paid by the produce of dungheaps. Thus, worse off than wild animals, many of which withdraw to a distance and conceal their ordure, the dwellers in these courts had converted their shame into a kind of money by which their lodging was to be paid.

The interiors of these houses and their inmates corresponded with their exteriors. We saw half-dressed wretches, crowding together to be warm; and in one bed, although in the middle of the day, several women were imprisoned under a blanket, because so many others who had on their backs all the articles of dress that belonged to the party were then out of doors in the streets.

This picture is so shocking that, without ocular proof, one would be disposed to doubt the possibility of the facts; and yet there is perhaps no old town in Europe that does not furnish parallel examples.

DR NEIL ARNOTT's account of Glasgow slums; P.P. 1842, Lords, vol. 26, p. 24.

7

'Only nicknames, like dogs'

The indiscriminate mixture of workpeople and their children in the immediate vicinity, and often in the same rooms with persons whose character was denoted by the question and answer more than once exchanged, 'When were you last washed?' 'When I was last in prison', was only one mark of the entire degradation to which they had been brought.

The working classes living in these districts were equally marked by the abandonment of every civil or social regulation. Asking some children in one of the rooms in which they swarmed in Glasgow what were their names, they hesitated to answer, when one of the inmates said, they called them ——, mentioning some nicknames. 'The fact is,' observed Captain Miller, the superintendent of police, 'they really have no names. Within this range of buildings I have no doubt I should be able to find a thousand children who have no names whatever, or only nicknames, like dogs.'

E. CHADWICK, account of visit to the wynds of Edinburgh and Glasgow; P.P. 1842, Lords, vol. 26, pp. 132–133.

8

Back to Back in Liverpool

All the better class of houses in Liverpool are furnished with proper necessaries, and in many of the courts there is a due provision of such conveniences, but a large proportion of these courts are wretchedly off in this respect. Some have no privies at all; in others these buildings are in a dilapidated state, in many instances caused by the inhabitants themselves, who destroy them and burn the doors and windows as firewood, and if repaired by the landlord, they would not be allowed to remain whole for a month. There are no public necessaries . . . The courts and alleys are not cleansed at all by scavengers, being considered private property. There are no dust-bins, properly so called, but in the old borough or parish of Liverpool every morning dust-carts go round for the reception of dust, etc., that may be brought out by the inhabitants.

As in all large towns, the borough of Liverpool has its share of courts and alleys for the working population. Many of these, constructed within the last 10 or 15 years, are open, and afford comfortable dwellings, are well drained and clean, and are consequently healthy; others are of a very different class . . . The houses are generally built back to back, but this does not prevent a sufficient ventilation, as each room has three openings, viz. a door, a window, and a chimney; some of the courts are closed, some open; the cleansing of the courts is left to the inhabitants themselves, and some of these will be found to be as clean as the most favoured parts of any town, whilst others, inhabited by the idle and dissolute, are as filthy. The Irish population of Liverpool, by the census consisting of nearly 60,000, and those of the lower class, are so notoriously dirty in their habits, that the better class of English workmen will not reside in the same courts.

P.P. 1845, vol. XVIII, p. 84.

9

'I could not believe this at first'

There is one circumstance which very much affects the atmosphere in those districts [in Liverpool] in which the cellars are particularly; there is a great deal of broken ground, in which there are pits; the water accumulates in those pits, and of course at the fall of year there is a good deal of water in them, in which there have been thrown dead dogs and cats, and a great many offensive articles. This water is nevertheless used for culinary purposes. I could not believe this at first. I thought it was used only for washing, but I found that it was used by the poorer inhabitants for culinary purposes.

Was that owing to the want of a supply of water?—There is a good supply of water for the poor, if they had the means of preserving it. The water is turned on a certain number of hours during the day, four hours, perhaps; the poor go to the tap for it; it is constantly running; and each poor person fetches as much as they have pans to receive; but they are not well supplied with these articles, and in consequence they are frequently out of water. It is not sufficient for washing, or anything of that kind.

J. RIDDALL WOOD, in evidence; P.P. 1840, vol. XI, p. 132.

IO

Birmingham Features

The courts in Birmingham are extremely numerous; they exist in every part of the town, and a very large portion of the poorer classes of the inhabitants reside in them . . . The courts vary in the number of the houses which they contain, from four to twenty, and most of these houses are three stories high, and built, as it is termed, back to back. There is a wash-house, an ash-pit, and a privy at the end, or on one side of the court, and not unfrequently one or more pigsties and heaps of manure. Generally speaking, the privies in the old courts are in a most filthy condition. Many which we have inspected were in a state which renders it impossible for us to conceive how they could be used; they were without doors and overflowing with filth. We have also seen the privies of many of the manufactories in an equally disgusting condition, and have observed that those for the men and the women, both in the courts and the manufactory yards, were generally situated close to each other, and often so placed that it is impossible to go to them without being observed by and exposed to the remarks of the persons employed in the workshops . . .

Contagious fever, extending from house to house, and ravaging whole streets, and abiding almost constantly in certain localities, as it is described to do in some other large towns, is a condition so rare that it may be said to be almost unknown to the inhabitants of this burgh. On this subject we feel unable to do more than to point out a few circumstances in which Birmingham, perhaps, differs from most of those large towns in which fever constantly prevails, and in which its ravages are so formidable. These are—the elevated situation of the town —its excellent natural drainage, and its abundant supplies of water—the entire absence of cellars used as dwellings—the circumstances of almost every family having a separate house—and, lastly, the amount of wages received by the woiking classes, which may be regarded as generally adequate to provide the necessaries of life.

From a Report on the State of the Public Health in Birmingham by a committee of Physicians and Surgeons; P.P. 1843, vol. XIV, f 176–181.

II

'Most Filthy' Bradford

The general state of the surface of the streets of Bradford is respectable, but in most of the inferior and cross streets, chiefly inhabited by the working classes, the condition is quite otherwise. Few of those are paved at all; none of them properly. In some streets a piece of paving is laid half across the street, opposite one man's tenement, whilst his opposite neighbour contents himself with a slight covering of soft engine ashes, through which the native clay of the subsoil is seen protruding, with unequal surface, and pools of slop water and filth are visible all over the surface. The dungheaps are found in several parts in the streets, and open privies are seen in many directions. Large swill-tubs are placed in various places by pig-feeders for collecting the refuse from the families, for which they pay in some cases from 1d to 2d per week.

The chief sewerage, if sewerage it can be called, of the inferior streets and of the courts, is in open channels, and from the rough and unequal surface of the streets, the flow is tardy and the whole soil is saturated with sewage water. The main sewers are discharged either into the brook or into the terminus or basin of a canal which runs into the lower part of the town. The water of this basin is often so charged with decaying matter, that in hot weather bubbles of sulphureted hydrogen are continually rising to the surface, and so much is the atmosphere loaded with that gas, that watch-cases and other materials of silver become black in the pockets of the workmen employed near the canal. The stench is sometimes very strong, and fevers prevail much all around. Taking the general condition of Bradford, I am obliged to pronounce it to be the most filthy town I visited.

Report on the Sanatory Condition of Bradford, by JAMES SMITH, of Deanston; P.P. 1845, vol. XVIII, Pt. 2 Appendix, p. 315.

12

Sheffield Smoke and Grime

Sheffield is one of the dirtiest and most smoky towns I ever saw. There are a quantity of small forges without tall chimneys. The town is also very hilly, and the smoke ascends the streets, instead of leaving them. It is usual for children to wash before they go to bed, but not universal, and their bodies imbibe continual dust and grime. One cannot be long in the town without experiencing the necessary inhalation of soot, which accumulates in the lungs, and its baneful effects are experienced by all who are not accustomed to it. There are, however, numbers of persons in Sheffield who think the smoke healthy.

J. C. SYMONS; P.P. 1843, vol. XIV, E 11, 93.

13

The Filthy Yards of Leeds

The general arrangement of the streets and alleys of Leeds are in the older parts very much as in all old towns, somewhat irregular and narrow; but, fortunately for Leeds, the main street is of ample width ...

The row of streets running parallel to the river are, however, narrow, crooked, and irregular. Streets more recently formed are more ample in width, and there are many cheerful, open streets where the better classes reside. The lower classes here, as elsewhere, inhabit the less comfortable and less healthy localities along both sides of the Addle Beck . . . A number of dwellings which, from the damp and the pestilent effluvia arising from the decaying matter in the bottom of the Beck, combined with the smoke and fumes arising from the various works, are most unhealthy.

But by far the most unhealthy localities of Leeds are close squares of houses, or yards, as they are called, which have been erected for the accommodation of working people. Some of these, though situated in comparatively high ground, are airless from the enclosed structure, and being wholly unprovided with any form of under-drainage, or convenience, or arrangements for cleansing, are one mass of damp and filth . . . The ashes, garbage, and filth of all kinds are thrown from the doors and windows of the houses upon the surface of the streets and courts . . . The privies are few in proportion to the number of inhabitants. They are open to view both in front and rear, are invariably in a filthy condition, and often remain without the removal of any portion of the filth for six months. The feelings of the people are blunted to all seeming decency, and from the constantly contaminated state of the atmosphere, a vast amount of ill-health prevails, leading to listlessness, and inducing a desire for spirits and opiates; the combined influence of the whole condition causing much loss of time, increasing poverty, and terminating the existence of many in premature death.

Report by JAMES SMITH; P.P. 1845, vol. XVIII, pp. 312–313.

14

Halifax Fights the Dirt

The town of Halifax is in part very ancient, but has been greatly extended during the last thirty years . . . by the prosperity of the manufactures of the place, chiefly worsted spinning and weaving . . .

The streets are in general steep, and being, upon the whole, well paved, they are much washed by rain . . . There being little traffic . . . they are clean and tidy, with the fault, however, of much of the sewerage water having to run in open gutters.

Near the margin of the river there are some damp, wretched-looking dwellings, and there is in some localities a class of dwellings for the lower orders called *Folds*, which are a sort of courts or enclosed spaces. Most of these folds are very damp and filthy; the seats of poverty and disease. Such localities in every town are invariably found to be inhabited by the lowest grade of the working people, but who, in the case of Halifax, though in the midst of filth, and with a low state of finances and morals, are nevertheless inclined to be cleanly and tidy, but are kept in a depressed condition by the outward filth and effluvium which assails them at every step. Houses of this class generally belong to public-house keepers, or a class of operatives who have contrived to save a little money, sometimes in building clubs.

The water is of fair quality, and upon the whole rather abundant; though far short of the supply necessary for thorough cleansing. I found that the people of Halifax use water more liberally for washing their windows and floors, and even in some instances their lanes and streets, than in any other town I visited.

From JAMES SMITH's report; P.P. 1845, vol. XVIII, p. 317.

15

Nottingham's Insanitary Labyrinth

I believe that nowhere else shall we find so large a mass of inhabitants crowded into courts, alleys, and lanes, as in Nottingham, and those, too, of the worst possible construction. . . . The courts are almost always approached through a low-arched tunnel of some 30 or 36 inches wide, about 8 feet high, and from 20 to 30 feet long . . . They are noisome, narrow, unprovided with adequate means for the removal of refuse, ill-ventilated, and wretched in the extreme, with a gutter, or surface-drain, running down the centre; they have no back yards, and the privies are common to the whole court: altogether they present scenes of a deplorable character, and of surpassing filth and discomfort. It is just the same with lanes and and alleys . . . In all these confined quarters, too, the refuse is allowed to accumulate until, by its mass and its advanced putrefaction, it shall have acquired value as manure; and thus it is sold and carted away by the 'muck majors', as the collectors of manure are called in Nottingham.

The houses . . . are for the most part singularly defective, being erected in parallel ranks, three stories high, side to side and back to back, with one apartment in each storey, about 11 feet square, exclusive of a narrow staircase, under which is a small closet used for keeping victuals and coals. The lower room is used for all ordinary day-purposes; the second, generally is a bedroom; and the upper, very frequently as a workshop, occasionally both as a workshop and bedroom . . . It is common to find privies constructed under the dwellings, and equally common to find them exposed to the public gaze of the inhabitants of the courts, lanes, and alleys . . .

From J. R. MARTIN's report; P.P. 1845, vol. XVIII, pp. 250–253.

16

'Low and grovelling'

As a general characteristic of the working classes within my district, I should do them injustice were I to pronounce them intemperate. There are, however, too many instances wherein the pressure of poverty, inability to maintain decent appearances in clothing and household comforts, have led to a low and grovelling mode of living; and much immorality—especially immorality of language—prevails amongst the young of both sexes, more especially those who are employed in factories.

MR POOLE, reporting on Coventry; P.P. 1845, vol. XVIII, p. 263.

17

Not Enough Water in Bath

An epidemic smallpox raged at the end of the year 1837, and carried off upwards of 300 persons; yet of all that number I do not think there was a single gentleman, and not above two or three tradesmen. The residences of the labouring classes were pretty regularly visited, disease showing here and there a predilection for particular spots, and settling with full virulence in Avon-street and its off sets . . . Everything vile and offensive is congregated there. All the scum of Bath—its low prostitutes, its thieves, its beggars—are piled up in the dens rather than houses of which the street consists. Its population is the most disproportioned to the accommodation of any I have ever heard; and to aggravate the mischief, the refuse is commonly thrown under the staircase; and water more scarce than in any quarter of the town. It would hardly be an hyperbole to say that there is less water consumed than beer . . .

A permanent feature in the midst of this mass of physical and moral evils is the extraordinary number of illegitimate children; the offspring of persons who in all respects live together as man and wife. Without the slightest objection to the legal obligation, the moral degradation is such that marriage is accounted a superfluous ceremony, not worth the payment of the necessary fees; and on one occasion, when it was given out that they would be dispensed with, upwards of 50 persons from Avon-street, who had lived together for years, voluntarily came forward to enter into a union . . .

I have been rendered familiar with these places by holding a curacy in the midst of them for upwards of a year . . . I think these facts supply us with important conclusions. Whether we compare one part of Bath with another, or Bath with other towns, we find health rising in proportion to the improvements in residences; we find morality, in at least a great measure, following the same law.

REV. WHITWELL ELWIN; P.P., Lords, 1842, vol. 26, pp. 169–170.

18

'Windsor is the Worst'

Extensive as the improvements in the state of drainage of almost every town in these counties might be, there is no town amongst them in which there is so wide a field for improvement as Windsor, which from the contiguity of the palace, the wealth of the inhabitants, and the situation, might have been expected to be superior in this respect to any other provincial town.

Such, however, is not the case; for of all the towns visited by me, Windsor is the worst beyond all comparison.

From the gas-works at the end of George-street a double line of open, deep, black, and stagnant ditches extends to Clewer-lane. From these ditches an intolerable stench is perpetually rising, and produces fever of a serious character . . . The ditches of which I have spoken are sometimes emptied by carts; and on the last occasion their contents were purchased for the sum of £15 by the occupier of land in the parish of Clewer, whose meadows suffered from the extraordinary strength of the manure . . .

From the report on the counties of Berks, Bucks, and Oxon; P.P., Lords, 1842, vol. 27, p. 94.

19

Holyrood Not Fit for Her Majesty

In the thickly populated districts of Edinburgh, are there any common sewers open ?—Not in the town itself, but immediately in the suburbs; and it is the foul water from these ditches which is sprinkled over the land to irrigate it.

Is this for market gardens?—No, for grass; it is cut two or three times a year.

Have you heard of any consultation, or reference to the opinion of medical men, with regard to the evils of this practice to the inhabitants of the royal palace?—Lately, about two years ago, the Lord Advocate asked the opinions of the surgeons and physicians of the Queen in Scotland, with reference to the health of Holyrood in consequence of this practice, and they gave it as their opinion that it would not be a fit habitation for Her Majesty on that ground . . .

DR JAMES SIMPSON, examined before the Committee on the Health of Towns; P.P. 1840, vol. XI, p. 120.

20

Greenock's Monster Dunghill

In one part of Market Street is a dunghill—yet it is too large to be called a dunghill. I do not misstate its size when I say it contains a hundred cubic yards of impure filth, collected from all parts of the town. It is never removed; it is the stock-in-trade of a person who deals in dung; he retails it by cartfuls. To please his customers, he always keeps a nucleus, as the older the filth is the higher is the price. The proprietor has an extensive privy attached to the concern. This collection is fronting the public street; it is enclosed in front by a wall; the height of the wall is almost twelve feet, and the dung overtops it; the malarious moisture oozes through the wall, and runs over the pavement.

The effluvia all round about this place in summer is horrible. There is a land of houses adjoining, four stories in height, and in the summer each house swarms with myriads of flies; every article of food and drink must be covered, otherwise, if left exposed for a minute, the flies immediately attack it, and it is rendered unfit for use, from the strong taste of the dunghill left by the flies.

DR LAURIE; P.P., Lords, 1842, vol. 26, pp. 46-47.

21

A Nice Town, Inverness

Inverness is a nice town, situated in a most beautiful country, and with every facility for cleanliness and comfort. The people are, generally speaking, a nice people, but their sufferance of nastiness is past endurance. Contagious fever is seldom or ever absent; but for many years it has seldom been rife in its most pestiferous influences. The people owe this more to the kindness of Almighty God than to any means taken or observed for its prevention.

There are very few houses in town which can boast of either water-closet or privy, and only two or three public privies in the better part of the place exist for the great bulk of the inhabitants. Hence there is not a street, lane, or approach to it that is not disgustingly defiled at all times, so much so as to render the whole place an absolute nuisance. The *midden* is the chief object of the humble, and though enough of water for purposes of cleanliness may be had by little trouble, still as the ablutions are seldom, MUCH filth in-doors and out of doors *must* be their portion. When cholera prevailed in Inverness, it was more fatal than in almost any other town of its population in Britain.

DR J. I. NICHOL, Provost of Inverness; P.P., Lords, 1842, vol. 26, p. 43.

22

Homes and Habits of the Scottish Colliers

A few of the colliers' houses are good, but the great mass of them is very bad. The roof is frequently insufficient, admitting wind and rain in wet and windy weather . . . In some the rafters and thatch are quite rotten and decayed. I was in one house, shortly before I left Tranent, where the rafters were infested with bugs, which occasionally dropped down. In

329

the worst kind of these houses the apartment is ill supplied with light, the windows being only partially supplied with glass, and its place supplied with paper, bundles of rags, and old hats. In some of these houses the windows cannot be opened . . .

In the better houses of the colliers the furniture is ample, and in some is kept with great neatness and cleanliness; but in others, even where the furniture is good, there prevails a shocking amount of uncleanliness. . . . In some of these houses the females are so lazy and so filthy in their habits that they carry their ashes and cinders no farther than to a corner of the apartment, where they accumulate and have their bulk swollen by the addition of various impurities.

This wretchedness does not arise from want of money. These colliers are in receipt of 20s and 30s per week, and I have been informed by their employers that they might earn much more, would they turn out to work on Monday, instead of drinking, as they commonly do on that day, and even on others . . .

The floors of the cottages inhabited by colliers are composed generally of beaten earth. These floors are very dirty, and so uneven as to make a stranger almost fall. It is not uncommon to see holes and depressions in these floors that would contain a peck or two of sand. These holes have been formed in the course of time by various causes, by the wear and tear produced by heavy shoes, the breaking up of coals by the poker, and by the presence of water spilt upon the floor. No attempt is made in many cases to fill up these cavities, although this might be done at very little expense and trouble. The bedstead is generally covered with dust, and with innumerable fly-marks. In summer, bugs in multitudes may be seen, more especially at night, when the light of a candle is suddenly thrown upon the bedstead. The odour of these apartments is most offensive and sickening, from the long-continued presence of human impurities . . .

The dress of the great mass of the colliers, and more especially of the women and children, is extremely dirty, ragged, and highly disreputable, like that of beggars. Many of the men, on the other hand, dress tolerably well, when off work, and there are several, indeed a good many, who dress like respectable master tradesmen on Sundays, with clean linen and woollen clothes in excellent order . . . The children of the dissipated are very ill-clothed; many have scarcely enough to cover them; girls go about with apparently only a frock, often so torn as to disclose their naked limbs, and without shoes or stockings.

The moral condition of the collier population is on the whole very bad. A large proportion of the colliers is remarkable for ignorance, prejudice, and apathy in almost everything, except whiskey, cock fighting, and the like . . . They work only because they find it necessary. The chief occasions on which they are aroused from their sottish and apathetic condition are riotous dances, lasting, perhaps, with little intermission, for several days, raffles, shooting-matches, cock-fights, and scuffles amongst themselves. Political, social, religious, and all great and national questions are totally uninteresting to the majority of these degraded men . . .

R. SCOTT ALISON, M D, report on the sanitary condition and general economy of the town of Tranent, and neighbouring district in Haddingtonshire, Scotland; P.P. Lords, 1842, vol. 27, pp. 85–96.

23

Merthyr's Inconvenienced Females

The great proportion of the houses in Merthyr is occupied by those who are employed in the iron works . . . The best of the workmen's houses are, for the most part, those erected by the different iron companies, for such as labour in connection with their establishments . . . Speculators of various kinds seem to have built courts, alleys, and rows of houses wherever opportunities presented themselves, in order to meet the demand for the rapid increase of the town, entirely without regard to any order or system, and without any control as to lines, the form of streets, or to arrangements for drainage. The result is a very straggling town . . .

The rarity of privies is one of the marked characteristics of the town. Even many recently erected houses are unprovided in this respect . . . In some localities, a privy was found common to 40 or 50 persons and more, . . . and from its neglected state, it might well be doubted if it were of advantage, further than to conceal the inhabitants frequenting it from view. Even the houses of small but respectable tradespeople were found unprovided in this respect at Dowlais, and in consequence the females of the families were put to much inconvenience.

From the number of persons congregated together, and the scarcity of privies, not much regard to decency is paid by the mass of poorer persons, though some of the women are described as suffering much from constipation, brought on by their attempts to avoid exposure. The cinder heaps, as the lines of refuse slags from the iron works are termed, and the river sides are frequented by persons of all ages and sexes, who manage in the best way they can.

This system produces much indifference to personal exposure, and may in some way account for the not uncommon practice of the workmen, on their return home from their labour, stripping, and being washed and rubbed down, while naked, by the females of the house, or who may be in at the time, usually, as it is stated, without much regard to their being married or unmarried.

Notwithstanding such exposures and practices, however, the inhabitants of Merthyr are stated by competent and highly credible witnesses to be no more immoral than the inhabitants of other towns in South Wales, and to be not at all remarkable for freedom of intercourse among the sexes.

Report on Merthyr Tydvil, by SIR H. T. DE LA BECHE; P.P. 1845, vol. XVIII, pp. 144–146.

24

'Extreme of human misery'

If I thought it desirable to describe minutely some of those extreme instances of human misery I have met with when visiting the dwellings of the poor, I think I should take them from the hand-loom cotton-weavers . . .

Weaving, as a domestic occupation among the hand-loom cotton-weavers, is carried on in circumstances more prejudicial to health, and at a greater sacrifice of personal comfort, than weaving in any other branch. The great majority of hand-loom cotton-weavers work in cellars, sufficiently light to enable them to throw the shuttle, but cheerless because seldom visited by the sun. The reason cellars are chosen is, that cotton requires to be woven damp. The air, therefore, must be cool and moist, instead of warm and dry. Unhappily, the medium which might be preserved without injury to the constitution, and which is preserved in the best power-loom factories, the impoverished hand-loom cotton-weavers are obliged often to disregard.

I have seen them working in cellars dug out of an undrained swamp; the streets formed by their houses without sewers, and flooded with rain; the water therefore running down the bare walls of the cellars, and rendering them unfit for the abode of dogs or rats. The descent to these cellars is usually by a broken step-ladder. The floor is but seldom boarded or paved; a proper place for coals and ashes, but less fitted for a workshop than even an Irish hovel, because under ground.

*   *   *

A great mistake prevails in the minds of many persons as to the extent to which factory labour . . . is unfavourable to the health or morals of a community, or the happiness of a domestic life. With regard to health, having seen the domestic weaver in his miserable apartments, and the power-loom weaver in the factory, I do not hestitate to say that the advantages are all on the side of the latter.

The one, if a steady workman, confines himself to a single room, in which he eats, drinks and sleeps, and breathes throughout the day an impure air. The other has not only the exercise of walking to and . from the factory, but, when there, lives and breathes in a large roomy apartment, in which the air is constantly changed.

It has been said that factory labour is unfavourable to the happiness of the community, as far as it depends upon domesticity. But domestic happiness is not promoted, but impaired, by all the members of a family muddling together and jostling each other constantly in the same room . . .

w. e. hickson, reporting on the condition of the Hand-loom weavers; P.P. 1840, vol. XXIV, pp. 7, 43.

25

The 'Health of Towns' Report

By reference to the Population Returns it appears that, from the beginning of the present century, the whole population of Great Britain has increased at the rate of nearly 16 per cent every ten years;

from 1801 to 1811, thence to 1821, and again to 1831; and there is every reason to believe about the same rate of increase will be found to have taken place next year, when the next decennial return will be made. Whilst, however, such has been the increase in the population of the kingdom at large, reference to the same returns shows, that the augmentation of numbers in the great towns of the realm has been much more rapid: thus, whilst the increase of population in England and Wales, in thirty years, from 1801 to 1831, has been something more than 47 per cent, the actual increase in the number of inhabitants of five of our most important provincial towns has very nearly doubled that rate; being Manchester 109 per cent, Glasgow 108 per cent, Birmingham, 73 per cent, Leeds 99 per cent, Liverpool 100 per cent, giving an average increase of almost 98 per cent in five cities, whose united population in 1831 amounted to 844,700, and at the present time may be calculated at not less than 1,126,000. Far the larger portion of this vast body of persons are engaged constantly in occupations connected with manufactures or commerce . . .

Your Committee do not wish to go here into details as to the miserable and neglected state of the dwellings of the poorer classes in various districts of the metropolis and other large towns, but refer to the evidence . . . in which statements of the most melancholy and appalling nature will be found. It will there be seen, that the sewerage, draining, and cleansing is (in many places inhabited by dense masses of the working classes) greatly neglected; that the most necessary precautions to preserve their health in many cases appears to have been forgotten; that in consequence fevers and other disorders of a contagious and fatal nature are shown to prevail to a very alarming extent, causing widespread misery among the families of the sufferers, often entailing weakness and prostration of strength among the survivors; and becoming the source of great expense to the parishes and more opulent classes . . .

Your Committee would observe, that it is painful to contemplate, in the midst of what appears to be an opulent, spirited, and flourishing community, such a vast multitude of our poorer fellow subjects, the instruments by whose hands these riches were created, condemned, for no fault of their own, to the evils so justly complained of, and placed in situations where it is almost impracticable for them to preserve health or decency of deportment, or to keep themselves and their children from moral and physical contamination; to require them to be clean, sober, cheerful, contented, under such circumstances would be a vain and unreasonable expectation. There is no Building Act to enforce the dwellings of these workmen being properly constructed; no draining Act to enforce their being efficiently drained; no general or local regulation to enforce the commonest provisions for cleanliness and comfort.

It appears to Your Committee . . . that where such evils are found to follow from the neglect or inability in these respects of local authorities, that it is the duty of the Legislature to take efficient steps to protect so numerous and valuable a portion of the community . . .

Report of Select Committee on the Health of Towns; P.P. 1840, vol. XI, pp. iii–ix.

(b) CHADWICK THE SANITARY REFORMER

Few men have deserved so well of posterity as Edwin Chadwick, although History has been in no hurry to acknowledge the debt. He was one of the first and the greatest of the Sanitary Reformers, without whose work, and the work of the men whom he chose and inspired and prodded and ordered about, the towns that had been spawned by the Industrial Revolution must surely have perished, suffocated by their own growth, poisoned by their own waste products. It is only fitting that this section should open with the famous outburst in which he tried to shame the Victorians into a realization of their disgusting condition and arouse in them a resolve to do something to remedy it (No. 1).

Born in 1800, in a village near Manchester, Chadwick lived until 1890. His father was a journalist, and what little he remembered of his mother was summed up in his phrase, she was 'a sanitarian *pur et simple*'. He went to London as a boy, got a job in an attorney's office, wrote for the reviews and was called to the Bar. An article of his on 'Preventive Police' brought him to the favourable notice of Jeremy Bentham, and he was that very practical philosopher's secretary in the last years of his long life. Already the idea of eradicating the diseases of poverty and squalor had taken possession of his mind, and he spent much time in visits of investigation of the fever dens of the metropolis. In 1833 he was appointed to the Factory Commission, and he was the chief author of its report. In the following year he became the secretary of the Poor Law Commission, and as a Civil Servant he soon made his mark. He had a passion for facts—and there were so few of them in the social sciences. He set about finding them, most especially facts about the living conditions of the labouring population.

Among his first successes was the inclusion in the measure

providing for the official registration of births, marriages, and deaths of the direction that the cause of death should be entered upon the death certificates. Then in 1838, when there had been an exceptional number of typhus cases in the east end of London, he induced his superiors to dispatch into the most affected districts a mission of inquiry. It was composed of three doctors, all convinced 'sanitarians', viz. J. P. Kay, Southwood Smith, and Neil Arnott. Arnott and Kay explored Wapping and Stepney, while Southwood Smith investigated Bethnal Green and Whitechapel. Typical of what they found was given in Southwood Smith's report, given in the preceding section. Many people (though not Chadwick) were surprised to learn that the ill-health of the London poor was attributable not so much to their own fecklessness as to the abominable conditions in which they were compelled to exist. In the following year the Bishop of London, Dr Blomfield, using Southwood Smith's report as his text, moved in the House of Lords for the institution of an inquiry into the sanitary condition of the labouring classes. This was agreed to, and Chadwick was put in charge.

For the next three years he pursued his enquiries with characteristic vigour, and in 1842 his Report on the Condition of the Labouring Population of Great Britain was published. The 'his' is thoroughly justifiable: not only had Chadwick collected much of the material but his official superiors in Whitehall, realizing what offence the report was likely to give in some most influential quarters, granted him permission to sign it.

Several of the descriptions of the country's most insanitary places have been included in the previous section, and now we give passages illustrating more general aspects of the problem, including jerry-built houses (No. 2) and the lack of piped-water supply (No. 3). The document quoted in No. 4 is Chadwick's rejoinder to those who argued that the public would be bound to make nuisances of themselves if they were allowed access to gardens, etc., and in No. 5 he counters the plea that the sanitary reforms he advocated would be bound to cost an impossibly large sum of money. In a town such as Bury, he pointed out with grim exactitude, where there were cases of six people sleeping in one bed, the money spent on drink would be sufficient to meet the rent and rates of several thousand houses for the working classes. Chadwick's general Conclusions and Recommendations are given in No. 6.

In retrospect, the Report is seen as an epoch-making document, but at the time it was felt that still more evidence was required before Parliament took action. In 1843, therefore, the Conservative Government of Sir Robert Peel set up a Royal Commission to inquire into the State of Large Towns. The Commissioners appointed included Southwood Smith and Neil Arnott, but not Chadwick; he had, however, proved himself so indispensable that he was left to 'run' the Commission. The first Report was published in 1844, covering fifty of the largest towns in the country, in most of which the drainage and the water supply were deficient or terribly bad; most of this Report was written by Chadwick. The Commission's second Report followed in 1845. Among Chadwick's 'star' witnesses were Mr Hawksley (No. 7), who demonstrated that a Company operating for profit could provide a supply of piped water at a very reasonable cost, and Mr Thorn (No. 8) who gave an illuminating description of the methods of refuse collection in London. A corollary to this is the account of Liverpool's 'reckless nightmen' in No. 12.

While doing two or three men's work for the Royal Commission, Chadwick still found time to produce a report of a special inquiry that he had instituted into the 'Practice of Interment in Towns', extracts from which are given in No. 13.

In due course Chadwick was called in to draft a public health bill, and the first Public Health Act was put on the Statute Book in 1848. A Board of Health was appointed, of which Chadwick was a member, and it fell to him to get the local boards established throughout the country. Naturally he made many enemies and not a few mistakes, and after four years of intense activity he was sacked—on a pension of £1000 a year. Prince Albert the Prince Consort, who appreciated his worth while realizing his being difficult to work with, got him the C.B., but he was not knighted until 1889, the year before his death. Long before that time he had become recognized throughout the world as the first and perhaps the greatest exponent of the 'sanitary idea'.

I

Chadwick's Famous Outburst

Such is the absence of civic economy in some of our towns that their condition in respect to cleanliness is almost as bad as that of an encamped horde, or an undisciplined soldiery . . .

The discipline of the army has advanced beyond the civic economy of the towns. In the standing orders given and enforced by the late General Crauford there are the following from Article 2, on the interior regimental arrangements on arriving in camp or quarters:—'It must be explained to the men, as a standing order, that when no regular necessaries [i.e. latrines] are made, nor any particular spot pointed out for easing themselves, they are to go to the rear, at least 200 yards, beyond the sentries of the rear guard; all men disobeying this order must be punished . . .'

The towns whose population never change their encampment, have no such care, and whilst the houses, streets, courts, lanes, and streams are polluted and rendered pestilential, the civic officers have generally contented themselves with the most barbarous expedients, or sit still amidst the pollution, with the resignation of Turkish fatalists, under the supposed destiny of the prevalent ignorance, sloth, and filth.

From EDWIN CHADWICK's General Report; Sanitary Condition of the Labouring Population, 1842; vol. 26, p. 43.

2

Jack Straw's Houses

An immense number of the small houses occupied by the poorer classes in the suburbs of Manchester are of the most superficial character; they are built by the members of building clubs, and other individuals, and new cottages are erected with a rapidity that astonishes persons who are unacquainted with their flimsy structure. They have certainly avoided the objectionable mode of forming under-ground dwellings, but have run into the opposite extreme, having neither cellar nor foundation. The walls are only half brick thick, or what the bricklayers call 'brick noggin', and the whole of the materials are slight and unfit for the purpose.

I have been told of a man who had built a row of these houses; and visiting them one morning after a storm, found the whole of them levelled with the ground; and in another part of Manchester, a place with houses even of a better order has obtained the appellation of 'Pickpocket Row', from the known insecure nature of the buildings. I recollect a bricklayer near London complaining loudly of having to risk his credit by building a house with 9-inch walls, and declared it would be like 'Jack Straw's House', neither 'wind tight nor water tight!' His astonishment would have been great, had he been told that *thousands of houses* occupied by the labouring classes are erected with walls of $4\frac{1}{2}$-inch thickness.

The chief rents differ materially according to the situation, but are in all cases high; and thus arises the inducement to pack the houses so close. They are built back to back, without ventilation or drainage; and, like a honeycomb, every particle of space is occupied. Double rows of these houses form courts, with, perhaps, a pump at one end and a privy at the other, common to the occupants of about twenty houses.

MR MOTT's evidence; Lords Sessional Papers, 1842, vol. 27, p. 240.

3

The Worst Smell of All

No previous investigations had led me to conceive the great extent to which the labouring classes are subjected to privations, not only of water for the purpose of ablution, house cleansing, and sewerage, but of wholesome water for drinking, and culinary purposes . . .

Mr John Liddle, one of the medical officers of the Whitechapel union, after describing the deplorable condition of the dwellings of the labouring populations in that part of London, states, that—'In connexion with this state of things is the deficiency of water which is not laid on to any of their houses. They get it for the most part from a plug in the courts. I cannot say whether it is the actual scarcity of water, or their reluctance to fetch it, but the effect is a scarcity of water. When I have occasion to visit their rooms, they have only a very scanty supply of water in their tubs. When they are washing, the smell of the dirt mixed with the soap is the most offensive of all the smells I have to encounter. They merely pass dirty linen through very dirty water. The smell of the linen itself, when so washed, is very offensive, and must have an injurious effect on the health of the occupants. The filth of their dwellings is excessive, so is their personal filth. When they attend my surgery, I am always obliged to have the door open. When I am coming down stairs from the parlour, I know at the distance of a flight of stairs whether there are any poor patients in the surgery . . . If I cast my eye over the whole district at this moment, I do not think that one house for the working classes will be found in which there is such a thing as a sink for getting rid of the water. There is no such thing in the poorer places as a house with the water laid on. There is also a want of cess-pools; there is only one or two places for a whole court, and soil lies about the places which are in a most offensive condition . . .'

Supplies of water obtained from wells by the labour of fetching and carrying it in buckets or vessels do not answer the purpose of regular supplies of water brought into the house without such labour, and kept ready in cisterns . . . and it is observed, that when the supplies of water into the houses of persons of the middle class are cut off by the pipes being frozen, and when it is necessary to send for water to a distance, the house-cleansings and washings are diminished by the inconvenience.

EDWIN CHADWICK; P.P., Lords, 1842, vol. 26, pp. 63–64, 69–70.

4

Queen Victoria's Wedding Day

On the holiday given at Manchester in celebration of Her Majesty's marriage [10th February, 1840], extensive arrangements were made for holding a Chartist meeting, and for getting up what was called a demonstration of the working classes, which greatly alarmed the municipal magistrates. Sir Charles Snow, the Chief Commissioner of Police, induced the Mayor to get the Botanical Gardens, the Zoological Gardens, and other institutions thrown open to the working classes at the hour they were urgently invited to attend the Chartist meeting. The Mayor undertook to be personally answerable for any damage that occurred from throwing open the gardens and institutions to the classes that had never before entered them. The effect was that not more than 200 or 300 people attended the political meeting, which entirely failed, and scarcely 5s worth of damage was done in the gardens or in the public institutions by the workpeople, who were highly pleased. A further effect produced was, that the charges before the police of drunkenness and riot were on that day less than the average of cases on ordinary days.

EDWIN CHADWICK; P.P., Lords, 1842, vol. 26, p. 277.

5

Six to a Bed in Bury

In the town of Bury, with an estimated population of 25,000, the expenditure in beer and spirits is estimated at £54,190 annually, or £2 3s 4d for each man, woman, and child, a sum that would pay the rent and taxes for upwards of 6,770 new cottages at £8 per annum each.

But on an inquiry made from house to house by the agency of the Manchester Statistical Society into the condition of the labouring population of this town, with such an expenditure on one source of dissipation and ill-health, it appeared that of 2,755 of their dwellings examined, only 1,668 were decidedly comfortable; that a smaller number were well furnished; that the number of families in which there were less than two persons sleeping in one bed were only 413; that the number in which on the average there were more than two persons to a bed was 1,512; that the number of families who had not less than *three* persons in a bed and less than four, was 773; that the number of families in which there were 'at least four persons, but less than five persons to one bed', was 207. There were 63 families where there were at least five persons to one bed; and there were some in which even six were packed in one bed, lying at the top and bottom—children and adults. Similar results as to misapplied means and numbers crowded together would be ascertained from similar inquiries into the state of the population in other districts ...

EDWIN CHADWICK; P.P., Lords, 1842, vol. 26, p. 228.

6

Chadwick's Conclusions and Recommendations

After as careful an examination of the evidence collected as I have been enabled to make, I beg leave to recapitulate the chief conclusions which that evidence appears to me to establish.

First, as to the extent and operation of the evils which are the subject of this inquiry—

That the various forms of epidemic, endemic, and other disease caused, or aggravated, or propagated chiefly amongst the labouring classes by atmospheric impurities produced by decomposing animal and vegetable substances, by damp and filth, and close overcrowded dwellings prevail amongst the population in every part of the kingdom, whether dwelling in separate houses, in rural villages, in small towns, in the larger towns—as they have been found to prevail in the lowest districts of the metropolis.

That such disease, wherever its attacks are frequent, is always found in connexion with the physical circumstances above specified, and that where those circumstances are removed by drainage, proper cleansing, better ventilation, and other means of diminishing atmospheric impurity, the frequency and intensity of such disease is abated; and where the removal of the noxious agencies appears to be complete, such disease almost entirely disappears ...

That the formation of all habits of cleanliness is obstructed by defective supplies of water.

That the annual loss of life from filth and bad ventilation are greater than the loss from death or wounds in any wars in which the country has been engaged in modern times.

That of the 43,000 cases of widowhood, and 112,000 cases of destitute orphanage relieved from the poor's rate in England and Wales alone, it appears that the greatest proportion of the deaths of the heads of families occurred from the above specified and other removable causes; that their ages were under 45 years; that is to say, 13 years below the natural probabilities of life as shown by the experience of the whole population of Sweden ...

That the ravages of epidemics and other diseases do not diminish but tend to increase the pressure of population.

That in the districts where the mortality is the greatest the births are not only sufficient to replace the numbers removed by death, but to add to the population.

That the younger population, bred up under noxious physical agencies, is inferior in physical organization and general health to a population preserved from the pressure of such agencies.

That the population so exposed is less susceptible of moral influences, and the effect of education are more transient than with a healthy population.

That these adverse circumstances tend to produce an adult population short-lived, improvident, reckless, and intemperate, and with habitual avidity for sensual gratifications.

That these habits lead to the abandonment of all the conveniences and decencies of life, and especially lead to the overcrowding of their homes, which is destructive to the morality as well as the health of large classes of both sexes.

That defective town cleansing fosters habits of the most abject degradation and leads to the demoralization of large numbers of human beings, who subsist by means of what they find amidst the noxious filth accumulated in neglected streets and bye-places ...

Secondly. As to the means by which the present sanitary condition of the labouring classes may be improved:—

The primary and most important measures, and at the same time the most practicable, and within the recognized province of public administration, are drainage, the removal of all refuse of habitations, streets, and roads, and the improvement of the supplies of water ...

That for the prevention of the disease occasioned by defective ventilations, and other causes of impurity in places of work and other places where large numbers are assembled, and for the general promotion of the means necessary to prevent disease, that it would be good economy to appoint a district medical officer independent of private practice, and with the securities of special qualifications and responsibilities to initiate sanitary measures and reclaim the execution of the law.

That by the combination of all these arrangements, it is probable that the full ensurable period of life indicated by the Swedish tables; that is, an increase of 13 years at least, may be extended to the whole of the labouring classes . . . I have the honour to be, Gentlemen, Your obedient servant, EDWIN CHADWICK.

P.P. Lords, 1842, vol. 26, pp. 369–372.

7

Nottingham's Water Supply

Mr Thomas Hawksley, Civil Engineer; designer, constructor, and resident engineer of the Trent Water-works at Nottingham, when asked 'What has been the effect produced on their habits by the introduction of water into the houses of the labouring classes ?' replied:

At Nottingham the increase of personal cleanliness was at first very marked indeed; it was obvious in the streets. The medical men reported that the increase of cleanliness was very great in the houses, and that there was less disease. There was also an advantage in the removal of the assemblages round the public pumps. At Newcastle-on-Tyne, where they have common fountains, and where young girls are brought into contact with every description of characters, the effect is highly objectionable.

When, on the return home of the labourers' family, old or young, tired perhaps with the day's labour, the water has to be fetched from a distance out of doors in cold or in wet, in frost or in snow, is it not well known to those acquainted with the labourers' habits that the use of clean water, and the advantages of washing and cleanliness, will be foregone to avoid the annoyance of having to fetch the water?—Yes; that is a general and notorious fact; when the distance to be traversed is comparatively trifling, it still operates against the free use of water.

Before water was laid on in the houses of Nottingham, were the labouring classes accustomed to purchase water?—Before the supply was laid on in the houses water was sold chiefly to the labouring classes by carriers at the rate of one farthing a bucket; and if the water had to be carried any distance up a court a halfpenny a bucket was, in some instances, charged. In general it was sold at about 3 gallons for a farthing. But the Company now delivers to all the town 76,000 gallons for £1; in other words, carries into every house 79 gallons for a farthing, and delivers water night and day, at every instant of time that it is wanted, at a charge 26 times less than the old delivery by hand.

My own observation and inquiry convince me that the character and habits of a working family are more depressed and deteriorated by the defects of their habitations than by the greatest pecuniary privation to which they are subject. The most cleanly and orderly female will invariably despond and relax her exertions under the influence of filth, damp, and stench, and at length ceasing to make further effort, probably sink into a dirty, noisy, discontented, and perhaps gin-drinking drab—the wife of a man who has no comfort in his home, the parent of children whose home is the street or the gaol. The moral and physical improvements certain to result from the introduction of water and water-closets into the houses of the working classes are far beyond the pecuniary advantages, however considerable these may under certain circumstances appear.

Report on State of Large Towns; P.P. 1844, vol. XVII, pp. 302–321.

8

The Economics of Refuse Collection

William Thorn, of the firm of Stapleton & Thorn, cleansing contractors; contractor for cleansing and dust collection in the south-western division of St Pancras, the Foundling Estate, the Doughty Estate, the

Pancras Union; and the St Mary's division of Mary-le-bone for dust only.

Is not there an increasing difficulty in finding places where filth may be deposited in the vicinity of the populous parts of London?—I should say that it was the general feeling of the inhabitants of London not to have a lay-stall nearer to them than can possibly be avoided.

Is not there a rapid increase of buildings in the vicinity of London gradually covering over those places that were formerly used for such purposes?—Yes; they drive us out.

And the inhabitants make an objection to your coming there?—Yes; they say they do not like our men, and they do not like our carts; we are not very pleasant sort of people . . .

The ashes and breeze are used in the manufacture of bricks. For what purpose is the remainder of the stuff used?—If we mix the street-sweepings with horse-dung and cow-dung, we get rid of it to the farmers, who use it for fallow lands for manuring, for turnips and wheat, and all their produce in fact. If we sell it alone without mixing it with horse-dung and cow-dung, it is put upon meadow-land after the first crop of hay is off.

Do you also carry night-soil [contents of privies, cess-pools, etc.]? —We have one place to which we can carry it, over the canal-bridge, about 500 yards on the same road. We lay it there in the midst of a very large field; the person who allows us the privilege of shooting it there (Mr Clarke) bakes it, I believe, and sends it over to the West Indies . . .

What is the average cost of cleansing out a cess-pool?—It is done by the load. Our average is generally 10s a one-horse and 15s a two-horse load. A load is as near a cubic yard as possible. The houses we are most in the habit of removing night-soil from are lodging-houses, with a family on every floor. That is about five loads. We cleanse those once a year, or once in 18 months. It is impossible to say it exactly, because they do not employ the same person twice, if they can get it done a shilling or two cheaper by another . . . During the last 13 weeks of the St Giles' contract we were paid 5s a week for keeping the inhabitants in Lascelles-court, Holborn, decent; preventing them making use of a small place which had seemed to have been originally a watch-box, and a place of filth it was. We used to send a barrow in at 4 o'clock in the morning, and take it away.

So that they had no convenience at all?—No. At that time they threw the dust into the night-soil, and rendered it worthless. We were paying a large sum for the dust, and it was a great loss to us. We generally find a market for the dust with the brick-makers . . .

How do you dispose of the bones and those things?—Our general plan is to contract; we underlet our work of sifting to a man, and we give him everything that it produces except the ashes and breeze. He gets the rags and bones, and other things. The oyster-shells belong to us; he sells the bones . . . The bones are always sold to the Jews; and they send them away in barges, and they are taken and boiled, I believe, in the country somewhere, and ground and used as bone-dust for manure. The fine rags are washed; and if they can be made anything of they are taken and disposed of to the papermills for the purpose of manufacturing paper. The woollen coarse rags are taken into the country and laid down till they moulder away, and then the rag-dust is sold to the hop-farmers in Kent. It is a most excellent thing to prevent the fly in wine. Oyster-shells, broken crockery ware, and everything that we call 'hard core' is sold to the contractors for roads . . . There is no better thing in existence . . .

Can you state how much dust and ashes in a year a house of a given size produces on an average—take the house of a tradesman in Tottenham-court-road, who is there all the year?—I think that, on the average, it is about a load and half a year . . .

Do you pay extra wages to the men who get out the night-soil?—Yes, we pay so much a load to the men. For a fair night-job we send out five men and a cart, and I generally send a foreman with them when I cannot go myself, because I am very particular. I do not like such a thing as spilling it on the road, or the men getting drunk. We pay the men 6d a load to each of the five men, and for an average job that is half-a-crown to each man. For that they work till five in the morning generally, not quite so long as five, because it must be done by four o'clock . . .

Are they paid rather more in consequence of the employment being disagreeable?—A third more at least.

Do they drink a good deal?—Yes. It is a very disagreeable occupation, and I do not wonder at their drinking . . . They come in as lads; they come from the country about 16 or 17, and if once they get into a nightman's yard they never leave it . . . We have got a man now that is 67. They live to a good age in general . . .

P.P. 1844, vol. XVII, pp. 274–278.

9

The Builder's Fancy

From the absence of any systematic and compulsory arrangements, every man has built as it has pleased his own fancy, and little precaution has been taken as to drainage. There are thousands of houses and hundreds of courts in this town without a single drain of any description; and I never hail any thing with greater delight than I do a violent tempest, or a terrific thunderstorm, accompanied by heavy rain; for these are the only scavengers that thousands have to cleanse away impurities and the filth in which they live, or rather, exist.

In Liverpool . . . the soil is subdivided into a multitude of holdings, and a man runs a new street, generally as narrow as he possibly can, through a field, not only to save the greater expense of soughing [drainage] and paving, which, in the first instance, falls upon himself, but also that he may have a greater quantity of land to dispose of. The next owner continues that street, if it suits him, but he is not obliged to do so, and . . . the growth of narrow thoroughfares, the utter neglect of proper sewerage, the inattention to ventilation, and that train of evils which is so much to be deplored, is the inevitable consequence.

SAMUEL HOLME, builder; P.P. 1844, vol. XVII, p. 186.

10

Queuing Up for Water

Joseph Quick, Engineer to the Southwark Water Company, when asked to explain what were the evils he had spoken of resulting from the system of water supply by stand-pipes instead of one carried into each house, replied: The labour of fetching the water, the loss of time in waiting for what they call their turns, and the demoralization from the numbers brought and kept together. I have seen as many as from 20 to 50 persons with pails waiting round one or two stand-pipes; the strongest pushing forward, and the pails, after they are filled, being upset. In the winter time the inconvenience is increased by the liability of the cock being frozen, and injuries to the health from the weather, and getting wet-footed. It also happens frequently that the man and woman are out at work during the time the supply is on the common tap. When they return home there is no supply, and this may occur from day to day: if the man has work he is generally out, and a large proportion of the women work from home.

P.P. 1845, vol. XVII, p. 397.

II

Buried in a City Sewer

Richard Kelsey, Surveyor to the Commissioner of Sewers for the City of London, when asked if he knew of any drains in London that stood above the level of houses, replied: I think I could mention one which has been exposed, but which is covered by the floor of the basement story; that is one that was built by St Bartholomew's Hospital long before the Fire of London, which passes under the houses in Hosier-lane, and that is covered with the floor of the houses, but it is covered substantially; it is not open at all.

Do you happen to know whether there is any smell through the structure of the drain?—Not through the drain itself; but unfortunately that sewer being extremely ancient, and being built over by very old houses, has been exceedingly ill-used, so much so, that in endeavouring to rout out all the sewers, to make a plan, we found part of a bedstead in that sewer, and we have even found dead bodies, or at least coffins, in sewers. In one which passed under a churchyard we found that it had been used for sepulture; that they had broken into the sewer and put bodies in it.

Who do you imagine had done so?—The sexton or somebody, surreptitiously . . .

P.P. 1845, vol. XVII, p. 209.

12

Reckless Nightmen

The infrequency of scavenging, and the neglected state of the courts and alleys, has given rise in Lancashire to a practice unknown in the metropolis, viz., the forming of open cesspools, dunghills, or 'middens', as they are termed, as places of deposit for refuse from all the houses in the court . . . And the consequence of which is, that there are no systematic arrangements for their removal. This circumstance has called into existence in the large towns a wretched set of men . . .

'The nightmen', says Mr Moore, president of the Agricultural Society of Manchester, 'are very filthy in their appearance and habits, and being often assisted in their labours by their families, their houses are usually most offensive and wretched abodes.' Nightmen are paid 3s for a load of 2 tons, and to obtain this quantity, two men, with some assistance from their families or from the carters, may be able to load two carts from 3 a.m. to 9 a.m.; they, therefore, generally frequent those places where most manure is to be procured with the least labour, neglecting to visit districts in which this is not the case. But the inhabitants of districts frequently visited by these reckless men complain of them as an intolerable nuisance. Mr Rishton, the town surveyor of Liverpool, states that . . . 'many of the privies are damaged and rendered useless by the nightmen wilfully breaking up the floors and seats to get out the soil; they will pull down one side of the bog-hole that their work may be done with more ease. In this way they cause considerable damage to property, and it is too often left in the same state for a considerable time, and the place becomes one open mass of filth from daily accumulation.'

P.P. 1845, vol. XVIII, pp. 14–15.

13

Interment in Towns

In the metropolis, on spaces of ground that do not exceed 203 acres, closely surrounded by the abodes of the living, layer upon layer, each consisting of a population numerically equivalent to a large army of 20,000 adults and nearly 30,000 youths and children, is every year imperfectly interred. Within the period of the existence of the present generation, upwards of a million of dead must have been interred in these same spaces.

A layer of bodies is said to be about seven years in decaying in the metropolis . . . In some of the populous parishes, where, from the nature of the soil, the decomposition has not been so rapid as the interments, the place of burial has risen in height; and the height of many of them must have greatly increased but for surreptitious modes of diminishing it by removal, which, it must be confessed, has diminished the sanitary evil, though by the creation of another and most serious evil, in the mental pain and apprehensions of the survivors and feelings of abhorrence of the population, caused by the suspicion and knowledge of the disrespectful and desecration of the remains of the persons interred [i.e. by 'body-snatchers' for hospital dissection-rooms].

*   *   *

In a large proportion of cases in the metropolis, and in some of the manufacturing districts, one room serves for one family of the labouring classes: it is their bed-room, their kitchen, their wash-house, their sitting-room, their dining-room; and, when they do not follow any out-door occupation, it is frequently their work-room and their shop. In this one room they are born, and live, and sleep, and die amidst the other inmates.

The condition in which the remains are often found on the occurrence of a death at the eastern part of the metropolis are thus described by Mr John Liddle, the medical officer of the Whitechapel Union: 'Nearly the whole of the labouring population there [dock labourers, navigators, brick layers' labourers, and the general description of labourers inhabiting Whitechapel and lower Aldgate] have only one room. The corpse is therefore kept in that room where the inmates sleep and have their meals. Sometimes the corpse is stretched on the bed, and the bed and bedclothes are taken off, and the wife and family lie on the floor. Sometimes a board is got on which the corpse is stretched, and that is sustained on tressels or on chairs. Sometimes it is stretched on two chairs. When children die, they are frequently laid out on the table. The poor Irish, if they can afford it, form a canopy of white calico over the corpse, and buy candles to burn by it, and place a black cross at the head of the corpse. They commonly raise the money to do this by subscriptions amongst themselves and at public-houses which they frequent.

'The time the corpse is kept varies according to the day of the death. Sunday is the day usually chosen for the day of burial. But if a man dies on the Wednesday, the funeral will not take place till the Sunday the week following. Bodies are almost always kept for a full week, frequently longer . . .

'What I observe when I first visit the room is a degree of indifference to the presence of the corpse: the family is found eating or drinking or pursuing their usual callings, and the children playing. Amongst the middle classes, where there is an opportunity of putting the corpse by itself, there are greater marks of respect and decency. Among that class no one would think of doing anything in the room where the corpse was lying, still less allowing children there.'

*   *   *

The causes which influence this practice amongst the greatest number of the population appear to be, first, the expense of funerals—next, the delay in making arrangements for the funeral—the natural reluctance to part with the remains of the deceased, and occasionally a feeling of apprehension, sometimes expressed on the part of the survivors, against premature interment. Mr Byles, the surgeon, of Spitalfields, in reference to the delay of interments, states: 'The difficulty of raising the subscription to bury the dead is . . . one chief cause of the delay. When, in the instance of the death of a child, I ask why it cannot be interred earlier, the usual reply is, "we cannot raise the money earlier".' Mr Wild, the undertaker, states: 'The time varies from 5 to 12 days. This arises from the difficulty of procuring the means of making arrangements with the undertaker, and the difficulty of getting mourners to attend the funeral. They have a great number to attend, neighbours, fellow-workmen, as well as relatives . . .'

The nature of the expenses of interment in London . . . are most fully developed in the examination of Mr Wild. ' . . . The average price of funerals amongst the working classes for adults will be about £4. This sum generally provides a good strong elm coffin, bearers to carry the corpse to the grave, pall and fittings for mourners. For children the average cost is 30s, but these charges do not include ground and burial fees . . . In benefit societies and burial clubs there is generally a certain sum set aside for the burial, which sum is, I consider, frequently most extravagantly expended. This arises from the secretary, or some other officer of the club, being an undertaker . . .'

* * *

The desire to secure respectful interment of themselves and their relations is, perhaps, the strongest and most widely-diffused feeling amongst the labouring classes of the population. Subscriptions may be obtained from large classes of them for their burial when it can be obtained neither for their own relief in sickness, nor for the education of their children, nor for any other object . . .

The burial clubs of the labouring classes are generally got up by an undertaker and by the publican at whose house the club is held . . .

Mr Robert Hawksworth, the Visitor to the Manchester and Salford District Provident Society, recently stated to me: 'Here, the mode of conducting the funerals—the habits of drinking at the time of assemblage at the house, before the corpse is removed, renewed on the return from the funeral, when they drink to excess, the long retention of the body in one room, are all exceedingly demoralizing. The occasion of a funeral is commonly looked to, amongst the lowest grade, as the occasion of "a stir"; the occasion of the drinking is viewed at the least with complacency.' A minister in the neighbourhood of Manchester expressed his sorrow on observing a great want of natural feeling, and great apathy at the funerals. The sight of a free flow of tears was a refreshment which he seldom received. He was, moreover, often shocked by a common phrase amongst women of the lowest class— 'Aye, aye, that child will not live; it is in the burial club.'

From E. CHADWICK's Supplementary Report on the results of a Special Inquiry into the Practice of Interment in Towns; P.P. 1843, vol. XII, pp. 27–71.

(c) RECREATION AND AMUSEMENTS

Right at the end of our survey is not an inappropriate place for a glance at the way in which the working population spent such leisure as was theirs. For those who had the ordering of their lives thought this a matter of very small importance. As Sir James Graham, the Home Secretary in Peel's Government, told the House of Commons, 'throughout this world of sorrow and of care, the lot of eating, drinking, working, and dying, must ever be the sum of human life among the masses of a large portion of the human family'. What had 'the masses' to do with leisure, still less with pleasurable ways of spending it? Theirs but to toil, and produce a fresh generation of toilers to take over when they were getting past it . . .

What was the outcome of this gloomy philosophy will be clear enough from the documents given here. Fortunately there were some in all classes who not only refused to believe it but took steps to ameliorate the situation. Need it be said that one of the earliest was Dr Kay, and his letter (No. 1) to the chairman of a Select Committee appointed to consider the question of providing 'public walks' is quite in keeping with all that we have read before from that energetically benevolent gentleman's pen. Samuel Smiles, the industrious preacher of 'self help', advocates Reading (No. 9), and an intelligent engineer expresses the opinion that what he had witnessed of the Continental Sunday made it decidedly preferable to a state of affairs in which the English workman got 'beastly drunk' (No. 10). Not at first, and not for a long time, but eventually, it came to be accepted that every man and woman, and every child, has a right to leisure, to recreation and amusement, for only then can they attain to the fullest development—physical, intellectual, moral—of which they are capable as members of the human family.

I

Manchester Wants Parks

The operative population of Manchester enjoys little or no leisure during the week, the whole available time being absorbed by their occupations. The few hours which intervene between labour and sleep are generally spent either at the tavern, or in making some necessary family arrangements. On Sunday the entire working population sinks into a state of abject sloth or listless apathy, or even into the more degrading conditions of reckless sensuality.

At present the entire labouring population of Manchester is without any season of recreation, and is ignorant of all amusements, excepting that very small portion which frequents the theatre. Healthful exercise in the open air is seldom or never taken by the artizans of this town, and their health certainly suffers considerable depression from this deprivation.

One reason of this state of the people is, that all scenes of interest are remote from the town, and that walks which can be enjoyed by the poor are chiefly the turnpike roads, alternately dusty or muddy. Were parks provided, recreation would be taken with avidity, and one of the first results would be a better use of the Sunday, and a substitution of innocent amusement at all other times, for the debasing pleasures now in vogue.

Letter from DR J. P. KAY to R. A. Slaney, MP, chairman of the Select Committee on Public Walks; P.P. 1833, vol. XV, p. 66.

2

A Plea for Public Walks

During the last half century a very great increase has taken place in the population of large Towns, more especially as regards those classes who are, with many of their children, almost continually engaged in

Manufacturing and Mechanical employments. During the same period, from the increased value of Property and extension of Buildings, many inclosures of open spaces in the vicinity of Towns have taken place, and little or no provision has been made for Public Walks or Open Spaces, fitted to afford means of exercise or amusement to the middle or humbler classes . . .

Your Committee feel convinced that some Open Places reserved for the amusement (under due regulations to preserve order) of the humbler classes, would assist to wean them from low and debasing pleasures. Great complaint is made of drinking-houses, dog fights, and boxing matches, yet, unless some opportunity for other recreation is afforded to workmen, they are driven to such amusements. The spring to industry which occasional relaxation gives, seems quite as necessary to the poor as to the rich . . .

It cannot be necessary to point out how requisite some Public Walks or Open Space in the neighbourhood of large Towns must be; to those who consider the occupations of the Working Classes who dwell there; confined as they are during the week-days as Mechanics and Manufacturers, and often shut up in heated factories: it must be evident that it is of the first importance to their health on their day of rest to enjoy the fresh air, and to be able (exempt from the dust and dirt of public thoroughfares) to walk out in decent comfort with their families; if deprived of any such resource, it is probable that their only escape from the narrow courts and alleys (in which so many of the humble classes reside) will be those drinking-shops, where, in short-lived excitement they may forget their toil, but where they waste the means of their families, and too often destroy their health.

Neither would your Committee forget to notice the advantages which the Public Walks (properly regulated and open to the middle and humbler classes) give to the improvement in the cleanliness, neatness and personal appearance of those who frequent them. A man walking out with his family among his neighbours of different ranks, will naturally be desirous to be properly clothed, and that his Wife and Children should be so also; but this desire duly directed and controlled, is proved by experience to be of the most powerful effect in promoting Civilization and exciting Industry; and your Committee venture to remark, that it is confined to no age, or station, or sex . . . In conclusion, your Committee . . . hope that Public Walks may be gradually established in the neighbourhood of every populous Town in the Kingdom.

Report from the Select Committee on Public Walks; P.P. 1833, vol. XV.

3

'At home in their dirt'

How do the operatives of Manchester employ their Sunday afternoons?
—The whole Sunday is too frequently lost in either drinking or
inactive idleness. It is a most painful thing in Manchester, with the
full knowledge that there is a vast labouring population around you,
to observe that the whole Sunday is passing away without seeing the
great mass of the labouring classes, as you would see them here, with
their wives and children, walking out, and you wonder where they are:
they are too numerously at home in their dirt.

JOSEPH FLETCHER, secretary to the Hand-loom Weavers' Commission;
P.P. 1840, vol. XI, p. 75.

4

Skittles in Birmingham

The want of some place of recreation for the mechanic is an evil which
presses very heavily upon these people, and to which many of their bad
habits may be traced. There are no public walks in or near the town;
no places where the working people can resort for recreation. The
consequence is, that they frequent the ale-houses and skittle-alleys for
amusement.

Within the last half-century the town was surrounded by land which
was divided into gardens, which were rented by the mechanics at one
guinea or half a guinea per annum. Here the mechanic was generally
seen after his day's labour spending his evening in a healthy and simple
occupation to his great delight. This ground is now for the most part
built over.

P.P. Lords, 1842, vol. 27, p. 213.

5

Closed on Sundays in Sheffield

———

No manufacturing town in England is worse situated for places for public or healthful recreation than Sheffield. Thirty years ago it had numbers of places as common land where youths and men could have taken exercise at cricket, quoits, football, and other exercises ... Scarce a foot of all these common wastes remain for the enjoyment of the industrial classes. It is true we have a noble cricket-ground, but access to this must be purchased. We have also perhaps as beautiful botanical gardens as any in the kingdom, but these are opened only once or twice a year to the poorer classes, and they are admitted for sixpence each; and hermetically sealed on a Sunday ... the only day when members of the working classes have leisure to enjoy them. Many attempts have been made to open them in summer after service, but in vain; the X X X consider it would be a desecration of the Sabbath to permit the hard-toiled mechanic or tradesman to walk through these beautiful gardens on that day to view the beauties of creation in plants and flowers, such as the Saviour of mankind said that Solomon in all his glory was not to be compared with.

To the want of proper places for healthful recreation may be attributed, in a measure, the great increase of crime in this town and neighbourhood. Young people have no resort but the beer or public-house, and generally those of the worst character, for the most respectable houses will not suffer young men to drink in them; and young men of abilities and moral habits often get entangled with associates of the most profligate character.

JOHN WARDLE, cutler, aged about 50; P.P. 1843, vol. XIV, e 22/23.

6

Sunday in Wolverhampton

Sunday, March 14th. Walked about the town, streets and outskirts, during church-time. Met men, singly and in groups, wandering about in their working aprons and caps, or with dirty shirt-sleeves tucked up, and black smithy-smutted arms and grimed faces. Some appeared to have been up all night—probably at work to recover the time lost by their idleness in the early part of the week; perhaps drinking. Lots of children seen in groups at the end of courts, alleys, and narrow streets —playing, or sitting upon the edge of the common dirt-heap of the place, like a row of sparrows and very much of that colour, all chirruping away . . .

Boys fighting; bad language and bloody noses. Women, in their working dresses, standing about at doors or ends of passages, with folded arms. Little boys sitting in holes in the ground, playing at mining with a small pick-axe. Girls playing about in various ways; all dirty, except one group of about half-a-dozen girls, near Little's Lane, of the age of from 9 to 15, who are washed and dressed, and are playing with continual screams and squeaks of delight, or jumping from the mounds of dirt, dung, and rubbish-heaps, which are collected there, and cover a considerable space. Some fell with a sprawl; in a moment all were scuttling up the dirt-heaps again . . .

Adults seated smoking, or with folded arms, on the threshold of the door, or inside their houses, evidently not intending to wash and shave. Many of them sitting or standing in the house, with an air of lazy vacancy—they did not know what to do with their leisure or with themselves. One group of five adults very decently dressed; they were leaning over the rails of a pig-sty, all looking down upon the pigs, as if in deep and silent meditation—with the pigs' snouts just visible, all pointing up to the meditative faces, expecting something to come of it. No working men walking with their wives, either to or from church or chapel, or for the sake of the walk—no brothers and sisters. Until the issuing forth of the children from the Sunday-schools, with all those adults who had attended some place of worship, nothing seen but squalid disorder, indifference, and utter waste, in self-disgust, of the very day of which, in every sense, they should make the most. With all this, no merriment—no laughter—no smiles. All dulness and vacuity. No signs of joyous animal spirits, except with the girls on the dirt-heaps.

'Copied verbatim from my note-book'; R. H. HORNE, sub-commissioner; Employment of Children Report, P.P. 1843, vol. XV, p. Q 21.

7

Liverpool's River

There is no public park . . . There is a public garden maintained by the Corporation on the south-east side of the town. Along the river front there are spacious walks. But the river and the convenience of steam navigation are the chief attractions, as frequently 20,000 persons pass over the river to Cheshire on a Sunday to enjoy their walk. The shores of the river at the north and south ends of the town are resorted to for bathing; and the Corporation have erected one set of public baths and wash-houses at the south end of the town for the accommodation of the poor and the working classes at a very small charge.

P.P. 1845, vol. XVIII, p. 86.

8

Pit-People's Hobbies

The general domestic state of the [Durham] pit-people may be said to be good . . . Their habits are cleanly, and their greatest vice is being addicted to drinking, which they are [at] generally once a fortnight, on their pay-days.

Their mode of spending their leisure hours differs very much; most of them have gardens, and many of them take great delight in the cultivation of flowers, and have 'flower shows' during the season. In winter they have no mode of employing their vacant time, and they spend it unprofitably; this may be accounted for from the small number of them who can read. The few who have had a little education are fond of reading, but they are mostly without the means of obtaining works, there not being circulating libraries, reading rooms, or mechanics' institutes . . . One of the most important things which could be done would be the establishment of reading rooms, with books of amusing though instructive character, as 'Chambers' Journal', the 'Penny Magazine', . . . and newspapers not particularly attached to any political body . . .

J. W. DAY, chairman of Houghton-le-Spring Poor Law Union; P.P. 1842, vol. XV, p. 719.

9

Wanted: Public Libraries

Samuel Smiles, editor for several years of a Leeds newspaper: stated that they had a sort of union of mechanics' institutes called the Yorkshire Union, and that all the 79 institutes composing the Union had libraries attached to them. The total number of members was about 16,000. There were 60,000 volumes in the libraries, and they were of all kinds: history, political economy, statistics to a small extent, and a large proportion of works of fiction. Fiction was principally read, but a taste for a better description of reading is evidently increasing. The numbers of issues of books on mechanics, philosophy, chemistry, and science is on the increase, and historical works have been much read of late years. I think the taste of the people is decidedly improving. Amongst those who read there has unquestionably been an improvement in their habits of order, temperance, and character generally . . . But the misfortune is, that but a small proportion of the population in our large towns, and probably also in the agricultural districts, read. The general deficiency we have to encounter in our neighbourhood is the want of elementary instruction to begin with. Even after the working people have learned to read, there is a want of opportunity of keeping up their reading. In the parish church at Leeds nearly one-half of the women who are married cannot sign their own names. But it is exceedingly probable that a large proportion of those women had learned to write then they were young, but had forgotten it for want of means and opportunity of practising it when they grew up . . .

There is a very large proportion of the working classes who are neither connected with any literary body nor any religious body, whom society does not look after in the slightest degree, who have no literary nor mental provision, and for whom libraries, or literary food of some description, is very desirable.

Select Committee on Public Libraries; P.P. 1849, vol. XVII, pp. 124–125.

10

The Continental Sunday

Edwin Rose, engineer, who had worked in France, Germany, Switzerland, etc. when asked, 'Should you say the French were a sober set?' replied, Yes, they appeared a very comfortable set of people. I did not see them get beastly drunk as working men here are inclined to do.

What amusement or innocent recreations has a working man here on a Sunday?—None at all that I know, but taking a walk in the country, which is not forbidden that I know of.

Judging from what I saw there, I should say that it was much better than the way in which people are forced to spend Sunday in England. Here a man can do nothing but go to the public-house on a Sunday, and he goes with the intention to get drink, as it were; and sit drinking glass after glass; there, people going out to dances and different games, and having different recreations at the places where they go, such as cards and dominoes, can cheerfully enjoy themselves, drinking but little. But here a man can do nothing at a public-house, if he goes there, but drink, and he can go nowhere else on a Sunday. It seemed to me that they went easier and happier to work again there than they do here . . .

P.P. 1833, vol. XX, D 1.

INDEX